THE QUEEN'S COUNTRYWOMEN

Other Books by
GODFREY WINN.

NOVELS:
Dreams Fade
Squirrel's Cage
The Unequal Conflict
Fly Away, Youth
Communion on Earth

ESSAYS:
I May be Wrong
Personality Parade
A Month of Sundays
For My Friends

WAR BOOKS:
On Going to the Wars
The Hour Before the Dawn
The Kind of People We Are
Scrapbook of the War
Scrapbook of Victory
Home From Sea
P. Q. 17

TRAVEL BOOKS:
Going My Way
The Bend of the River
This Fair Country

BIOGRAPHY:
The Younger Sister
The Young Queen

CORDIE

GODFREY WINN

THE QUEEN'S
COUNTRYWOMEN

HUTCHINSON
Stratford Place
London

Hutchinson & Co. (Publishers) Ltd.

London   Melbourne   Sydney
Auckland   Bombay   Cape Town
New York   Toronto

First Published · 1954

Printed in Great Britain by
William Brendon & Son, Ltd.
The Mayflower Press (late of Plymouth)
at Bushey Mill Lane
Watford, Herts.

For
ADRIANNE
in deep affection

CONTENTS

LIST OF ILLUSTRATIONS

ONE

THE SPLENDID JOURNEYWOMEN

EACH time that once again I start off on the adventure of writing a new book, there comes the same insistent flash of memory, intruding at first between myself and the blank page. A picture before my eyes that is at once a source of encouragement and a challenge. I see again the surgeon staring down at his workman's hands, as we stand there in the porch of the hospital, both blinking a little in the sun.

For we have been together in the clinical atmosphere of the operating theatre for long hours under the moon-white lights, while I have watched him perform a grafting operation that was a supreme demonstration of professional skill. From the patient's thigh he removed a razor-thin outer layer of skin which later he pressed, like pieces of putty, into the naked patches under the eyes. Skilfully, operation by operation, he would erase the war scars and give the anonymous airman who lay there like a mummy under the deep anaesthetic a new face and with it new hope for the future.

When at last this instalment was over and the surgeon had taken off his green mask and emerged from the theatre, a human being once again, I found myself asking him, on a sudden impulse, what more he wanted from life himself. Already his name was a legend in the world of surgery. He could command huge fees, when he would take them, and was infinitely beloved by all the hundreds of guinea pigs whom he had salvaged from being total war losses. What now? What did he seek from the peace?

Whereupon my chance question brought forth a reply that I have carried like a talisman ever since in my own journey along the road. Nor, I noticed, did he hesitate over giving it to me. Straightening his back with a gesture of unspoken weariness and glancing down at his hands, he confided that with all his success, all his fame, he still had one ambition that would stay with him all his days. "I want to be a good craftsman," he said.

I want to be a good craftsman. His words, engraved with the stamp

11

of ultimate truth, came back to me with a strangely compelling new force when I was invited to make an informal tour of the Spode-Copeland Works. These have been in existence on the same site at Stoke-on-Trent ever since that time, a century and a half ago now, when Josiah Spode and William Copeland first united forces. It has been well said that for beauty of design combined with lasting usefulness, the craftsmen of the eighteenth century set standards which remain unchallenged to this day. However, the name of Spode lives on magnificently in the china that, on my last visit to the United States, I saw displayed in the front window of a Fifth Avenue Store, labelled MADE IN BRITAIN. Not surprisingly I still recall the instinctive sense of pride that label gave me. While as for the other half of the partnership, the name of Copeland is very much alive today in the persons of 'Mr. Gresham', who might have stepped straight out of the pages of an Arnold Bennett novel, and his son, 'Mr. Robert', both affectionately regarded and respected as fellow-craftsmen, I was to discover, by every member of their thousand and more 'family'.

Of course, it is fashionable in some quarters to condemn out of hand all products of free enterprise. However, it has been my own experience in the course of many excursions to find that family businesses, especially when they possess a tradition stretching back across the centuries, are for the most part extremely well-run, with personal feeling and impersonal machinery nicely balanced, and the minimum of shoddy, careless work. Certainly this was my impression during my recent visit to the Potteries, that island of six towns in the heart of Staffordshire, which is a world unto itself, and which seems hardly to have altered, either as regards its physical contours, its kilns and its misty smoky climate, or its wary appraisal of outsiders, since the days when Arnold Bennett was a boy, living in the little pawnshop in Hope Street, Hanley, and being taken on Sundays to the Methodist Chapel on Swan Bank, Burslem.

For Mr. Sydney Smith, the personnel manager of Spode-Copeland, who can remember Queen Mary's visit in 1913, and how a lady from London came down specially the week before to teach the lasses how to curtsy in the yard, time has clearly stood still, too. Upright, alert, he bustled on ahead, and whenever we approached one of his contemporaries, who had started as an apprentice at the same time as himself and was now to a stranger's eyes clearly well inside the sixties, he invariably greeted him thus: "Now here is one of the boys I want you to meet."

The effect was most disarming. Usually after a couple of hours in any works I begin to flag and my feet grow weary and I long for lunch. But, instead, on this occasion, I felt more and more stimulated as the morning passed and my guide conscientiously—no that is not the right word—lovingly displayed for me the succession of processes by which the raw Cornish clay, after first being left for many months to weather on open ground and then magnetized to have all impurities drained from it, later has stone, water and flint added, if destined to be earthenware, and bone for such products as the precious 'Maritime Rose' china.

I was wondering whether I could explain that I was really more interested in people than in processes when we came upon a cup jollier at her bench who, for the last twelve years, had been making a series of cups from the plastic clay to insert inside the mould. It was my first exchange of conversation with a woman since my tour had started but Polly Leyland put me at my ease at once. Later I was to realize that I had never visited a factory where the men and women work so harmoniously and unselfconsciously side by side with mutual respect for each other's accomplishments. The fact is, just as that skill has been handed down through generations from father to son, so equally it has been passed on from mother to daughter: indeed, it is far more usual, in the china industry, for a young bride to go on working after her return from her honeymoon, than to give up her career, and her financial independence, on her wedding day. The seven years' apprenticeship which they have served, like the men, is far too precious to throw away.

"All the same, don't you feel very tired sometimes, in the evenings?" I asked this pleasant-faced woman in the very clean white overall and with the paste diamond ear-rings piercing her ears. "After all, you have to stand at your bench all day, and then go home and prepare the supper for your husband and get your housework done."

"Oh, I do sit down when we turn on the television. And then I have a nice sleep."

I was still smiling at the idea of television as the latest soporific, the new cure for insomnia, when I found myself standing beside a young potter who was most busily intent 'throwing' plates. In his case, the only one of five brothers to be apprenticed to the China

trade, Eric Beard assured me that he would choose the same road
if he had his time over again. And I could understand the conviction
in his voice as I watched the dumb eloquence of his hands. They
were so magically certain.

First he took a wire, like a grocer's assistant dealing with cheese,
and cut through a chunk of the block of moist clay at his side. Then
came the first act of the magician. Without weighing them he broke
up his slab into the equivalent of half a dozen mud pies, and each of
these balls was the exact amount needed to make the rough cast of a
plate.

"How do you know? How can you be sure?" I demanded.

The potter shrugged his shoulders, as with his right hand, he
picked up one of the balls and placed it on the spreader block. The
next instant, having touched a spring with his knee, the spreader
came down and automatically squeezed out the clay into the exact
thickness or rather, thinness, required for a plate. A moment later,
up went the spreader again and the human hand once more assumed
control. This time the left hand. Again and again I watched him
pick up the embryo plate—flabby, wet, uncannily alive—and fling
it down on one of the moulds. It had to fit like a glove, with
no bubbles of air underneath, or else the fashioning would be
a failure.

But the boy with the fair, curly hair never failed once. Yet
when he urged me to try myself, and handed over his apron, I need
hardly confess what a hopeless mess I made of everything, including
my clothes. "I suppose that's what being an expert at one's job really
means," I suggested ruefully. "To make it look as though anyone
could do it."

"Maybe," he agreed, adding a comment that was to echo in my
mind for the rest of the morning while I followed the steps by which
similar plates were receiving a first baking of seventy-six hours in a
biscuit oven and then were having transfers of their final patterns,
fastened round their edges, rolled off from a copper engraving. "I find
I learn something fresh every week," the potter had said.

Then I thought again of the surgeon's hands, of all true experts
in all trades, as with a growing sense of wonder, I gazed down over
the shoulders of a bevy of young ladies, who under the skilled and
critical eye of the forewoman, Miss Finney, were transforming the
transfers into their final floral patterns, painting each plate separately,

with delicate, intent precision. But why that darkish grey for the petals of a rose?

Whereupon it was explained to me that after this Ruskin plate had passed through the final processes of glazing and firing, its rose pattern would emerge a perfect, summer-like pink.

"Would you rather work here, or at X?" I asked one of the girls mentioning the name of another china works in the district, with a celebrated name. At once a vehement chorus of protest filled that quiet, light room. "Oh, we'd never want to work there. Why, it's all mass production now."

Her answer was a surprise but a pleasant one, and it was clearly a spontaneous one, and not cooked up in advance for the stranger's visit, any more than the catechism I was put through in my turn, as to how the records for the B.B.C's most obstinate success *Housewives' Choice* were chosen every morning. We want more Guy Mitchell, they cried, as though I had the power to give them what they wanted. I did not like to admit that I still trembled like a new boy every time I entered Broadcasting House. Better to switch the conversation before I was pinned down into any damning admission by the extremely pretty girl whose painting bench I had reached.

Miss Shingler, although only nineteen, had the sophisticated appearance of a young student in a fashion house. She wore an extremely elegant black grosgrain skirt, a white *broderie anglaise* blouse, while a band round her throat combined both colours. She would have stood out in any company, and I could not help asking her how she managed.

"Well, I average about five pounds a week wages," she told me, "and I hand it all over to my mother, and she buys my clothes. But I made my skirt, as a matter of fact, from a pattern."

Every Saturday evening Miss Shingler sets off in a special bus to Warrington, where she is one of the very carefully scrutinized hand-picked hostesses for the American servicemen, in their camp. It is a world, an adventure, apart. They can only mingle with their hosts, inside the dance hall. They must be content with soft drinks, and saying goodbye at a quarter to eleven when the same bus will bring all the girls home again. In their handbags they will carry, not the snapshots of their favourite partners, but a picture of themselves, with their official dossiers attached. Were they seeking to pass behind the Iron Curtain, they would not need a more meticulously documented passport.

A strange phenomenon of these uneasy times, when our island is invaded by foreign troops to a degree that never happened during the emergency of actual war. The infiltration looks like being a permanent one, though only occasionally are most of us brought face to face with the signposts of its urgent, vast and highly organized ramifications.

"I am sure the dances are great fun," I said, "but. . . ." I was recalling suddenly the faces of the G.I. brides waiting in a queue to shake my hand at the end of my lecture in Portland, Oregon. The more I reminded them of all that they had gained in their brand-new country, the more tearfully emphatic did they become in regard to all that they missed, all that they now remembered about their old homes and the land of their birth.

To lose your heart on a Saturday night in Warrington, and end up perhaps, in the wilds of Nebraska? I hoped it would not be so. Still, it was none of my business, and I retreated quickly into the next room where I found myself instantly capitulating to the charms of a young spinster of eighty summers. She sat there in an attractive, flowered smock, her neatly parted grey hair silhouetted against a frieze of Spode plates that she has faithfully been painting now for over forty years. She glanced up at me, smiling, and I thought: what a serene, what a happy face.

Cordie, as all her workmates affectionately call Miss Mary Caldwell, recently made her sixth pilgrimage to Lourdes, and I do not doubt that it is to the unfading reassurance of her faith that she attributes her splendidly youthful air. However, she did admit to being a little deaf now, though her hearing only really fails her at any suggestion that it is time for her to retire. Why had someone as delicately fashioned as her own beautiful china plates never found a husband for herself? That is the question which men in their vanity always ask. The answer I received was both more honest and more flattering than usual.

"Don't think because I have never married that I am a man-hater," Cordie exclaimed. "I think *some* men make very attractive companions."

As I went on my way, moving from the earthenware side of the works to the china, being introduced to one section after another,

"The Splendid Journeywomen"

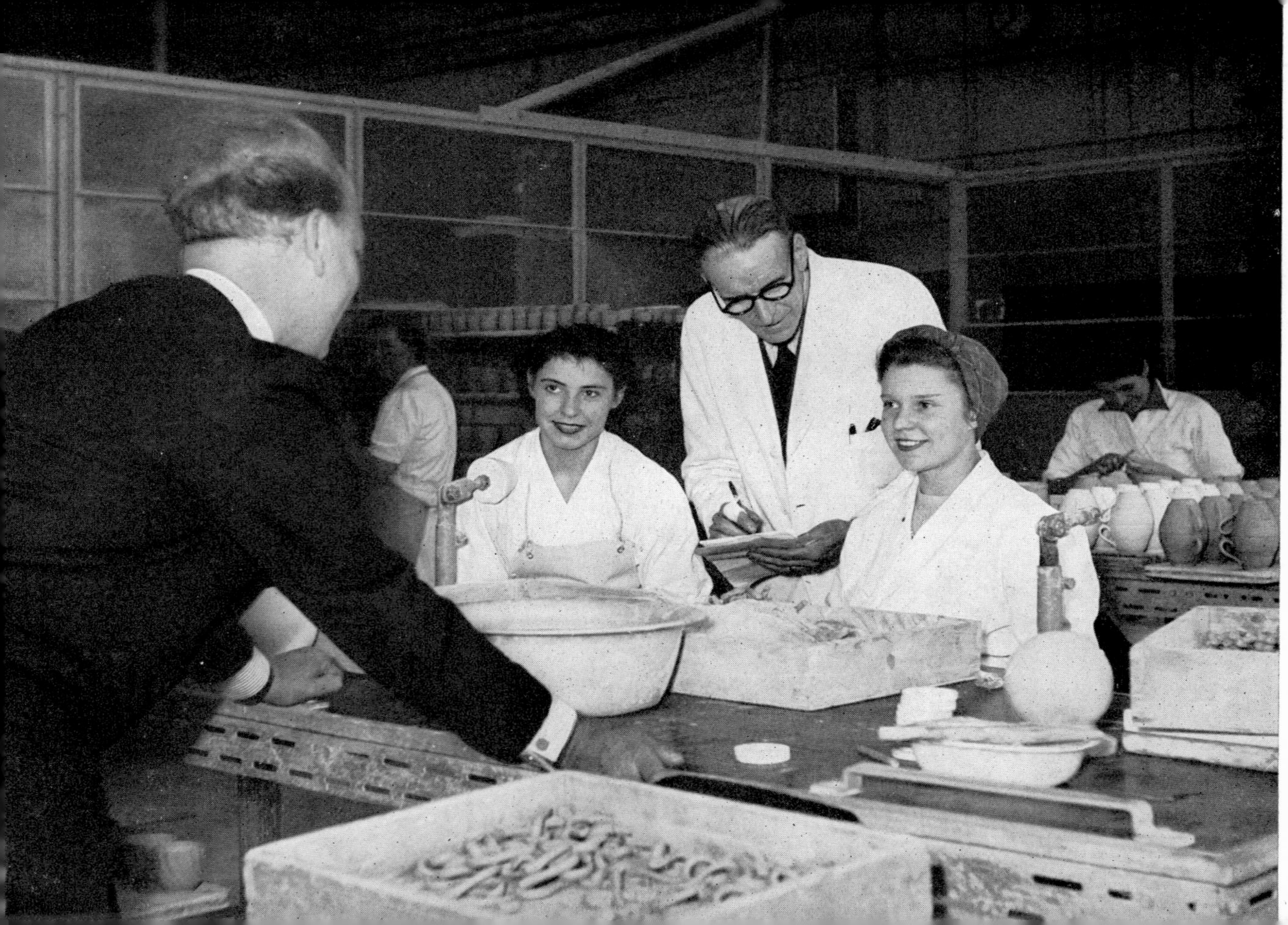

"Mr. Sydney Smith was my guide"

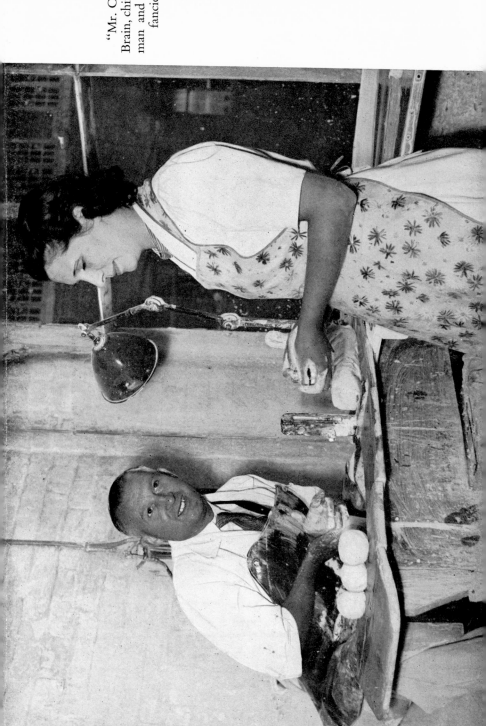

"Mr. Charles Brain, china fore-man and pigeon fancier"

The Brough family's teapot

Miss Shingler's plates

and each a completely civilized entity on its own, like the men in white caps, such as chefs wear, who dip the finished products into troughs of a liquid milky substance which is the final glaze, I found myself wondering how many of her male working comrades in other departments Cordie had ever met. And what her reactions would have been to the bundle of old silk stockings, pressed tight and flat, that Mr. Bill Clay showed me he carried under his cap to help support the weight of the packed plates, ready for the oven, in the 'sagger houses': or the strange and intricate motions that the strong arms of Mr. George Harrison made over the china glazing trough which would surely have defeated the 'What's My Line?' team: or the uninhibited welcoming smile of Mr. Charles Brian, china foreman and pigeon fancier, who, as he kneaded the clay crouching over the potter's wheel, with his legs wide apart, exuding strength and triumphant effort, while his handmaiden, Mrs. Dorothy Rudge hovered at his side, reminded me irresistibly of a rajah, wearing other fancy dress than his own.

Yes, he had the air of an omnipotent ruler, welcoming a visitor from far across the sea to his own sweet kingdom. Why did he need an assistant simply to hand him the balls of clay? Could he not reach out for them himself? He laughed at the suggestion, and his laughter echoed through the narrow shed like the glee of a giant. Why, the management had tried that for a time, and at once the output had sagged. So now dutifully a handmaiden once again fed the two potters' wheels presided over by Mr. Brian and his brother who worked a few yards away. Would the output have leapt again had they been served by a half-fledged youth? Did it in some mysterious manner subconsciously feed their male ego to know that while they sat there on their thrones a woman stood at their side to do their bidding?

I had no chance to ask for it was Charlie Brian who did all the talking and what good rich meaty talk it was. All about his eighty pigeons, mostly of the Harrison breed, and all the hundreds of pounds they had won for him in prize money, as one time champion of North Staffordshire: and how he would send them off racing to the four corners of Europe, but had not the slightest inclination or curiosity to follow in their tracks himself. The island kingdom of the Potteries was good enough for him: here was his space.

As for the tricks and the technique of being such an expert thrower that he had risen to be foreman of his whole department, his shining

B

teeth shut tight, his all-embracing smile momentarily vanished when
I asked whether a good craftsman could not be interchangeable
between the earthenware and the china side of the business. Oh
yes I had learnt by now that china, real china was translucent, and
when you pinged a plate, should make a sound like a church bell,
but. . . .

"It's all a question of the eyes," Mr. Brian interrupted the amateur
firmly. "Here on our side we see all sorts of minute flaws and stop
them before it is too late which the ordinary earthenware potter
would let by. Anyway, he'd expect them to come out in the wash,
and they probably would with him because of the coarser texture, but
not with us. . . ."

Again the china clay was so much more crumbling, so much
less malleable that it was a question of the hands, too. Indeed, there
were half a dozen important differences and the flights of the pigeons
were forgotten in the passion with which Mr. Brian expressed his
pride in his craft: indeed, I did not encounter such enthusiastic warmth
again until I came upon Mr. Jim Evans at the sweltering entrance to
his bottle-neck ovens that he has stacked week in and week out,
year after year, in a lifetime of service.

Three days of firing and three days for cooling off, the whole
process taking a week, and inside those narrow catacombs, soon to
be replaced by gas ovens, and where no handmaiden has ever trod,
what an agony of sweat. One did not have to have one's own imagination set fire to, to be conscious of that. Turning to my companion
at that moment, young Mr. Bob Copeland, the old fireman remarked
in the dry tones in which you make a statement of fact. "You know,
he worked as my odd man, feeding the fires for a week, and I could
not have had a better apprentice." How good it was to hear such
praise passing between master and man, both servants of a tradition
which had already, I reminded myself, outlasted the centuries.

As it happens, the firemen, despite all their outward solidity,
have the reputation of being the most temperamental men in the
trade, far more temperamental, strangely enough, than the artists
who create the new designs, or the gilders, who are the aristocrats
of the china industry, for as the winds change, so does the heat of
their fires raise or die down and thus, over-conscious that thousands
of pounds worth of goods lie in their sole charge, they feel the strain
far more than the excessive heat to which usage has accustomed them.

As for the golden embroidering of the china sets, I had been fascinated to see the ingredients in jars like pale brown bath crystals taken out of the safe in 'Mr. Gresham's' private office. Over two hundred pounds worth of pure gold dust, amalgamated with mercury and mixed with oil, is used every fortnight and they do not count the cost since behind the plate-glass windows of the show-room close by are examples of the craftsman's skill whose gilding is as fresh and clear as on the day of their creation in the reign of Josiah Spode the First.

Do their successors today ever seek to refresh their spirit by paying a visit to the Spode-Copeland Art Gallery, on their way home, in the evening? Perhaps their eyes are too tired by then to wish to gaze at anything, after the concentrated, patient hours they have spent, the devoted slaves of their pencil brush, moving with such infinite delicacy over the pattern which they are adorning.

No wonder the aristocrats work with their arm supported on a rest, I thought, as a climax to my tour, I was shown the entrance to the Aladdin's Cave where Mr. Tom Brough, the king of the gilders, was putting the finishing touches to his last plate of the day. A moment later, he was taking off his working glasses and putting on his homeward bound ones.

"I am sorry I have reached you so late. But there was so much to see, and I have been chatting to your sisters in the room below."

"Ah, the ladies are great talkers, aren't they?" he said, and his dry little chuckle exactly matched his neat, sparse figure. Even under the implacably bright lamp on his desk, he looked to be a still youngish man, so that I was astonished when Mr. Brough told me that he was sixty-three, having started as a lad of thirteen, fifty years ago.

"My two sisters and I have worked here all our lives as gilders, and our father, and our grandfather before us, here in this same works. Of course, I am past my prime now," he added, but I knew that his employers felt very differently, and what an example both he and his sisters set to the young apprentices who had just left school. And when he suggested that I should visit the Brough home and have tea with his family—"perhaps tomorrow would be best, to give my wife a little warning"—it was like a royal command, or one of those invitations which arrive impressively embossed in gold.

But though I went most eagerly to learn more about the skilled art of gilding china what I now recall most vividly about the party was Mrs. Brough's dark brown tabby of a teapot. That and something else, which happened at the end, when I was saying goodbye. But by that time we were all friends, not only my host, and his two sisters, Mrs. Edwards and Mrs. Wycherley, the one so pleasantly plump and fair, the other as slight and spare as her brother, but also Mr. and Mrs. Brough's three strapping sons, their two attractive daughters-in-law, and their two small grand-daughters.

Altogether it was quite a mustering of the clan in the front parlour of that semi-detached, snug house in the High Street at Fenton and, of course, that is where the huge brown teapot came in. It served as a kind of ice-breaker, when Mrs. Brough, who was clearly a most capable manager, gave a swift look of satisfied appraisal at her table loaded with home-made goodies and adorned with her best Spode tea service, and exclaimed to her husband. "It's all right, Tom. I haven't smashed the teapot which goes with your precious service. But you can see for yourself it would be far too small for today's party. So I hope you won't mind the family teapot," she added, pouring out the first cup for her guest.

Mind! I wanted to put my hands round it because it was so utterly, so solidly British, the counterpart of the outsize in teapots that you will find duplicated in thousands of kitchens all over the country, for use at all hours of the day and night. Always on the hob, always there, at moments of celebration and equally as a cure for moods of depression. The universal standby. And no one caring whether it is labelled, earthenware or china, or 'not for export', so long as what comes out of the spout is hot and strong.

However, to my host, though he kept silent, it was clear that there was a very fine distinction indeed. I watched the way that he touched with affectionate tenderness the cup out of which he drank and which he had decorated himself, and gazed with open pride of possession at what he called his 'heirloom' placed, under a glass dome, on the sideboard. It had been handed down, he explained, by his grandfather, himself a china printer in his day, who had helped to fashion the mugs which were struck to commemorate the end of the Boer War.

How many of them are left? Sometimes they find their way to the old antique shops in the Lanes at Brighton, or in the King's Road, Chelsea. But not this one which as a great privilege I was now allowed to hold. Was it not a symbol as well as an heirloom, this splendid example of the potter's craft, adorned by hand? With the image of

Queen Victoria painted on the outside, and inside the lip, all the names of her generals who had taken part in the campaign, together with such exemplary, confident slogans, enscribed as:

UNITY IS STRENGTH. EQUAL RIGHTS FOR ALL.
BRITANNIA, TOWER OF JUSTICE.

Assuredly, that bygone age, when everything seemed so utterly settled and secure and the sun never set upon the British Empire, has vanished for ever. Yet as I took another ham sandwich and started on my second cup of tea, the uneasy doubts that too often pluck at one's sleeve, concerning the prospects of a final and lasting peace in the civilized world, momentarily vanished. For there was something so reassuring in the unsung, unspectacular record of this brother and two sisters who between them had already knotched up well over a hundred years of far more than lip service to a tradition. As equally there was about their inarticulate feelings, not so much of satisfaction in their own skill, as of hatred for anything slipshod or slovenly.

Were a post-war generation of apprentices as eager and patient and truly humble as they had been? At once, a little to my surprise, the youngest of the trio, Mrs. Edwards, stood up fiercely for her own apprentice, a tall, handsome dark girl, Audrey Mould, whom I had met that afternoon, and who had been in her charge now for four years. "Audrey is a good girl and will make a splendid journeywoman," she exclaimed.

No one could tell me the precise origin of that title that is given after seven years' apprenticeship, but what an epitaph it would make —"A splendid journeywoman"—I thought, as I sat there between the two sisters, and the smaller one, who seemed only to peck at her food, confided in me that when the moment came for her at last finally to retire, it would make her so very happy if the firm gave a piece of the china she had spent so many hours holding preciously in her hands. She was a widow now, Mrs. Wycherley explained, and only worked part-time. But all those years she had had two jobs, so no wonder she seemed a little frail, and squeezed dry, though she had no complaints herself and her contented spirit shone forth like a lamp.

But what about their husbands? Hadn't they minded not being the sole provider? Hadn't that rankled and pricked their masculine self-esteem? I turned now to the other, younger sister, where the

problem was still a living one. "What do you do with your weekly
pay packet?" I asked. "Does it remain all yours, or does your husband
expect you to share it in the same way that he presumably shares his?"

"I should like to see him try," retorted Mrs. Edwards. Whereupon
there was universal laughter round the tea table, though it is not
really a laughing problem, this vexed and prickly question of the
age as to whether a woman's place, after marriage, is in the home.
And although in the china industry a very large proportion of the
women workers are married, I did come across one husband who dis-
agreed most emphatically with the idea of wives having two careers,
even if it did entail no television mast at home. Or other sacrifices
more stringent than that.

A very clean-cut young man he was, with reddish hair and an
engaging grin, whose business it was to place the 'saggers' of china
into the fire for their final roasting. His name was Walter Lambert
and they call him in the trade, a 'cod placer'. Working on shifts,
sometimes getting home at two o'clock in the afternoon, sometimes
at six in the morning, he was most emphatic that his wife should be
there always to greet him and look after his needs, and that no other
recipe for marriage could hope to succeed in the long run.

Certainly he himself gave the impression that he was a very happily
married man. Nevertheless, it is an extremely complex debating
subject at a time when the barometer of the cost of living has risen
so dangerously high that you have the anomaly of many wives
feeling that they must go back to work in order to give their young
children the same comforts as they themselves possessed at their age.
Has any husband the right to resent this argument?

Round our committee table of journeymen and women that
afternoon we all agreed that it must remain always a question of
individual choice. And if it was a hotly argued question in other
parts of the country, and one that had come to stay, it was scarcely
so in the Potteries where wives had always looked upon it as their
right to return to work and practise their skill again as soon as the
honeymoon was over. Nevertheless, all the time I had the feeling that
I was the guest of a particularly liberal and enlightened family especially when near the end of our party, I discovered that Mrs. Brough's
daughter-in-law, the one whose child had been sitting on her granny's
knee throughout tea, was a German girl, now happily settled in
what, so brief a time ago, had been an alien and enemy country.

Yet already she talked and looked like one of the Queen's country-women.

Potter's clay and human clay . . . how equally malleable they both can be, I thought, as I watched my new friends draw the other foreigner protectively within their family circle. "Have a cup of tea, my dear," Mrs. Brough said, reaching once more for her faithful, all-forgiving teapot.

TWO

THE MOTHER

THE law-encrusted voices, deliberately drained of all emotion, battled to and fro in the court, arguing legal points beyond a layman's head, until at last the leading counsel for the prosecution exclaimed: "Where does all this end?"

Then the judge as he lent forward pursing his lips, his face the colour of a wax-work model, seemed to sigh in agreement, and I found myself echoing that sigh. For although this was the Old Bailey, where the atmosphere alternates between the implacable coldness of a mausoleum and the dramatic intensity of a theatre, and although close beside me in the dock, another human being was fighting for his life, I did not feel somehow that here, too, was the heart of the matter.

The outward truth, the surface facts, of course, were clear enough. Two girls in their teens, Barbara Songhurst, and her friend, Christine Reed, both bubbling over with a zest for life, were cycling late at night along the river bank, near Teddington Lock, after having spent the afternoon and evening harmlessly larking with some youths who had set up a weekend camp. But the youngsters never reached the safety of their homes, because on the way, in the darkness of that early summer evening, they were set upon by a sexual maniac, raped and murdered and their bodies thrown into the water.

At once the tragic happenings of that Sunday evening in May became classified in the public consciousness as The Tow Path Murders, a tidy newspaper headline to take its place, in the crime records of the country, with the other sensational mysteries, finally resolved, like the Crippen case, and the Christie case, and the case of the murderer who cast the bodies of his victims into an acid bath.

On this occasion, for weeks after the discovery of Barbara Songhurst's body in the water, the police were completely baffled. They visited the café at Twickenham where the two girls had been seen in conversation with two strangers that weekend, they interviewed hundreds of possible suspects, they followed up every clue however improbable, they dragged the river waters, but their search produced little positive results. For they only found one of the bicycles and they never found the knife that had so savagely pierced the chest and lungs of the sixteen-year-old girl who, like a multitude of other teenagers, had always been so confident that she could take care of herself.

Finally, more by good luck than by good judgment, the police took into custody and had brought to trial a not unhandsome, heavily-built labourer of twenty-two, Alfred Whiteway, who had been identified as the assailant in another similar assault, this time upon a schoolgirl of fifteen, who was fortunate to escape with her life, when she was walking alone across Oxshott Common.

In the end, as it turned out, after another of those interminable wrangles between the prosecution and the defence counsels, with the judge acting as referee, had emptied the court, her evidence was not permitted to be given. However, it did not matter, for by now the police had collected sufficient circumstantial links to forge a chain for the defendant's neck, and not all the brilliant forensic skill of his counsel, an ex-guards officer, with the eloquence of a young Norman Birkett, could break asunder that chain, or rouse any feeling of emotion for the man in the dock. No pity at all.

No pity at all. Not for the first time, in these cases, one felt: let it end swiftly and let justice be done, and let the enemy of society make his peace as best he can with his God. On the other hand, all one's sympathies were engaged, one's imagination haunted by the fate not of the murderer who in due course has to hang by the neck until he is dead, but of the family left behind, especially the mother and father of the murdered girl, who must live on with their grief, and pray that time may deaden and blur the question marks in their mind.

If they had not permitted their daughter to go off on her own that sunny May afternoon, if they had made it an imperative command that she must always be indoors by half past ten at night. If, if. . . .

Was not there the heart of the matter? Now the question marks were stabbing at my own thoughts and when the court adjourned that day for lunch, after still another of those obscure lawyer's arguments based on dead judgements, on a sudden impulse, I took my car and drove away down to Richmond, following my memory over the bridge, for here I had spent part of my early childhood.

Thus there was little difficulty for me to find the tow-path at Teddington, where so often I had cycled myself, or the camping ground where the three youths had pitched their tents, and the two friends, Christine and Barbara, had spent their last carefree Sunday, alive.

It was raining now and the early summer promise was hard to conjure, though on the opposite bank white-painted boats still lay gracefully at anchor against the shore with private lawns stretching down to the water and a romantic façade of river| houses, as a background. Like a summer setting for an Edwardian musical comedy, I thought, and even that afternoon with the rain dripping off the trees and the leaves lying in melancholy heaps, there was still an untouched, timeless peace about the scene.

Certainly it did not look like a spot where murder, most foul and brutal, had been perpetrated on two who were still in the first freshness of their youth's joy. Thus the sense of unreality stayed with me, the feeling that I must have dreamed all the horrible details of the case in some monstrous nightmare, until I started to drive back, away from the river. Until I came to Princes Road.

Here at the end there was a row of neat and unpretentious council houses, all with freshly painted blue doors. Twenty houses in a row. Just like any other suburban road outside any other English town. While in the front garden a man was standing off-guard in his shirt sleeves. Short and slow-moving, with fine shoulders and an army belt round his waist. You could picture him on an early summer evening, talking to his neighbour over the fence, comparing the promise of their roses.

I was the neighbour today but we did not talk about flowers. Instead, we talked about his daughter, Barbara, whose constant smile and gay, confident voice, singing about the house had meant more to her parents than all the roses in the world. "At the chemist's shop where she worked, people used to go in, just to see her smile. They have told me so since," her mother said proudly, as she invited me indoors, to have a cup of tea in their homely kitchen, full of children, frisking round the fire, like puppies.

There were Edwin and John and Pamela, just home from school, big and sturdy for their ages, and eager to spread some paste upon the bread and margarine for their tea. And then there was the baby, Nina, who was only five years old, and had great solemn eyes which never left me while she played with Micky, Barbara's dog, and clutched to her heart the doll that Barbara had helped to save up for, the previous Christmas.

The children did not seem in the least shy of the sudden intruder in their midst and then I realized it was because ever since it happened their home had been invaded, night and day. First the police officers and then the newspaper men. Finally the long procession of the sympathetic and the curious. So what was one more new face among so many?

For my own part I was shy of discussing the details of their tragedy in front of Nina, until her mother said: "Oh Nina understands everything. Why, that Monday evening when I came back from identifying the body in the mortuary, she was sitting up for me, and she said: "Mum, don't worry, don't cry. Barbara is one of the stars now in Heaven." And every night before she goes to sleep, I have to lift her up to see the stars through the window, and she says, trying to comfort me. 'Look, there's Barbara, Mum.' "

Nina understands everything. I was beginning to understand, too, watching and listening, while the father and the mother struggled once again to put together, like the pieces of an unsolved puzzle, the sequence of events during that last weekend in their favourite daughter's life.

"For you know how it is," the mother confided, "I have had nine children, five girls and four boys, and they were all strong and healthy, and good boys and girls, too. But the one who goes, that is the one you seem to remember most."

Yes, I thought, and now until the end of their lives they would always remember how Barbara had come home that Sunday morning to change into slacks, telling her parents that she was off cycling with her friend, Christine, and later, in the afternoon, to the pictures. For just like other girls of her age, she loved the pictures and she loved dancing. Indeed, on the Saturday night, she had been to a dance, and because it had ended late, she had had permission to stay the night at Christine's home.

Usually, there was a tacit understanding that she must be in by eleven. However, when eleven o'clock came that Sunday night, followed by midnight, her parents did not worry unduly, imagining that she was again with Christine, two years her senior, and so went to bed themselves.

"I was always telling her, wasn't I, Mother, that she mustn't come in at all hours of the night," the father exclaimed. "But she used to smile back at me, and she had such a confident, open smile, and say: 'Don't you worry about me, Dad, I can look after myself. I promise you I can.' "

Then there was silence in that small, tidy room. A great wind, like the wind of eternity, beat at the window-panes, and then sank to a whisper. Even the younger of the children were still for a second, while the parents exchanged a long look across the family hearth. The father sitting down, because of the injury to his back that keeps him chained to the house and strip of garden, and unable to work, though he is rightly proud of his thirteen years service in the regular army, as well as his time fulfilling the duties of an air-raid warden in the war: the mother standing up, refusing to sit, even when I suggested it, as though her paper-thin body in its black coat and dress was stretched to breaking-point, so that only the courage which all mothers possess kept her sane, quietly getting through each day as best she could, feeding and clothing the living.

The living . . . when that Monday, the start of a new day, drew on to the afternoon and still no sign of her daughter, still no news from Christine's parents, with whom she had been in constant touch, a deadly fear began to press down upon the mother's heart, driving her at five o'clock to the local police-station.

It was after ten when she returned with a story like to the story that a Greek messenger in a play by Aeschylus might have to tell, with details so infinitely more terrible than anything the father could even have begun to imagine, as he sat in the kitchen waiting, and the last of the daylight drained from the sky.

"I talk about it, because it's better than not talking, than keeping it bottled up," the mother burst forth, "and if it serves as a warning to other mothers . . . though how any mother can be expected to watch her every child every moment of the day and night. . . ."

For a moment I thought that she was going to break down at last. The fine, grey eyes in her pale face clouded over but her voice was dry of tears as she went on to tell me how in the mortuary they showed her the great knife wound through her daughter's chest. As for the victim's face, battered in that frenzied mingling of desire and death, and later, immersed in the waters of the river. . . . "It was as though a woodpecker had been at it," she said.

It was then that the father rose with difficulty from his chair and went slowly from the room, returning with pictures to comfort his wife. First, the picture of their daughter, Rosie, taken on her wedding day a month before, Rosie who used to share a bed with Barbara and who looked, I thought, so very like a younger edition of her mother before life began to squeeze her dry.

Then there was also the picture of their twenty-year-old son, Arthur, handsome in his khaki, smiling cheerfully into the sun, with one eye, half-closed, as though in an unconscious wink that suggested that wearing a uniform had its compensations and its rewards. And finally the picture, enlarged from a snapshot, and later tinted, of Barbara herself in a gay, striped jumper and the pair of slacks that she was wearing the last time that they had seen her alive.

Looking at it reminded the mother suddenly of her ordeal in the witness-box at the Old Bailey. "I did not feel so bad," she whispered. "till they showed me the clothes that she had been wearing and asked me to identify them. Then it all came back in a great wave and I couldn't trust my voice." She paused and then continued in the same quiet monotone. "The police officers asked me what I wanted done with the exhibits afterwards, and I told them I didn't want to see any of them ever again. Except the trinkets that she was wearing. I would like to keep those. . . ."

On the table the father had brought and placed a white card-board box, which the mother opened now, and spread the contents before me. A shining, startlingly white rope of pearls, with two bracelets, and even ear-rings to match. Her brother Arthur, the one in the army, now stationed overseas in Germany, had bought them for his sister, out of his pay, to be a surprise for her, on his next leave.

But when he came home it was on special leave, for her funeral. It had become too late to give her the pearls, and they would stay now always in that box, the most macabre of family heirlooms.

"Whenever Arthur was at home," the father said, "he used to follow Babs around. He appointed himself her bodyguard. It was almost as though he had a premonition. She would get quite annoyed with him at times. But I used to hear him say to her, 'You never know what can happen to a nice-looking kid like you. . . .'"

Again there was silence between us until the mother, looking past me at the garden wreathed now in the autumn twilight, where in the spring Barbara had always been eager to do her share of work, said something in quite a different voice, a voice of happiness, a voice of pride. "The police told me right from the start that I was to stop worrying about one thing. Barbara was a *good* girl. The doctors could prove it for me."

Later I came to understand that there was something else which made her very proud, too, something utterly different, but, in another way, of equal importance if life was to continue in that house which is one of twenty in a row. And life does have to go on, I reminded myself, looking down at the book which the mother was holding out to me—the rent book for No. 75 Princes Road, Teddington.

"Look," she said, "it's paid right up to this week. What's more, we've never been a week behind all the eight years we've lived here. Not that it's been easy, mind you, with my husband not working now, because of his back, and Rosie married, so her money doesn't come in any more, nor the pound that Barbara used to give me every Friday night.

"I get £1 17s. 7d. relief each week, but £1 4s. 7d. of that goes for the rent and the rest in groceries. Still we manage it, don't we?" Now for the first time since I had been invited inside her home and her confidence she struggled to manage a little smile as though the very thought of giving way to self-pity was utterly abhorrent to her nature. "From his days in the army my husband is very good at making soup out of bits." And now her smile was specially for him. "So we have lots of soup. All the same," she added briskly, "I tell Nina she mustn't expect another doll like that, this Christmas, though if they all get a good meal on The Day, that will be something, won't it?"

At that moment the mother sounded like the head of any family, planning and making-do, as though no greater problem, no final loss had shattered their deep and happy sense of security. But it had and there was one more question which I still must ask if my portrait was to be complete. What were her feelings towards the maniac who had destroyed her daughter's life and future?

"I have no feelings left now," she said quietly. "When they told me first who they suspected, I just could not believe it. You see, we used to live only four doors away in the same road. Barbara was little Nina's age then and he would be twelve. We were good neighbours, and his mother and I would run down to each other's houses and borrow anything like tea or sugar, if we were short at the end of the week. If I saw her now. . . ." She paused, looking down at the smallest child, holding her black skirt. "If she came towards me down the street, I should not turn away. . . ."

Then truly there seemed nothing more to say, except that at the door, when they were bidding me goodbye and thanking me for coming, the father who had been working as a dustman before his back let him down, added, almost apologetically. "I am afraid we are not a very posh family."

'No,' I thought, holding the mother's hand, 'just any English family. It might have happened to anyone.' And the refrain, the bitter and implacable refrain kept on beating a tattoo in my mind, all the way back to my own home, in another street of twenty houses in a row.

THREE

'OUR PAT'

ONE has a strange feeling arriving at the House of Commons on a Friday afternoon, at half past four, and finding none of the usual queues, that *mélange* of constituents, excited schoolchildren, foreign visitors and cranks that gather from all corners of the globe outside St. Stephen's Entrance. It is like returning by accident to college on the first day of a vacation. In surprised silence my footsteps echoed up the grey stone staircase and then past the effigies of Chatham, Walpole, Fox and the younger Pitt. I had just paused to gaze up at Falkland, in his elegant cloak, leaning on his sword, to search once again for the mark where a certain militant suffragette, herself now a figure of history, is reputed to have chained herself, when there was a violent disturbance of the ether and of my reverie. The figure of a still young woman in navy blue, with brilliant Titian hair and the aura of having just got up in the morning, freshly dressed, came hurrying along the hall, which, until that moment had been so full of the dead past, of parliamentary ghosts. In an instant, flash, bang, I was back in the living present.

She said: "I was a minute late. Most unusual for me. I am so sorry. I meant to be waiting for you at the entrance. The House rose at four. It always has by then on a Friday. So we've got the place to ourselves. It's extraordinary how quickly everyone evaporates on a Friday afternoon. How I wish my day was over, and I had a free weekend, and I could get into the car, and drive to the sea."

"You'd soon get tired of sitting on the shore, and throwing pebbles. Much more tired than you do of living in a glass house where everyone throws stones."

"I suppose I would. But it always *seems* a nice vision on Friday afternoon. What would *you* like to do? Shall I be an Official Guide? Do you realize we are standing where Parliament used to sit, in Henry Eighth's reign, and at the time of the Guy Fawke's Plot. Later, after the fire, this was rebuilt on exactly the same spot, and to the same proportions, and you notice how narrow it is. Almost like a corridor.

I am sure that made for the introduction of the Two Party system." When I looked rather puzzled, she went on, in her clarion-clear, optimistic voice. "Don't you see how it could have happened? All the Members who were friends or came from the same social group, or had a particular axe to grind, getting together with their backs against the same wall, facing each other directly across the hall. It must have made a natural breaking-up of pressure groups. And from that you'd gradually get a bigger division. Do you think I make a good guide?"

"I think you are better when you are answering hecklers, and fighting mad on a platform, with your hair like a beacon. . . ."

"I don't believe you've ever seen me at that sort of meeting."

"No, but I can imagine it. After all, I have seen you canvassing, in your own division, at election time."

"Oh, yes, the day you came down to Chislehurst, at the last election, which I never thought I could possibly win, let alone become the youngest woman ever to be chosen to be a member of the Government. You know, I was just leaving, on a Friday afternoon like this, for a weekend's rest in the country, after the election was over, when my telephone rang, and I was told I was wanted by the P.M. at No. 10. Oh dear, I thought, I am going to be on the mat, for my election broadcast."

"But your election broadcast was an enormous success."

"In some quarters it was, in some it wasn't. After I had written it, the Central Office people tried to get me to cut out every reference to our Leader. But I refused, and took the script downstairs to Lord Woolton. He read it, and bless his heart, passed it, word for word as it stood. But all the same I decided, perhaps, the P.M. hadn't been pleased, but had been too kind to send for me to rebuke me while the battle was on. And then I arrived at No. 10, and it was like being in the anteroom outside the headmaster's study. Half a dozen of us waiting, and wondering what we were going to get. And then I was inside the P.M.'s room, and he was telling me that I had got the Ministry of Health. I was absolutely bowled over, but very thrilled because it would give me the chance to prove to our opponents, now in Opposition, that they are quite wrong in their assumption that Social Service is their exclusive prerogative."

Although I have always held that a writer should stand right outside politics, and for that reason had deliberately refrained, rightly

C

or wrongly, from voting in the last three elections, I could, as an unbiased onlooker, have considerable sympathy for that point of view. Indeed, I found the shyness engendered by my surroundings suddenly vanish and for the moment I became the speaker on the platform, instead of the expectant listener.

"On my last lecture tour in America," I exclaimed, "in several towns an English M.P. preceded me, speaking to the same society, usually a woman's club, and I was somewhat surprised to discover that she had assured her audiences there was a new aristocracy of babies in Britain: healthy babies *at last*. The assumption presumably being that all babies born under a Conservative Government had rickets. Which was palpably absurd and very typical, I thought, of the manœuvres of Party Politics. Facts twisted to suit their argument, every natural and inevitable step along the path of Progress purloined as the special contribution of one political section of the community. After all, if the Liberal Party were in power at this moment, and had been in power with a working majority since the war, I am quite certain that the National Health Act would equally have been placed on the Statute Book."

We had now emerged on to the Terrace and leaning against the stone balustrade had the noble façade of St. Thomas' Hospital facing us across the river, and I found myself recalling not all the other occasions when I had stood upon this spot, so evocative a symbol of our Commonwealth's heart, but the day when I had visited another hospital, St. Mary's at Paddington, to see the first child who had been saved by the use of the then miracle drug, M and B. The child had had acute meningitis. There would not have been the slightest hope for its survival, the doctors assured me, a few years earlier. It had been a most moving experience to look down over the cot's edge, at that small girl with her mass of fair curls, now able to play with her toys, so full of life again, so utterly unaware of her amazing good fortune. Unconsciously that moment had remained crystalized in my mind and I was quite surprised, in America, that the Member of Parliament hadn't gone one step further and suggested that it was her party, and not Professor Fleming who had discovered the power and properties of Penicillin.

"How I wish we could scrap the Party System altogether and have a Coalition, as we always do in the emergency of war. I would like to see the best brains of the country, irrespective of their political tinge, pooled." I had been speaking my instinctive thoughts aloud, and now I became conscious again, with a rush, who my companion was. "You know, Pat, what impressed me most about the day I watched you canvassing, were two things. First the wife, who was completely blind and possessed the cleanest house of any we visited on that new housing estate. I can see her now, in her spotless white overall, and all the washing out on the line, which she had already done herself that morning, by ten o'clock, after getting her husband off to work at Billingsgate. He was a porter there and she was one of your staunchest supporters. That combination intrigued me."

"Oh, that was Mrs. Starling. I sometimes think of her on Saturdays when I go down to the constituency and have private interviews with anyone who wants to ask my advice."

"You mean, you feel that sometimes your time is being wasted by people who don't appreciate when they are really well off. The kind of people who always expect something for nothing, in life."

"Yes. Mind you, if at the end of each Saturday, however tired I am, I can sincerely feel I have been able to help—or will be able to solve the problem—for even one family, then I know in my heart, it *is* worth while, and absolutely essential to hold these weekly private sessions. Occasionally, I feel almost like a priest, listening to the stories. I am someone to whom they can pour out their hearts, and know that their secret anxieties or grievances are safe with me. Of course, when I was first elected, and the Socialists were still in power, the problems were inevitably seventy-five per cent Housing, and it was heart-breaking to be so impotent. But these figures are dropping every week now, and I can't help being enormously proud, though it's not my personal Department. We *have* kept to our target and reached the 300,000 houses a year, which our opponents said was an electioneering lie."

As though she could sense my thoughts, she added quickly. "Stop me, if I start addressing you like a political meeting. I am always terrified of getting like that."

"To be quite truthful," I answered, "I was thinking how fresh you made the housing figures sound. Not a bit tub-thumping. As a matter of fact. . . ." and then I broke off, wondering if I could add what I wanted to do at that moment, admit how relieved and at the same time slightly surprised I was to find the Parliamentary Secretary to the Ministry of Health unchanged, uncorroded by her official status. Now if the friend with whom I was walking this early summer afternoon on what was almost holy ground had been a man, would not his entry into Parliament, let alone his impressive position in the Government have set him, markedly, on the other side of the fence? I had seen that happen so often. The moment a fellow countryman has the authority to place the letters M.P. after his name, he assumes divine rights: he starts to behave like a mortal, set apart, holding forth, in private company, in an Olympian manner on every subject under the sun, trying, even to give the impression that no Cabinet secrets are hidden from him, and that he and 'Winston' are on Christian name terms. He can become so easily, and in such a short time, an intolerable bore. How refreshing it was to discover that no signs of this metamorphosis were to be seen in the attitude of the woman at my side, who had started her living as a junior typist at the age of sixteen and had succeeded in supporting her widowed mother on the princely salary of three pounds, five shillings a week, in the last decade before the war.

"It's wonderful to see the change in the whole attitude to life of young couples, when they get away from their in-laws, or living in furnished rooms," she was saying, "and have a flat or place of their own at last. Of course, quite often, I know they have already made up their minds to vote for the other side in the next election, all the same, I can't help feeling immensely happy for their happiness. What does make me extremely angry, though, is another legacy which we have inherited from the six years our opponents were in power. They have encouraged the people to imagine that they have only got to ask for something and it will fall into their lap. Don't try to do anything for yourself, the Welfare State will provide. Just sit back and take and take and never count the cost or start to think who is going to pay for it all. Or how it is going to be paid for. We are up against that all the time in the Ministry, I wish you'd write an article about *that*, one day. The sooner, the better."

"But I never write about politics."

"I know, but this isn't politics: at least it shouldn't be. This is a national issue. How can we possibly hope to survive, if half the population of the country expect to do the minimum of work for the maximum of free gifts. Mind you, our side of the House feel just as deeply as the Opposition do about the need for increasing the Old Age Pension rates. (That's why I registered my vote most firmly against an increase in M.P.'s salaries.) But have you any idea what it would

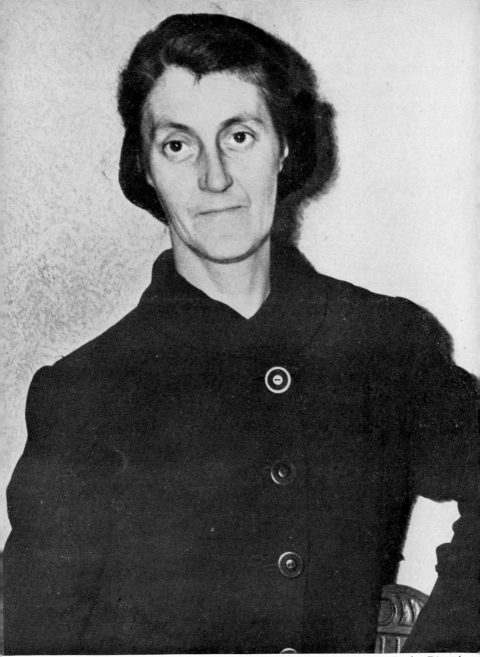

Sunday Dispatch

THE MOTHER

"The one who goes, that is the one you seem to remember most"

Dorothy Wilding

MISS P. HORNSBY-SMITH, M.P.

cost to do it properly as it should be done? That's one of the things I am going to talk about at Richmond tonight, so I won't give you the figures twice over." I was so engrossed by all that she was saying that I had been quite oblivious to the strangeness of having the whole Terrace to ourselves. No clusters of admiring visitors, no strawberries and cream: only the tubs of geraniums remained the same, giving colour, if not animation, to a setting that is so overwhelmingly English that I have often conjured it up, with a warming sense of security, when I had been unable to sleep in the insanitary heat of an American train, stifled by the odour of the green rep curtains of an upper berth.

"I shall never forget the first time I came out here, for a breath of air, after an all-night sitting. The dawn was just breaking down the river. After the stuffiness of the Chamber, the crumpled grey look of people who have been in violent argument hour after hour, to stand here, beside the balustrade and gaze at inanimate things was like a revelation, as though one had never been conscious of the beauty of Creation before. At the same time, it was brought home to me with overwhelming force, much more than when I stood up to make my maiden speech, that I really was a Member of Parliament, that it was part of my right to walk here, at any hour of the day or night. Can you understand that?"

"Yes, I can. Just to come here for half an hour as a visitor always seems to me a very special experience, one that never loses its impact. If I was an M.P. I should always slip away here to renew my confidence, to get rid of my staleness, whenever I was fed up with my colleagues, or my constituents. By the way, I never told you the other thing that struck me so much when I came down to Chislehurst. It was the way that you talked the same language to everyone we met. Whether they were your avowed supporters, probables, or votes already irretrievably lost to you. They still remained your constituents. And you treated men and women exactly alike. You were their Member of Parliament, you represented *all* their interests. You happened to be a woman, but you were doing a man's job in a man's way. You asked for no special favours because of your sex, and above all, you didn't start talking about, 'We women must stick together' as though you were in some sort of secret conspiracy against all men, whatever their political shades of opinion."

"Mind you, I do think that women should stick together, in that they should support their own sex, whenever possible. One of the reasons, in fact, I would say the chief reason why we have so few women candidates adopted is that at the weeding out stage it is the female not the male members of the Selection Committee who vote against having a woman candidate. However, the female element does this not so much from disloyalty to its own sex, as from a fear which, alas, has often been proved right that a woman candidate will approach her job from the completely wrong angle: she will imagine that if she is elected, she will be representing women's interests in the House, when she should be representing the *whole* community, the *whole* family. That's what I have tried to do from the start. It's not a question of unsexing oneself, it's surely a question of common sense."

As we turned once more to walk back along the Terrace, a faint but delicious aroma of perfume touched me like a summer breeze. One did not somehow connect a woman Member of Parliament with the feminine privilege of presenting a scented front to the world. If surprising, it was, nevertheless, I decided, a most intriguing combination. Whereupon another question came to the front of my mind that I very much wanted to settle. Later, perhaps. . . .

A group of the officers of the Richmond Branch of the Young Conservatives stood at the door of their hall to greet their ex-President that evening. She had added an elegant pair of longish, very white gloves and a small blue hat, with an edging of matching white, to the navy-blue ensemble in which she had greeted me at the House. The hat set far back like a bonnet, was both pretty and practical. It was now eight o'clock. In between the member for Chislehurst had returned to her Ministry to sign her letters and check some notes, then rejoined me at my flat for a very quick drink before driving down to the Borough where we had both spent so much of our childhood and which despite the introduction of a milk-bar near the 'Maids of Honour' shop and many new blocks of sky-scraper flats, remains surprisingly untouched in atmosphere. The view from the Terrace is still supreme; below the sweet Thames seems completely unconscious of the menacing beat of the traffic: The Lass of Richmond Hill remains a country pub. Nothing has shrunk, little has changed.

There had been no time for my companion to change her clothes had she wished to do so. In her case, it did not matter. Unlike an executive who had worked in the City all day, she still gave the impression of shining, immaculate cleanness. Nor as I struggled out of London through the rush-hour traffic did she deliberately conserve her voice, as many speakers would have done for the evening's solo performance to come. Instead she talked with passion and most moving eloquence about the desperate need for more trained personnel in the hospitals and institutions that care for mental defectives.

"We have recruited several thousand more nurses in the ordinary hospitals, since the Health Service started," she told me, "but we remain woefully understaffed, on the Mental side. What makes it so tragic is that our actual treatment of our mental patients is enormously in advance of all that I was shown in America, last year. There they still tie down the difficult or violent patients to the beds. Here we use the infinitely more humane process of the padded cell. While again the nursing staffs we have in Britain are absolutely superb. Many of them are Sisters, long past the retiring age, who have just stayed on because they cannot bear to leave a bigger gap, because they truly *care*. I have been more impressed with their devotion than with anything else since I came to the Ministry."

No wonder that in her own constituency, friends and political foes alike, they call her 'Our Pat', I thought. She has the power of making everyone to whom she speaks feel that whatever the subject, her crusade has become their personal responsibility, too. All the same, I could not help my thoughts wandering. The traffic lights at the corner of East Sheen were against us and the car had come to a standstill. I was remembering with a vividness that was almost like a pain all the times that I had bicycled from my home in Queen's Road, and turned down here, past the level-crossing and the gates of my uncle's brewery, to practise on the grand piano in the drawing-room at Guildford House, set back in an oasis from the slummy road and surrounded by a high wall. Hour after hour of dutiful scales that made all the photographs in their silver frames rattle. And to think that at that time there was a small red-haired girl, even younger than myself, living only a few roads away. Little had either of us imagined that thirty years later I would be driving her back to Richmond in my car to address a political meeting where her name would command a packed hall and be the star attraction of the season, or that an aunt of mine, herself a pioneer among women J.P.s, would give such a warm welcome that she still recalled it with a sense of gratitude today to an ardent young student serving on her first grown-up local committee.

"I had no idea till this moment that Mrs. Ludlow was your aunt. She was extraordinarily kind to me and impressed me deeply, for other reasons, too. She had an extremely good mind and a most decisive manner at committee meetings, and yet she remained so very feminine a personality that the men never seemed resentful when she argued with them or refused to accept their superior views. I learnt a lot from her on how to cope with men on committees. Believe you me, it is an art in itself."

"She was just as kind to me, as a small boy, and never smiled in a pitying way when I said I was going to be a famous playwright one day, though I suspect that she thought the practising was a waste of time. Which it was, of course. But if I put in so many hours, I was allowed to go to each change of programme at the cinema which used to be over there."

"Oh do you remember it, too? Look, there's one more Odeon standing there, now. The other was *very* different. My brother and I called it 'The Flea Pit'. All the same, it was my favourite treat. I saw *The Exploits of Elaine* there."

"So did I. How I adored Pearl White! No one has ever quite come up to her since."

"She was my brother's first heroine, too. Mine? Oh, I suppose my brother was my first hero: when he took my tiny tot's hand and conducted me across this corner to the magic entrance to the land of Make Believe."

The traffic lights changed. We drove on. A few minutes later, in the ante-room, where they made the tea, at the back of the hall, the Parliamentary Secretary to the Ministry of Health was shaking hands with each member of the committee, and accepting their thanks for having given up a precious Friday evening to come and speak to them again this year.

"But it's an annual event for me now," she exclaimed warmly. "It does me so much good to come back here, where I served my own apprenticeship. I explained to Mr. Winn that it was only a small meeting, in a way, but for me it is always one of my most important dates."

Her sincerity was transparent. The young men, in that dark little back room, glowed and expanded. I fell in behind them, as the

procession passed into the main body of the hall and the visitor in
her Parliamentary uniform went forward gracefully to the platform
while I slipped into the last vacant chair in the back row. The sexes
had divided themselves with shy determination. This was clearly more
a tilting than a mating ground. Looking round the room, I recorded:
had I not already known, I could not possibly have given a political
party label to the meeting. From the outward appearance of my
neighbours, it might just as easily have been a turn-out for a local
branch of any Young Labour League. The label 'Leisured Class' had
gone for ever, I thought, and a good thing, too. Tonight, the girls,
on the whole, were more *soignée* than the men. Mostly they were
dressed in neat coats and skirts and gave the impression that they
had been working all day in an office or behind the counter of a
shop. None of them wore hats and I was impressed by the universally
well-groomed look of their hair. So different from the young women
of the 'Flea Pit' era, but no different, on the other hand, from the
styles copied from Jean Simmons or Elizabeth Taylor that I would have
found equally echoed at a rally arranged by a Labour Association. The
good taste and high standard in modern clothes was something that had
stemmed partly from the influence of the films, partly from the
remarkable improvement in women's magazines, with a mass circu-
lation. In consequence, no political student, or eager convert to any
Party need any longer appear, to prove her single-mindedness, looking
either dowdy or dirty. And what a relief that was. Would it not be a
good idea, if the young men, whatever their party allegiance, now
followed suit?

We had reached the interval break for tea and biscuits, to be
followed by Question Time. Their former President had spoken to
them for an hour with enthusiasm and fervour about the solid progress
which unquestionably to her the Government in office were making.
True, she had been addressing the converted, nevertheless, it had
been an impressive performance. One felt that even in an important
debate in the House itself, she could not have taken more trouble
about her facts, her figures, or her manner of delivery. No hint
either of staleness, of condescension, or of platitudinous padding.
And it was remarkable the way in which the speaker reeled off rows of
figures and statistics, without ever faltering or having to glance down
at her notes. Was there any member of this junior branch here tonight

already chosen by destiny to follow in her footsteps? It was an exciting idea, no more fantastically improbable than the enviable success now hers would have seemed to that youngster with the flaming red hair when she stood up eagerly once upon a time to ask her own special question at a meeting, just like this. Tonight, instead, it was her rôle to be in the answerer's chair, when a girl, close to the platform, confessed what had happened to her during a recent essay in canvassing, during the local Municipal Elections.

"At one factory where I went in the lunch hour, a man brought up the question of Old Age Pensions. He said, did I think it would work. . . . I suppose he meant, would the Conservative Party agree to adding fourpence to the weekly insurance dues paid by all men and women in employment. Would that solve the problem do you think? And what should I say next time I am asked?"

"No, it wouldn't. Indeed it wouldn't." 'Our Pat' was on her feet in a moment. She had the air of someone who was not only prepared to answer a hundred hecklers, but to push them, one and all, over a very high precipice. The room was suddenly full of electricity. "I am so glad someone has asked me this question, because I had had every intention of dealing with it, in detail, in my talk to you tonight. And next time you are asked it"—now she was looking directly at the fair girl who had been on her feet a moment before—"you can say that if he—and everyone else—are willing to add four shillings— yes, four *shillings*, not four *pence*—to their weekly insurance cards, then we *might* be able to break even in providing the sum required to raise the pension rate from the present thirty-two-and-sixpence to the fifty shillings a week which is considered to be a more reasonable subsistence level.

"I know everyone in this room will agree with me," she went on, forming us all into marching order, "that we would all like to see the Old Age Pensioners having more, and personally I shall never understand how any Members on either side of the House were prepared to vote another five hundred pounds a year salary for themselves until this problem was at least partially solved. All the same, you will appreciate how complex and desperately difficult it is when I give you some figures. If the full claim was met at this moment, it would put us hundreds of millions in the red. At the end of the next twenty-five years of increased expectation of life—which you may or may not know is twelve years longer than at the beginning of the century—this claim would cost us over a thousand million more. Now if the Labour Party were back in power, would they be prepared to find that amount? And *how* would they find it? That is what you must ask next time you are questioned about Old Age Pensions. Of course, it isn't really a Party question at all, but a national one. Quote these figures and end up with—not four PENCE, but nearer four SHILLINGS extra every week. That's a figure, or perhaps a comparison of figures that most people can take in more easily."

It certainly was. If I had learnt nothing else that evening, my journey had not been in vain. For in my own correspondence, which ran into hundreds of letters a week, the tragic plight of so many Old Age Pensioners cropped up again and again, filling me with a sense of shame and impotent anger. Especially so since, whenever I had the honour to be invited to make a broadcast appeal on a Sunday evening, I invariably found that whatever the subject, whether the cause concerned men and sea, or invalid children on shore, always the biggest response came afterwards, in a few stamps or a postal order for a shilling, from those who could ill afford to spare a single farthing. Such is true charity.

Driving back to my flat afterwards for supper, I expected my companion to wilt at last, exhausted from all that she had given to her audience at the end of a grinding day's administrative work. After all, she had been almost continuously on her feet for two hours. Instead, she seemed refreshed by their enthusiasm and more charged with vitality than ever. I could only wonder and admire. And when we reached Ebury Street, and stood blinking in the lights of my living-room, I noticed that even her gloves, as she drew them off, were still surprisingly clean.

"I suppose that girl who asked the last question about the Old Age Pensions would be working somewhere in the neighbourhood, as a secretary?" I suggested.

"Probably. I was at her age."

"And had you any political aspirations—isn't that the usual phrase—yourself at that time?"

"Not really. I took a great interest in the Young Conservatives, of course, but I never dreamt that one day I would stand for Parliament myself." She lifted her glass of Dubonnet as if to drink a toast to the past and all that had happened since.

"Then what *was* your ambition?" I continued, leading her past the barrier of books in my library into the dining-room where, for once, the glowing colours of the Mathew Smith canvases on the wall were challenged by the brilliant aura of my guest.

"My ambition? Oh, I imagine it was to be a first-class secretary. After all, there are many grades in secretarial efficiency, though you would hardly imagine so from the salaries that youngsters demand for themselves today simply on the diplomas that guarantee their typing and shorthand speeds. Of course, that is simply the basis of their training, the groundwork, nothing more."

"And what really makes a first-class secretary, do you think?"

"Well, if you are visualizing someone who is the secretary to a politician, or for that matter, any other specialized career, my own view is that it is essential that a girl—or a man—should, whatever their college degrees, do at least a couple of years in some big commercial organization first. That will broaden them, prevent them from becoming intellectual snobs, and give them so much general experience that they will have the confidence and the facility henceforth to cope with any situation that may crop up. However, there's something else which, in my view, is infinitely more important than all that."

"Yes?" I had completely forgotten that I had a piece of asparagus suspended in my fingers, halfway from the plate to my mouth.

"You must believe that being a secretary—*or whatever your job may be*—is the most important mission in the world. I honestly think I did, and what's more, I should have felt just the same if I had been a shop assistant at that time. It might easily have happened. My father was a shopkeeper himself. I had to make my own way, right from the start, as soon as I left High School. There was no money to give me any Higher Education than that, and I don't regret it a bit now, looking back. I might have got false and fatal ideas about my own importance in the labour market. As it was. . . ."

She broke off, dipping a piece of asparagus in the melted butter on her plate. She seemed to relish the rite, as though it was the first time this season, as though she did not have to attend at least two

The Miner's Wife

"I always believed that things would be better tomorrow," Mrs. Lewis said

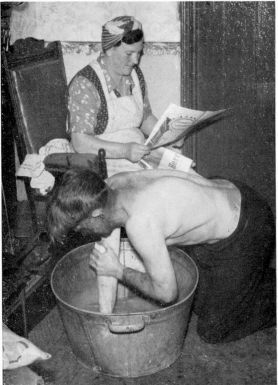

public functions every week, dutifully eating her way through a four-course meal, as the official representative of her Ministry. Despite the richness of it all, that must be the most boring part of her work, I thought. And how she must long sometimes for a scrambled egg on a tray in her bed, fussed over by the aunt who now keeps house for her and tells you on the telephone, at half past eight in the morning, that Miss Hornsby Smith has already left for the office.

"As a matter of fact, that was a white lie. I had left for an early session, *en route*, with my dressmaker. Being a man, you can't appreciate quite what a complication that is for me. Trying to ring the changes on my clothes—especially my evening dresses—so that with all the parties that I *have* to attend, I don't hear too many people saying behind my back: 'Oh, she's got the same dress on that she wore at the Hospital Ball last week.' Luckily with my hair I can wear a lot of black at night, and that helps a good deal. Of course, it's all part of my job, and when I have had a bad day, as we all have sometimes, when everything seems to go wrong, I remind myself of a very sobering truth. Ninety per cent of the men and women who go out to work, for their living, end up in *cul-de-sacs*, facing a blank wall, the dreams that they once had, stifled. Whatever they do is their bread and butter: they *must* stick at it, they *must* bring home a wage packet on Friday nights. In consequence, most of the time, they go through the motions of their work, like a sleep-walker. They just aren't interested, and it is not difficult to understand why. All the same, I swore to myself right from the start that I wouldn't be like that, even if for the rest of my life I had to exist on three pounds five a week. So I took a passionate interest in any extra sources of knowledge which came my way, in the course of my duties, in the vague hope that one day the break would come, and these extra facts and figures, tucked away, would just tip the scale. Which they did. You hear people hold forth about so-and-so having been so jolly lucky in their life, but it isn't luck, really. Or rather, good luck goes to those who are ready and prepared for the moment, *when* it comes."

"And you think it does come to everyone, *once* in their life, but most of us don't notice it, because we aren't ready and prepared, as you suggest?"

"Yes, I do. Take my own case. When I was put in the short list of prospective candidates for the Chislehurst Division, I had to go down and make a political speech in front of the committee, as you always do. But when I came into the room, I found that they had changed the usual format, and wanted something quite different, an imaginary eve of the poll address. I was blazing mad then, because I was certain in my mind that the other candidates, who were local young men, had been warned of the change. So I let them have it good and strong, and I must have shaken the committee, because after having warned me, 'no more than ten minutes, please' they kept me with them for three-quarters of an hour, hurling questions at me, and it was then that I got my chance. One of the things they asked me about was the Education Act, and as I had been secretary to Lord Selborne, who had piloted it through the Lords, I had much of it written out in my mind. With the result that when I had gone out of the room, the committee decided that it would only be fair to ask the other candidates the same question, which hadn't been in the original schedule. And they all floundered, apparently, though I didn't know, of course, at the time. When they dismissed me and told me that they would be getting in touch with me, I was certain it was the usual polite brush-off."

"And then what happened?" I asked with a growing sense of excitement, for unlike some after-dinner speakers this story-teller possessed the rare quality of making everything seem as though it was really happening at that moment.

"Well, at one o'clock the next morning at home, the telephone rang, and it was the agent on the other end. 'You're selected,' he said. I made him repeat it, because I thought I must be dreaming."

My guest smiled, as she lifted her brandy glass, and gently swirled the contents round the bottom of the glass, with the familiar antici-patory gesture of a man. "I shall never forget the Adoption meeting. At the last moment, my mother said she would like to go, too. The place was packed out but they found a seat for her somewhere in the middle of the hall. When my name was announced, and I stood up, the emotion of the moment, the reality at last, was more than she could cope with and she burst into tears. Whereupon the woman behind her gave her shoulder a sharp shake, and shouted in her ear. 'Why aren't you clapping? Don't you like "Our Pat".' 'She was My Pat, first' was all my mother could whisper. . . ."

I could have gone on listening all night, I had no desire for sleep, since this was the very stuff that dreams are made of but, alas, tomorrow's timetable was like Big Ben ringing in our ears. Still, there was one more question that I wished I might ask before my guest drove her own neat, grey car away from my front door over the bridge to Battersea.

"I am the only Member of the Government who lives on the wrong side of the river," she exclaimed with some relish.

"But aren't you sometimes tired of your bachelor state? Wouldn't you like to get married? After all, many of the women M.P.s are married."

"Yes, but they were all married *before* they entered the House. You never hear of anyone marrying from the House, unless they are a widow. I think, Jennie Lee was the only exception."

"You believe it scares the men as much as that?"

"Yes, I do. A woman M.P. is the symbol of all Career women, with a capital C. Still, as they have moved another six thousand people into my constituency, it could be that I shall no longer be a Member of Parliament after the next election."

"And then?"

"Oh, I suppose I could take up a commercial post again. One good thing about having such a small majority, I never get wrapped up in cotton-wool, or lulled into a false sense of security, which makes some of us in the House get smug and lazy, and over-rate our own importance in the universe. I am so very conscious that I may be out on the pavements of Westminster, looking for a job, tomorrow."

"You know, you haven't really answered my question."

"Very well, then, as I have had such a very good supper, and you drove me all the way down to Richmond and back, I will answer it for you. So often the men who have wanted to marry me, expected me to protect them: they gathered from my career to date that I was that kind of woman. They didn't seem to appreciate that because I had had to fight so hard for myself, I longed to lean on someone else's shoulder, for a change. I only seem to attract the weak and. . . ."

"If you do, surely it's only because you never show a moment's weakness yourself," I interrupted, watching her draw on her long white gloves, and being once again struck by their uncreased whiteness.

"Well, it's too late for us to start the evening all over again, with a discussion on Psychology," she said crisply.

Afterwards, I watched her drive away down the street and my heart was full of gratitude. For had I not just spent one of the most stimulating evenings of my life, so very different from anything I had ever conjured up in the days when a schoolboy at Richmond had saved up his pocket money for the next instalment of *The Exploits of Elaine,* and his neighbour, in the ninepennies, may so easily have been a small podgy girl, with two scarlet plaits.

FOUR

THE MINER'S WIFE

I T is an odd sensation when getting up in the morning a man looks
into the mirror to shave and sees there not his own face but the
cloudy image of someone whom he hopes to meet before the day
is over. So it was with me that spring morning in the Cardiff hotel,
where I had arrived the evening before in search of the material for yet
another portrait to add to my gallery of the Queen's countrywomen.

This time it was to be a miner's wife. I pictured her with the look
of someone who had suffered through the bleak, bitter times of the
depression in the thirties, but whose scars were hidden now because
her children had sufficient food in their stomachs and their father no
longer walked in fear that there would be a closure at the pit and he
would be back again on the dole. She was standing at the doorway of a
semi-detached house, with grey tiles on its roof, but no television aerial,
tilted against the side of the mountain: a scarf was tied round her
head, not in mill-girl fashion, but like a turban, and she had the soft
melodious speech, and the dark, melting eyes of the southern Welsh.
She would be what an older generation always called a bonny woman
though she would no longer be young. Yet meeting her would give
me a sense of rebirth, of warm hope that the shameful words, 'Distressed
Area' were for ever erased from the map of Britain.

And then behind her head, in the mirror, I saw, in a sudden
close-up, the mountain itself and its scars were not hidden, the
patches of scraped surface, where in their desperation whole communities of mining folk had dug with their bare hands for the semblance of coal, for anything that would burn in their starving
grates. Nothing would hide those scars ever, no matter how clothed
in summer green the valley might seem when the procession of royal
cars drove slowly up Rhondda Fawr, in a few weeks' time. And would
anyone point out to Her Majesty what those marks, like sores on the
open face of the mountainside, really meant?

It was, I reminded myself, as I dressed, a coincidence with some
point that I should happen to return to South Wales, just before

D   49

the official visit of the Queen, after her Coronation ceremonies, since my last tour had taken place in the wake of the Duke of Windsor, then Prince of Wales. Despite the loyal cheers that greeted him, he had been so overwhelmed by the feeling of hopelessness everywhere that he had made the statement from his heart which was to become history, and which was to affront the conventional-minded politicians who preferred to stay in London. "*I promise you something shall be done.*" So unconstitutional, they whined, it will do us so much harm in our own constituencies, and were thankful to see him go. They did not know—and doubtless would not have cared if they had—that in one of the villages through which he drove where the pit was closed down and everyone was on the dole, a man came hurriedly out of a cottage, pulling on his jacket, and forcing his way through the crowd, stood in the royal path.

"She is in la-bour! My poor wife, afraid in her heart she is, mon. Come you on in, I do beg and beseech. She won't be afeared no more then, see? Nor I shan't be fretting for her."

Whereupon the Prince, with the aura of gold to his head, went into the cottage where there were blood-red smears on the walls that he would not recognize as the marks of bugs, and sat down in the foetid atmosphere beside his unknown countrywoman until the doctor arrived and, while they waited, soothingly he held her hand as though she were a member of his own family.

That child if he was a boy, would be of an age to go down a mine himself now, I thought, remembering how the Duke himself had looked, the night I watched him drive out between the gates of Marlborough House, an hour after his mother's death. The hair still gold, but the face shrivelled into the mask of an old man, whom life has defeated. But today in the mining villages of South Wales, you will still find the pictures of him on the parlour wall, as he was then. And to them he is still their Prince.

Nevertheless I ate my breakfast in a mood of doubt. Had I been wrong to come? Would I find my optimism unjustified? What a contrast there was between Cardiff itself, so imaginatively planned, with the most beautiful civic centre in the whole of our country, and the villages, some of them almost on its outskirts, that were thrown up like eruptions of lava overnight, as one after another, the rich mine shafts were sunk into the virgin green of the Rhondda.

Queen Elizabeth was, of course, no stranger to the splendours of the Welsh capital, the hall-porter reminded me proudly. Was it really the Welsh capital? I did not like to argue. Instead I recalled how in 1948 when as Princess Elizabeth she received the Freedom of the City, she delivered a speech to the people of Wales that so far from seeming just one more official address, is doubly apposite today. For referring to the undoubted fact that fixed standards of morality have become unfashionable all over the world, she added these words.

"We cannot blame children whose upbringing in some cases hardly gives them a chance to know the difference between right and wrong. It is often conditions at home which are responsible. I myself have been extremely lucky in this respect and I can speak with feeling of the advantages which a happy family life brings to a child."

Would I find these same advantages in the homes I hoped to visit before the day was over? Deliberately I had given no warning of my coming. I would just knock on any door. That was my plan. But would I be able to carry it out?

Fortunately I had provided myself with two excellent guides and bodyguard loaned to me for the day by their employer, an old friend of mine with considerable business interests in Cardiff. Kenneth Davies had explained to me that one was a J.P., and the other the youngest Rugger International to be capped by Wales. "The best judges of the game swear that no better stand-off has ever turned out for us." What seemed of more importance from the point of view of our mission was that one had been a miner in his youth, the other was the son of a miner. Therefore I took it to be an omen that the sun was shining brilliantly as I stood on the hotel steps, waiting to be hailed by my good companions.

I knew it was going to be like that the moment the mettle-some chariot drew up that looked as though it was used to climbing mountains and out of it stepped a man with the benign air of a bishop, followed by a youngster with a mane of black hair, piercing dark eyes and a wide grin that scarcely left his face for the next ten hours, except when we were listening to the Treorchy Male Choir, practising for yet another Eisteddfod. But that was far ahead, a final climax to the outing of which as yet I had no inkling. At that moment we were fully occupied introducing ourselves, and packing back into the car. "I am Mr. Hopkins, and this is Cliff . . . Cliff Morgan . . . and he's very happy to have the day off."

"And so is Mr. Hopkins," retorted Cliff, with no respect for the other's grey hairs.

"And so am I," I echoed with no respect, for once, for the truth. For, after all, this had been planned as a working party though it was to turn out quite differently, one of those halcyon days you remember all your life. Soon I was surrendering most happily to the joyous laughter of Cliff that ran like a vein through the conscientious texture of Mr. Hopkins' local lore. First he tried me with reference to Anticlinal and Bituminous coalfields, but when we reached Llantrisant which, from the distance across the fields, has the air of a mediaeval French hill town, to my secret relief, he descended unconsciously to my own level of comprehension. As our car swung to the right at a corner, he pointed out a house standing back a little from the road. "That is where Doctor Price lived."

"Which Doctor Price?" I asked.

"The one who started as a villain and ended as a hero. There is a plaque up there on the wall. The date is 1885, I think. They tried to stone him to death on one occasion, and a huge crowd collected at this corner, and broke all his windows. And afterwards there was a big trial that created world-wide attention. The doctor wanted it that way. He was prepared to be a martyr for what he believed."

"And what did he believe?" Cliff and I both asked this time in unison.

The answer was a surprise. "He believed in cremation. He offered cremation to his patients. He even administered it to his five-months-old child, whose body, after its death, he burned in a barrel half filled with paraffin oil. Why he should have chosen a Sunday evening between seven and eight when the townspeople were returning home from chapel, no one seems to know, and we can only assume that he intended to create as much publicity as possible, and be taken to court."

"And what happened to him in the end?" I asked, my curiosity now passionately aroused. "Did he go to prison? Was his right to practise taken away from him by the Medical Council of the day?"

"The case was sent to Cardiff Assizes and heard before Mr. Justice Stephen who delivered his now famous pronouncement that 'I am of the opinion that a person who burns instead of burying his dead does not commit a criminal act unless he does it in such a manner as to amount to a public nuisance at Common Law.'

"Doctor Price was himself cremated at Llantrisant, and on that day twenty thousand people visited the district and the legend—for it is a kind of legend now—is that many of them even took away cinders as souvenirs. Anyway, he made cremation legal for all time in this country—to the everlasting glory of Wales."

"And didn't he, Mr. Hopkins," broke in Cliff, "once graft a piece of bone taken from the leg of a calf, on to a miner's leg?"

"He did, indeed, and he was also the master of seven languages, and the leader of the Chartist Riots in these parts, so that on one occasion, he had to escape to the Continent dressed as a woman."

"I thought that was Bonnie Prince Charlie," I exclaimed, and once more Cliff dissolved into laughter. Mr. Hopkins bore our levity with good humour, and when we passed through his own home town of Tonyrefail patiently informed me that Ivor Novello's grandfather had been a Methodist minister there.

"And no doubt at all, that's where the fervour came for his passionate belief in everything he wrote, so that he never minded the scoffers, and you won't find many in these valleys. It was the Celtic fire in him. A Welshman never escapes from his own destiny. Why, even young Cliff here, though you wouldn't believe it to listen to him, or to the language that some of his supporters use when they shout out advice to him from the touchline, still teaches in Sunday School—don't you, boy?—and goes to choir practice twice a week, with his parents."

I am afraid I was only half-listening. To hear that other name mentioned unexpectedly against this background had roused in me a sudden awareness of the perpetuity of the pattern. The last musical play in which the author and composer wanted to act himself was to have been set against these same hills and in these same valleys, where his own childhood roots lay deep. There can be no doubt that it would have been tinged with a very special emotion, far removed from the love scenes that with his indestructibly romantic profile turned towards the matinée audiences who never rattled their tea-cups when he was on the stage, he had played against a succession of Ruritanian settings. It would have been a fitting climax to a career whose upward graph had never wavered; indeed, Ivor Novello told me of the project that he was nursing to his Welsh heart the last weekend I ever stayed with him at his country home. Yet I was filled with fear, not because he was changing the formula at last, but for himself.

He looked so grey and worn, he could only speak in a whisper, and kept on falling asleep beside the fire.

Something very strange happened that Sunday morning of which I could not speak now to my two chance companions with the spring sunshine warming our bones. I had been urging my friend that he must take more care of himself, and be less prodigal of his generosity and his goodness—for he was, that rare thing, a good man—whereupon he had replied that I was not to worry, because he would be on top of the world again as soon as he had had a holiday in the Jamaican sun (in actual fact, he returned from that breathing space only to die a few days later) and then suddenly rousing himself to lean forward in his chair beside the fire of the long living-room where he had composed so many of his songs that have already proved themselves to be less mortal than their creator, he exclaimed: "Have you ever played the game, Godfrey, of where you would want your funeral procession to call on its way to the cemetery?"

I was too startled to reply.

"I haven't any doubts where I shall want mine to call. Starting from my flat in the Aldwych, it would go first to Drury Lane, because of *Glamorous Night*, and then to the Palace, because that's our new home, and we all love it, and then to the Prince of Wales, because that's where I had my first big success, on my own, in *The Rat*—do you remember, you came to see it at your family theatre in Birmingham and sat in your family box and felt so grand, though you were still at school—and then to The Ivy, for all the gay and glorious lunches I've had there, and then. . . ."

But I did not hear the rest of the list, for looking into his face, I saw only the dry bones of a skull. In the evening, he tried to recapture some of his usual buoyant good spirits, and when another old friend, Terry Rattigan, arrived, played for us the music that he had written for Cicely Courtneidge, with its hit number 'Vitality' that was to stop the show on the first night. Alas, his own vitality was ebbing fast and the other production that was to be the sublimation of all the dreams of his youth and of all the music that he had breathed in at his mother's knee was never given its final shape.

What was it that he had said to me once when I asked him the secret of his eternal youth, and almost to the end, he had remained untouchably young? "I shall never grow really old," he had answered, "because I was never bored when I was young."

As young as Cliff Morgan, who had halted the car in his own village of Trebanog and was leaping across the road, as though half the English pack were at his heels. We had stopped outside one of those terraces of houses, all linked together, with their grey roofs, that are so much a feature of the mining villages. We were half-way up the hill-side: below was the plain, behind the strips of back-garden flowered into the wilderness. How bleak it must be in the winter, I thought, as I watched Cliff bend down and push something under the door. "I am telling Mam, we will be back for tea. She will be out doing her shopping now."

With a certain measure of relief it crossed my mind that if our quest failed elsewhere I should have the satisfaction of meeting one miner's wife at tea-time, even though, in a way, she would be set apart, because of the glory of her son's fame as a footballer. How-ever, soon we were to strike a seam of good fortune, because pushing on through Tonypandy, we were hailed in the High Street of Gelli by a supporter of Cliff's, a local sports writer, named Mr. Tudor James, who immediately was roped in to the search party. What advice had he to offer? No, mon, not about next Saturday's match. Which village was most likely to throw up gold?

As we chattered there in a group on the pavement, a little crowd collected, staring at Cliff, with the same expression of awe as though he was another Prince of Wales. However, he seemed not to notice what was happening and was not in the least embarrassed by the succession of complete strangers who asked if they might shake his hand. Because of a shared love for Wales' national game, they were all his friends. It was as simple as that. I found myself wishing that some of the spoilt little starlets that make such a nuisance of themselves at the so-called Gala Premières of West End films, hogging the cameras and wearing ridiculously outrée clothes could have been there. How badly their noses would have been put out of joint. This was real hero worship, instead of a phoney brand of whipped-up hysteria. As for myself, I must confess it was a moment of secret consolation when a housewife, emerging from James and Evans' shoe shop, made the exception of recognizing me, and started talking to me at once about the Queen's visit.

Mrs. Lani Powell of Ynys Wen Road, Treorchy, had a grievance, but neither Mr. Hopkins, on his magistrates' bench, nor Cliff with the kind of fame that opens any door in Wales, nor myself with my pen, could hold out any hopes of solving her problem in the way that she longed for it to be settled.

"You see, Mr. Winn, the moment I heard, I thought, here is my chance to get the front of the house done up at last. And I'd got all the paint stripped off the front door, before my husband came home and said: 'You needn't worry, the Queen's not passing our door, after all.' Don't you think if it was explained to her, she would have the route changed again? Anyway, I mean to shame *him* into finishing the job, just the same!"

What an amusing and touching film story could be written about all the dramas that go on behind the scenes before a Royal visit, I thought, as once again we moved on, with an addition to our own *entourage*. Mr. James was arguing fiercely that we should go and pay a call on his butcher—"don't you see, mon, he will be able to tell us from the ration cards, who has a big family and you want a proper family, don't you?"—when we almost ran over a middle-aged man, in an old mackintosh, who was carrying a plant in his hand.

At once there were shouts, and cries of recognition, and somehow or other, he, too, was packed into the car, and immediately the butcher was forgotten because the newcomer turned out to be the local M.P. and everyone assured me that Mr. Thomas was the oracle of all oracles. By now I was quite silent, and thankful to leave it to my good companions to explain what we were searching for on that spring morning, nor did the saga lose anything in the telling. "There is a family in my constituency I should like you to meet," Mr. Thomas said at the end. "The husband works at the same pit where I myself worked for many years, in my youth, and his wife, I think you will agree, is a very exceptional person, indeed. A woman in a thousand."

He was utterly right: what a fascinating haphazard business life is. For if our chariot had not swung round the corner at that second, and if a grateful constituent had not stopped her Member of Parliament in the road, a moment before, to give him a plant, we would have gone our separate ways, completely in ignorance of each other's near presence, without ever meeting. Nor would I have found myself a quarter of an hour later outside No. 28 Tallis Road, Cwmparc, shaking hands with a woman who bore a startling resemblance to the image I had conjured up that morning in the wash-stand mirror of my Cardiff hotel.

Elizabeth Mary Lewis was just coming home from the grocer's where she stocks up with provisions twice a week as though her grey-stoned house at the top of the road which winds down into the valley was a ship at anchor, and she wore the turban bound closely round her hair because of the wind that was blowing off the sea, and there was a crew of husky young men to feed.

There is a crew, she agreed at once, but they were all her sons. Eight of them, and two young daughters thrown in for good measure, "though it would have been nice," she exclaimed, "if Mary—she's ten—had come when Brian did—he's seventeen—because by now Mary would have been a real help in the house."

She looked so much a woman in her prime who would have made a splendid figurehead for the prow of a ship that I was frankly amazed when she assured me that she had grown-up children, and how many she had, so that we proceeded to check over their names, like a roll call. Cliff—the eldest—was twenty—two years younger than his namesake in our party—and working like his father, a chargehand, earning eight pounds a week today, in the mine, whose upcasts and surface machinery was as much the dominating feature of the landscape as the clock of Big Ben is to those who consider that Westminster is the centre of their world. Next came Eric, aged nineteen, followed by Brian—he was at home, having been on night shift and at first was very shy of the invasion and hid away in the kitchen as though we were heralding a return to the bad old days, when the arrival of strangers usually meant stony questions about how the relief money had been spent—and finally there was Emrys, making a quartet of sons, all quite contented, their mother volunteered, to be following in their father's footsteps.

That was a hopeful sign, I thought: that conditions were more stable, more civilized at last and future prospects, the long-term policy was winning adherents from a new generation who had been weaned in an atmosphere of utter revulsion from the uncertainties and hardships of a miner's calling. Indeed, how many times have I heard these men who belong to a race of their own interbreeding, stubborn, brave, isolated, misunderstood, declare with passionate conviction that they would rather maim their sons than allow them to go down any mine.

Yet here were four lusty young sons doing precisely that, and clearly with their mother's blessing. For Mrs. Lewis showed no signs of dismay that half her family should be already working underground, though she did add that the next boy, Gareth, who at fifteen, had just left school, had broken away from the tradition and had chosen to apprentice himself in a grocer's shop. "But I don't know how long he will stick to it," she added, as though The Parc was only waiting for a sign of weakening to draw him below into a world of dark mysteries, unknown to women.

The other children were still at school: Brynley, aged fourteen, who following in another tradition had joined the Silver Band and, coming home for his dinner, was persuaded first to give us as an appetiser, his rendering of 'The Old Hundred' on his instrument that was a revered and polished ornament in the front parlour; and Myrddin who at the time of our visit was only seven. Yet already he had shown himself to possess a talent both rare and greatly to be welcomed in any family, but especially in one of such proportions as this. He really enjoyed washing-up and drying the plates after every meal as much as other small boys of his age like rushing off to fish for tiddlers. "He is the only boy who always volunteers," Mrs. Lewis said.

At the same time she swore that she had no favourites, not even the five-year old baby, Keri, trotting home from nursery school, and like any small animal, ravenous for his feeding hour, and what was there to eat in all this chatter, chatter, nor the two little girls, Mary and Gillian, who one day may be content to stay at home and be domesticated though at present they pursue quite a different rôle: it is they who bring their mother tidings from the outside world she has herself so little time to visit. "Your sweetheart's on at the pictures," they cried out in unison the moment that they were inside the house.

Then it was that I discovered that Mrs. Lewis' favourite actor was Jeff Chandler, though her face did not really light up until she began to speak of her husband whom I was not to meet. However, I felt his personality strong upon this home where love and faith dwelt. All during the years when he and his wife were together in the valley of darkness, unable to get a home of their own, living in the two rooms where all their children were born, and no money coming in each week except the meagre allowance grudgingly allowed by the Means Test, never once in his moods of savage doubt had he made her own burden intolerable.

Now today all that is behind them: and the war years, when in the raids, the brood of children would take refuge with their mother, in the same shelter. "I tried to persuade her to put some here, and some there, just in case there was a direct hit," Mr. Thomas, the political godfather who finally had got them a home of their own, broke in, "but Mrs. Lewis used to say, didn't you, that if it had to be, you would all want to go together, not some spared and others taken. To be left without their Mam."

Now today the father, like the boys, hands over his pay packet intact to Mam every week. Yet even with five wage packets coming in, she needs it all when one remembers that her grocer's bill alone is eleven pounds a week. Would the blue-print planners of the brave new world approve the manner in which she ran her household? To me her arms gave away the secret of her whole life. They were a woman's arms, and yet so immensely strong and developed that I was no longer surprised when she took me through the kitchen into the scullery where there were no less than eighteen shirts hanging up to dry. Eighteen!

How often did she do the washing? On Mondays and Thursday and again on Saturdays. "My husband and the boys, who are now working, always bring back their pit clothes. And they've got to be washed over the weekend and mended. That's why there isn't time for me to go to Chapel on Sundays. Sunday is often my heaviest day of the week. All the same I do believe in One Above. Even when the children were small and it seemed as though we should never get a place of our own, let alone one with four bedrooms, and there used to be so little coming in to feed them on, I still always believed that things would be better tomorrow."

And now that tomorrow has come. Not only to the Lewis family, but surely for the majority of the mining communities in South Wales. If only the bitter memories did not lie so deep beneath the surface. And sometimes the unforgiving hatred. Though here in this home, so crowded and yet miraculously scrubbed, I could sense the atmosphere of security, as at other times one is equally conscious of fear and disillusionment. Moreover it all sprang, I felt, from the mother who showed no signs of suffering, of all that she had endured, upon her own face. Was it because women fundamentally expected less from life than men that their faces showed fewer scars?

It was quite a different question that I now finally asked this woman whose ten children, like the Queen in her childhood, were clearly having all the advantages of a good home. "If you could have one wish that you were absolutely certain would come true, what would it be?"

As I asked, I wondered whether she was going to say, like the pretty fair woman I had met earlier in the morning, that she longed for Her Majesty to drive up Tallis Road, and stop outside her own front door; yet that proved not to be her secret wish at all.

"I have never had a proper holiday since I was married," Mrs. Lewis said, in her soft, gentle voice. "An occasional day's outing with the Mothers' Union or the British Legion—once we went to Weston-super-Mare, that was lovely—but what I would really like, what I dream about sometimes, is one whole week in London . . . and everything brought to me, on a tray!"

We were standing in the little backyard that opened on to the free mountain. A few yards above us, sheep were grazing, clinging to the loose stones, picking what they hardily could from a rather barren pasturage. With her back to the pit, Mrs. Lewis shielded her eyes and looked to the horizon beyond. It was as though the whole of the day had flowed towards this moment of significance and then the children came clamouring for their dinner and the spell was broken.

However, the day was only half spent, and I was to recapture the mood at tea-time, when, after the other Cliff's mother had produced her best Crown Derby china and we had had a delicious meal of cold ham, Mrs. Morgan shooed us into the little front parlour, and we instinctively gathered round the piano.

On the walls hung pictures of their famous son, in his rare cap, with his team mates, on the wing, captured by the camera, in that split second of tingling ecstacy, when the ball has just been heeled out of the scrum, and the vital pass is given which, with a rippling movement down the field, promotes the scoring of a try. Otherwise, the parlour was identical with hundreds of others past whose trim, grey fronts we had driven that day. And so was the piano which is not only the most prized possession, but regarded as far more of a necessity than a washing machine, in any Welsh cottage.

Cliff sat down and started vamping, singing and humming as he found the theme of the latest number of the 'Hit Parade'. Suddenly his mother, in stature a much smaller woman than Mrs. Lewis, but with exactly the same aura of philosophical calm that all wives of miners seem to possess, came unobtrusively from the other room. "Now, son, let's have a hymn," she said, not scolding, not coaxing, but immediately without a trace of self-consciousness or demur, he struck the opening chords for the Twenty-third Psalm. At the same instance, all laughter had left his face, and his dark, fervent eyes became filled with the Celtic twilight. This could only be happening in Wales, I thought. This might, long ago, have been Ivor and his Mam. And I remembered how I had read in Thomas Firbank's *A Country of Memorable Honour* that the quality of the Welsh character was like that of the harp. Touch the strings with a violent and untutored hand and there is discord: stroke them with gentle fingers and there is harmony.

Here in this front parlour was the same harmony as I was to discover later that evening in a school classroom in Treorchy, after Cliff had insisted first on showing me over his own school, the magnificent modern grammar school at Tonyrefail. The corridors were empty, there was only an old janitor and ourselves. In the course of our tour, we found ourselves standing in front of the picture of Cliff, in pride of place in the library, but that was not why we had come. It was touching to see his pride and gratitude for his Alma Mater. Within these walls, another generation, born and growing up since the arid starved years of the depression, were being stinted of nothing that could help to earn them a place in the sun. They might find it increasingly difficult to speak their native tongue, but the strength of the Latin tag remained. *Mens sana in corpore sano*. This was the new Wales.

Just as in the classroom at Treorchy, commandeered for a musical practice, out of school hours, I found an emanation of the old Wales, and in a different way, was equally stirred. Here were boys from the mines, the echoing image of Mrs. Lewis' sons, who had come straight from their pithead bath, clerks from offices, a sprinkling of other industrial workers, and all ready to sacrifice their summer evenings, four times a week, just for the honour of the choir, just for the pleasure of lifting up their voices. And the large room was packed, while the discipline was that of a picked corps. But no weapons to kill and destroy, only the baton of the honorary conductor of the Treorchy Male Choir, Mr. John Davies, himself a schoolmaster.

At the previous year's Eisteddfod, when they had finished their rendering in Welsh of the 'Twenty-third Psalm', the adjudicator had exclaimed, "If they sing as well in Heaven, I am ready to go there now." I had the same reaction when, as a special favour, they repeated their performance that evening. The years slid from my shoulders. I felt washed clean and I had the sensation of being carried far into another realm of spontaneous feeling, muted glory.

It was the same when they sang a different kind of anthem, like the traditional 'Counting the Sheep', or broke into the challenge of Stanford's setting for 'Songs of the Fleet'.

'Now the fleet's a fleet again, bound upon the old ways,
Splendour of the past, comes shining in the spray. . . .'

Outside the schoolroom windows the spring twilight darkened into night, and the hills disappeared from view. One had the feeling that nothing else existed in the world except this room, this hour, this blessed hour, snatched from Time. It had been such a generous, sunlit day, even with the coming of the darkness I did not want it to end. Cliff was completely held in thrall by the old magic, but each time Mr. Hopkins politely caught my eyes, between songs, I shook my head. My instinct told me that the best was still to come and I was right. Once again they sang it in the speech of their forefathers, but afterwards, when we were having a night-cap with Tony Thomas, the proprietor of The Prince of Wales, someone translated those soaring, triumphant sounds, upon the back of an old envelope.

'The dawn is not distant, nor is the night starless.
Love is eternal.
God is still God, and His Faith shall not fail us.
Christ is Eternal.'

It is called NIDAROS they said, and when I repeated the word awkwardly, I was suddenly aware, gazing from one to another of their faces in that crowded taproom, where so many of the older men had the blue stigmata of their calling upon their forehead, that I had spent the day in a foreign country, and tomorrow must cross the frontier again. A pang touched my heart.

Almost in silence we drove back to Cardiff, which in itself is another world from the Rhondda, and saying goodbye to my two companions, who had held out the keys to so many doors, I shook hands quickly and disappeared into my hotel. There were no words left. I hope they understood. But the night porter did not know that I was any different from the guest he had greeted the night before.

"Will you have breakfast in your room again?" he asked politely.

"Yes, I want everything brought to me on a tray," I said.

But, of course, he could not appreciate the reference.

"Very good, sir. And what time?"

And I thought of the father and his four sons, starting off down the road towards The Parc, singing perhaps as they went, if there was no early mist to catch in their throats, with their 'snap' in their pockets, and the mother getting the breakfast for the other children, packing them off to school and then the scrubbing and the washing until another day was gone.

"I'd like to be called at seven, and I'll come down to breakfast."

The night porter did not look in the least surprised by the sudden switch. After all, all foreigners were a bit funny, weren't they now?

FIVE

THE LAST VICEREINE

HAVE you ever stood outside a house at night, its windows brilliantly
alight, wondering about the lives of the people within? Were they
happy? Were they pleasant folk? Did they know where they were
going?

Of course, the façade of any house can be very different from its
interior: with an even greater difference again from the living personality
of its occupants. It is easy to make mistakes, to be satisfied with super-
ficial judgments, I decided that evening when we drove up the long
avenue at Romsey towards the pillared mansion where once upon a
time Palmerston used to live and which had known Florence Nightin-
gale so well.

That night, because of the floodlighting, it was as though one
was approaching the Palladian façade for the first time. And certainly
I had never seen the drive before parked with rows and rows of cars.
However, something I noticed at once, a symbol of our times, as
well as a symbol of the Mountbatten legend. Many of the cars were
small ones that did not look as though they would fetch much in
the second-hand market. Again there was only a small knot of
chauffeurs, watching the rest of the guests arrive. So different from
how it would have been at a party in the old days, someone com-
mented to me later.

The old days? I was not sure if my companion, as we danced to
the tune of 'Diamonds are a girl's best friend' was referring to a way of
life, once current in certain social circles, or to the way of living of
our host and hostess in that far-off era of the rich and roaring twenties
when the Duke of Windsor was still very much the Prince of Wales
and his cousin, young Lieutenant Mountbatten, R.N. was chosen to
be his A.D.C. on his world trip in *The Renown*. And whether Lady
Louis Mountbatten wore a cloche hat like the heroine of *The Green Hat*,
or a briefer beach-dress at Deauville, her appearance was accepted as
being the most fashionable silhouette of the moment.

But these were the 'new days' and as I waited my turn with the other guests to be received by the woman who even in her ceremonial robes as the last Vicereine had never looked more handsome than she did at this moment in her sea-green dress with the billowing bouffant skirt and the family emeralds at her throat, standing beside the man who always stares at you as though he can glimpse the sea beyond your head, my mind went back two years to a rather different party.

It had happened informally at a Butlin's holiday camp. A wet Saturday in July. All afternoon, as a climax to a two-day tour, the superintendent-in-chief of the St. John's Ambulance Brigade had taken the march past at a huge rally in Lancashire. Later she arrived at the Filey aerodrome, still in her neat black uniform. When I remonstrated with her for not changing out of her wringing wet clothes (through which not surprisingly she caught a bad chill) she said simply: "If the cadets and all my colleagues can stand and march past in the rain, I can inspect them all and take the salute. In any case, there wasn't time to change."

Instead, she changed as soon as she reached her chalet in the long line of chalets. She did not seem in the least surprised by the set-up. The wash-houses labelled 'Lads' and 'Lassies': the fact that she would have to walk a hundred yards to a communal bath tub. Why should she have been surprised? It had been her own desire to see this experiment in living, and in any case it was luxury of the 'old days' compared with the conditions she had encountered in the Far East at the end of the war, when, from a sense of passionate urgency to save human lives, she had flown, as the official representative of S.E.A.C. Red Cross, into Java and Sumatra, even before any allied troops had landed.

Later, on a goodwill tour of Australia with her husband, she received a letter from the first man with whom she had shaken hands in Praitcai P.O.W. camp in Thailand. It is touching to read what Walter Eales, now home once more in Loftus Street, Katoomba, wrote to someone who had already become for him a legendary figure.

"I was too overcome on that day to express my deep feeling of gratitude and pride in knowing that, through the horrors of war, the world and the Empire in particular still produced women like you who could take their part in a huge war effort and still retain their womanly qualities."

E

One can understand a letter like that meaning so much more to its recipient than all the pomp and ceremony of official honours, I thought, as the music stopped and my partner suggested that we walk upon the lawns and watch the iridescent plumes of the fountains, assuring us that the war was over. And now we were at peace again, albeit an uneasy kind of peace, and the Mountbattens in honour of their younger daughter's coming of age, were giving their first private party since their return from India, where they had, indeed, found an uneasier atmosphere still. This the man, whom his troops had affectionately called 'Supremo' had tried to combat by declaring to Pundit Nehru: "I want you to regard me not as the last Viceroy winding up the British Raj but as the first to lead the way to the New India."

To which his visitor in the teak-lined study of Viceroy House replied: "Now I know what they mean when they speak of your charm being dangerous."

However, if his charm could be dangerous, hers would always be contagious, I decided, recapturing that moment pinpointed by the News Reel cameras for all time, when Gandhi after posing informally on the lawns at his first meeting with the last in the long line of Viceroys, turned to go indoors and placed his hand in a sudden reaching out of warmth, on his hostess' shoulder. It was a spontaneous gesture of which the reverberations went round the world and I found myself fighting many battles over that gesture. For there is still a type of English society woman who, in her vociferous clamour that there should be a rigid line of demarcation between the black and white races, has become the unconscious enemy of the survival of her own class.

Out in India, some of the English might delight to scoff at the Mountbattens behind their backs for choosing to greet Indians, on occasion, the Indian way, with hands pressed together: others, again, might sneer when it was reported that on her visits to Gandhi the Vicereine sat on the floor side by side with her host. (If there was no chair where should she sit?) However the records remain to be judged not by partisan feeling, not by political prejudice, but by posterity. Such as the records of the film of that afternoon when they joined the great concourse beside the river after the Mahatma's assassination and watched the flames of the funeral pyre, so close to where they were seated in the anonymous throng of mourners that they were almost scorched.

Once when I questioned the woman who had come home again at last, as to the most outstanding man she had ever met in all her journeyings, she replied without a second's hesitation that it was Gandhi, and that the funeral of the Mahatma was her most dramatic and heart-moving experience. Even more so than that moment when paying their first frontier visit, she and her husband arrived at Peshawar to be warned by the English Governor that a huge Moslem League demonstration was on its way and the police would be powerless to stem its advance without dangerous bloodshed. What would one have done oneself under such circumstances? This is what they did. At once together, both dressed alike in bush shirts, they went forth to meet the surging, shouting crowd of a hundred and fifty thousand strong. They could not speak to them, they could only stand there, he at the salute and secretly pray that the message of their presence would prevail. And miraculously it did. Soon the violent shouts of "Pakistan Zindebad" turned to "Mountbatten Zindebad" and the day was saved.

Later, when the Vicereine was asked whether she was not frightened, she replied simply. "I have always felt as much at home in India, as in my own country."

And one has no doubt that she was recalling the worst as well as the best: not the scarlet and the gold of the Vicereine's throne, so much as the back streets of Bombay which she insisted on visiting and the Punjab after the tragic riots, and, most of all, the refugee camps full of flotsam, so utterly forlorn and desperate that they tore at her heart. But tears achieved nothing: she had learnt that lesson long ago. So she set to work, organizing and improvising and not even the blazing, pitiless sun could quench her spirit.

As Nehru said, in his farewell speech. "Wherever you have gone, you have brought solace, you have brought hope and encouragement."

Both his words and hers came back to me, as I walked with my partner beneath the trees. There could be no more English, no more evocative scene than this. For once Nature was being kind. It was a hot, still August night. The scents of the garden drifted and merged into the echoes of the music, now muffled, now clear again, with its timeless beat of jazz, taking one back to the days when the Charleston was all the rage and Fred and Adèle Astaire in *Stop Flirting* the toast of London, and Edwina Ashley, whose deep, wide-set questioning eyes set her apart from the other pretty-doll *débutantes* of her year, had been summoned, at the age of seventeen, to go and act in London as hostess for her grandfather, Sir Ernest Cassel, the close friend of Edward the VII.

Her mother had died when she was still a child, she had been brought up by the father whom she adored in this house where we were dancing, but though at nineteen, she was to inherit a tremendous fortune, on trust, it was not true, she has often told me, that she never had to worry about money, never had to count the silver spoons. In actual fact, up till the time of her engagement, she had received an allowance of exactly a hundred a year from her family and had had to manage on it entirely. For clothes, railway fares, tips, everything.

In consequence, she has never forgotten the occasion when she was accompanying her future husband to the port where his ship was lying. As a naval officer he had to travel first-class, whereas she always travelled third. What was she to do? It was a long journey and she simply hadn't the money in her bag to pay the difference. So in the end the girl who, in years to come was to traverse paths where few white women had previously trod, sank her pride and allowed a young naval lieutenant to pay for her.

Having done that, she went further. She borrowed the boat fare from a romantic-minded great aunt to follow him out to India that winter where he was acting as A.D.C. to his cousin, the Prince of Wales on his world tour. Before she left Miss Ashley gave out that she was hoping to do some tiger-hunting. It didn't prove such a mis-statement, after all. For when the moment came and the test was to hand, the young man in a topee was to prove himself a tiger in battle.

They came back to be married at St. Margaret's, the bride's gift to the bridegroom was a Rolls-Royce, and the wedding reception was held at Brook House, that great mansion at the top of Park Lane, which has now, with the tide that beats upon the economic shore, been turned into flats but had at that time been left to Lady Louis—as she is still called by all those who work for and with her—by her grandfather.

Although the major part of his enormous fortune had become hers, on trust, income tax was such in that era that she was still left with a prodigious yearly income, and no need, if she wished, to spend it on anything except her own pleasures. What saved her? What turned her into the strong, self-disciplined character she has become whose chief desire in life today is to be of service to the community?

It is a question which many people have asked, including several of my partners that evening, and to them all I gave the same answer, which was the answer that our hostess had given me herself. "Edwina always points out," I explained, "that she inherited not only wealth and position but also responsibility and a tradition."

And it is true that she did: for what people forget when they compare the life of the Mountbattens at the time when they first were married with the kind of existence they lead today and show so much apparent surprise that they should no longer want to go to night-clubs or give a private party themselves, except for a very special occasion, is that she possessed a grandfather who grew into one of the great philanthropists of his age.

Moreover, just as the story of the last Vicereine is the story of a self-made public figure, so is the story of Sir Ernest Cassel that of a completely self-made man. For landing as an emigrant in Liverpool, as a boy of seventeen, from Germany, young Cassel's first job brought him fifteen shillings a week. Later, when he had made his fortune he was to found, in memory of his wife and his mother, both of whom died of tuberculosis, the famous sanatorium at Midhurst and also to be one of the guarantors behind the settlement at Papworth which has equally done noble pioneer work. While again on her father's side, Lady Mountbatten's great-great-grandfather was that Lord Shaftesbury who at the most difficult moment of the nineteenth century succeeded in getting the Factory Act passed which was the beginning of improved conditions, especially for children, throughout industry.

"With such a legacy behind her," I explained to one of my partners, "it was inevitable that sooner or later she was bound to feel that she must try to play her part, too. Besides, as she so frankly tells one herself, there is her mixed blood."

"Mixed blood? You make it sound most sinister!"

"It isn't in the least sinister. But altogether she has English, Scottish, Irish, German, Jewish and Red Indian blood in her veins."

"Red Indian?"

"Yes, Red Indian," I repeated. "For she can trace her descent directly back to the Princess Pocahontas who, coming to England in the seventeenth century, married an Englishman, John Rolfe, and their child, in turn, was affianced—I think that's the word they used in those days—to a member of Edwina's family."

I have little doubt myself that it is this mixing of many bloods that has given Edwina Mountbatten today her passionate interest in finding out how the rest of the world lives. And doing something constructive about it, though in the first years of her marriage, she was expected, in the conventional pattern of the young naval officer's wife, to follow her husband dutifully from port to port. And she can never hear the name of Plymouth mentioned without seeing again the hotel where she lived for months on end, restlessly waiting for her husband to come ashore. "The other day I went back for a luncheon on one of my St. John's tours and it was all I could do not to make straightaway for *my* bedroom," she told me not long ago.

Another year she diligently pursued her husband along the coast of France and Spain, hoping and praying that he would sometimes be able to get a weekend ashore. On one occasion, not content with all his own sea-time, Lord Louis took his wife on a weekend trip from Gibraltar to Morocco. Missing the boat back, and terrified of being 'Absent without Leave', he hired a small and perilous craft and it was their luck to run into a considerable storm.

This had a sequel, the after-effect of their second daughter (later to be christened Pamela Carmen Louise) being born nearly two months before she was expected. I wonder if Pammy tonight is remembering the flap that happened then, I thought, and how nearly this party was cancelled, at birth.

For in Barcelona, her father, for once taken by surprise and unable to control the situation, was unable to locate a gynaecologist. Frantically, he rang through to his cousin, the Queen of Spain, to be answered on the phone by Alphonse XIII. "My wife is having a baby," he yelled. "My wife is having a baby." Whereupon the king promised to have a guard of honour placed round the hotel at once, when all that the distracted parent-to-be desired was the name of a first-class doctor.

A day or two later a friend, arriving at the hotel to inquire after the new infant's health, found its father seated on the side of the bath, with his trousers turned up, watching with solemn concentration the progress of a diminutive toy boat propelled by a jet of carbide gas. The naval inventor brushed aside the congratulations of his guest. "Come and watch the way this craft does its stuff," he exclaimed, in the tones of a proud parent.

And all the time his wife was longing, like many other wives before her, for equal opportunies to employ her own driving power, her almost masculine brain, her immense adaptability. She seized any chance, however unconventional, that came her way. As early as the General Strike of 1926 she had volunteered to be a telephone operator in a Fleet Street newspaper office: the Abyssinian crisis, nine years later, found her acting as a radio announcer, in Malta.

In between, whenever her husband had been away on distant cruises, she had used the gap of freedom to go off exploring herself, travelling light along the road to Teheran with only a tent and the clothes she stood up in. On another occasion she crossed the Andes on horseback, but the adventure that delights her most in retrospect is the trip that she made as a member of the crew of a trading schooner plying between Tahiti and the Polynesian islands of the South Pacific. On board it was her job to cook and look after the cargo of livestock which did not like it any more than she did when they hit a hurricane. Finally they reached Rapa, a remote island on the other side of the world, and her face lights up still when she speaks of the happiness she found in those uncharted journeys, especially those that had an archaeological flavour.

Then she would return to the more charted life of that fabulous pent-house they had created on the top of Brook House. The lion cub or the wallaby that she had collected on her last trip would be added to the family circle while she would concentrate once again on the children, on the social business of polite entertaining, on doing much charity work for such worth-while organizations as Toc H, and being at her husband's side whenever he came on leave. It was still a family with one career, not two careers of equal prominence, for the final metamorphosis was still to come.

"I've been to parties all the season, and this is my last before I go to Scotland, but it's much the best. There are so many people here with interesting faces. A different sort of crowd to the ones you usually see at dances. I mean, you'd never discover Malcolm Sargent, or the Hartley Shawcrosses at a Debs' Ball. And all those lovely saris, and Anna Neagle looking just like she does on the pictures. It must be thrilling to be the Mountbattens and know that everyone you ask will come. But I wouldn't like to be Pamela."

"Why not?"

"With such a mother to live up to? She hasn't a chance."

I had never thought of it from that angle before, because I knew them to be such a devoted family, and that the parents, despite their panoply and power had no terrors for their two daughters, who mercilessly debunked them at the first sign of a manner *plus royale que royale*, which, in any case was rare, indeed.

Passing through the hall, on the way to the supper-room, we found some late arrivals being greeted by our hostess. Michael Wilding and Elizabeth Taylor. I had last seen her in Hollywood, still a school-girl in a plain skirt and Fair-isle jumper. Now she was dressed up with elaborate sophistication, but because the occasion was so very different in atmosphere from a film *première*, one could sense that she was decidedly, if momentarily, ill at ease.

I watched the softening process, the instinctive way in which the older woman found exactly the right words with which to smooth the nervous fears of her guest who was no longer standing in her own world. No Harley Street doctor with an anxious patient could have taken more trouble or displayed a more expert technique. It happened at that moment that Lady Mountbatten's nephew was also crossing the hall with his partner. At once his aunt called to him, in a firm voice, placing her hand on his arm, as though he was still the junior naval officer, who had been so glad of a bed at her London house, on weekend leave during the war. "Oh, Philip, I would like to present Miss Elizabeth Taylor, who is English, you know, though she has been winning great fame in Hollywood." For a moment the star was so overwhelmed, looking up into the face of someone whose looks were so infinitely more dazzling than those of any of her leading men, that she forgot to curtsy. Her happiness and her evening were complete.

The tableau was over. We ourselves moved on into the supper-room, and sat down at the one conspicuously empty table. A moment later, we realized why: it was being tactfully reserved for the Duke and Duchess of Edinburgh. Far more overcome than Miss Taylor had been, we forgot our hunger and, recalling thankfully that there was a champagne buffet in the garden, did not wait upon the order of our going, but went.

"Has she changed much, do you think?" my companion asked when we were at last safely in obscurity again, under the trees.

"Who? Elizabeth Taylor?"

"No, our hostess."

"Well, I thought tonight she looked as dazzling as ever. There is a sort of timeless aura about her, to me she gives the same sort of illusion of being everlastingly at her best, like Gertrude Lawrence always did. All the same, I did also think that she looks very much thinner than when I first knew her. Which isn't surprising considering the ruthless timetable she *makes* herself keep up. One always gets an answer to a letter by return, for the simple reason that she has herself woken at six every morning, however late she is the night before, so that she can cope with her personal mail, before she has breakfast, and starts her official duties."

"Does she do as much now as she did in the war?"

"Oh yes, quite as much. Too much in a way. But then women are always more conscientious than men. If they really take up a cause, they don't play at it, they give the whole of themselves. And what I admire so much about Edwina is that she will never accept any information that comes to her second-hand. She insists on seeing everything for herself. Look what happened after the war in Europe had ended. She was out East with the forgotten armies. She insisted on travelling long distances third-class with the troops, and then having seen, for herself, the filthy condition of the wooden compartments, the hopelessly inadequate lavatory and washing accommodation, and the practically non-existent facilities for canteens at the railway junctions, she sat down and wrote a scorching and sizzling report. An eye-witness report. I was so impressed with it, when one of her secretaries showed it to me, that I memorized the last paragraph by heart. It went like this:

'The medical and welfare services in India and South-East Asia and the troops themselves do not expect the impossible: they do, however, rightly demand essentials and a definite improvement all round.' "

"And was there a definite improvement?"

"You bet there was. Unlike some generals, she always wins her battles. I would not like to have to fight her on any administrative problem."

"You make her sound rather tough . . . one of those unsexed women who care only about their careers."

"She's not a bit like that, in fact she's ultra feminine. I mean she always manages to remain feminine, under any circumstances, even when in India she used to fly off in the dawn, in a bush shirt, to visit the refugee camps. All day she would stay there, handing out hospital supplies, giving personal advice, letting the people touch her for comfort and then fly back again, with half an hour, in which to change and descend the staircase at Viceroy House, to greet her official guests, wearing one of her dresses by Worth, and looking as though she had rested all afternoon, behind closed shutters. It was the A.D.C.s half her age who wilted."

"How old were you yourself when you first met her?"

"Oh, it's nearly twenty years ago now. Her stepmother, Mollie Mount Temple asked me to come here, for a weekend. They had a shooting-party, which wasn't my cup of tea at all, and it was a bitterly cold Saturday afternoon. I had to stand patiently behind the guns, and without talking—you can imagine what that meant for me—and even the arrival of the Mountbattens, on the scene, didn't warm my blood, at first. I had heard so much about their legendary glamour, and there they were in anonymous tweeds. And like everything else he does, Dickie took his shooting madly seriously. Fortunately her Sealyhams caused a diversion. The were called Mizzen and Gib, and came sniffing at my trousers, because they could smell the scent of my own Mr. Sponge. Being an ardent Sealyham fancier provided a bond between us from the start. You know how silly people are about dogs. You automatically think that anyone who likes the same breeds as you do must be wise and understanding and very, very nice."

"So you made up your mind there and then, on the spot, and never deviated since?"

"No, not exactly. I only made friends with the dogs that afternoon. It was two years before I was to surrender myself completely to her spell and understand why every man on the lower deck of any ship in which he has served would gladly die for him."

Was the champagne making my speech over-enthusiastic? But it was the truth, it had been a surrender, I reminded myself, seeing again in my mind's eye, the luxurious spaces of their pent-house in Park Lane, that afternoon when I had been asked to tea, and my hostess made me feel that I was the only other person in the room, and my host had shown me his bedroom, decorated like a destroyer cabin, and in his study next door the map of the world on the wall with the British Empire marked in scarlet against a background of Mediterranean blue.

The sky had been the same colour outside, that deceiving June day, without a single cloud to spoil the illusion of peace, and my host had come fresh from playing polo at Roehampton. But he was still a sailor, at heart, now and for ever, and suddenly he started to talk about the war that lay just below the surface in everyone's mind. Again and again, he dinned into my ears that the way to stop successful dive-bombing attacks at sea was to pack ships with small light guns that have a deadly explosive range at 2,000 feet. "No dive-bomber would survive such a barrage," he exclaimed passionately.

I listened, deeply impressed not only by his prophetic words, but by the way that his whole personality had changed before my eyes. His magnetism and his power of leadership were very strong at that moment, though, alas, not strong enough at first to make the Admiralty adopt the Oerliken gun in which he believed with all his heart. For he was very conscious that time was running out and when a few weeks later he was given the command of *The Kelly*, for which there had been 3,000 volunteers at Chatham, he assembled the crew he had finally picked, and at the dockside addressed them thus:

"I will give you not three weeks but three days to get this ship ready to sail. None of us will take off our clothes or sling our hammocks until the job is done. Then we'll send Hitler a telegram, saying, '*The Kelly's* ready—you can start your war.' "

It was the sort of speech the Navy understands and loves. Ironically, though, the ship's first commission of the war was to cross to Havre, so that they could bring back to these shores the captain's cousin and his wife, the Duke and Duchess of Windsor. What must have been the silent thoughts of the two cousins, when, the ship berthed safely at Portsmouth, they had a farewell dinner in the captain's cabin. All that had happened to them since the light-hearted peacetime days of their world cruise in *The Renown*. All that was to happen to them both before they were to meet again.

As for the woman, already at her first-aid post in blacked-out London, she admitted to me, when we were discussing that period in her life: "Oh, of course, like every other service wife, I was pretty worried about what lay ahead."

At the same time she was worrying equally about something else: how to achieve an all-embracing wartime job that would consume her burning vitality and give her a sense of real fulfilment at last. However, long before *The Kelly* was to be in mortal combat with the enemy, her captain's wife had found the road that was to bring her leadership of a great army of volunteers, and a completely new working timetable of existence.

In assessing her stature in the contemporary scene, it is important to realize that she started as a member of the ranks working with the Kensington unit. Then she rose swiftly through her now proved qualifications to become first, Deputy Superintendent of St. John's, and finally, in 1942, Superintendent in Chief, the 'queen-bee' position which she still holds, not simply because of her untiring organizing ability, but because she possesses an asset that is rare among career women, she is able to handle her own sex, without creating jealousies and emotional situations.

During the war, turning night into day as far as her work was concerned, acted in some strange way as a kind of sedative to her nerves. Thus she was able by her constant presence to inspire every member of the organization to look upon themselves as soldiers in the raids, to think only of the casualties, never of their own safety. Perhaps it was that she herself was already through familiarity becoming immune to shock, just as the family's pre-war secretary was used to a buoyant masculine voice ringing her up from some unknown quayside call-box, and starting: "Hello, Nancie, break the news gently to Lady Louis, but we've had another 'party'. . . ."

There were four of them altogether, and on one of the earlier occasions the family reunion had taken place in the Station Hotel at Newcastle. That night as they travelled south again, too thankful to try to sleep, the sailor, home from sea, had taken his wife not through every phase of the battle just over, but through all the questions that she might be asked in the next St. John's examination looming ahead of her. You've *got* to pass, he commanded her. And she did. "I wouldn't have dared confess to Dickie if I hadn't," she told me with the re-evoked smile of the young girl who always swears that she pursued her future husband half-way across the world to propose to him.

Then came the last 'party' off Crete, and the only time that he had not brought his ship somehow back into harbour. *The Kelly* was gone: only the legend remained. What would happen now? As I walked that night, in the gardens at Broadlands, I was remembering how in a wartime summer, in such a different atmosphere, a naval captain and his lady (who was herself of considerable rank) had spent a few snatched days of respite, at their Hampshire home.

Most of Broadlands had been turned into a hospital, but one small corner they kept for their very rare reunions when they could put on mufti, and walk beside the river. Had they any premonitions? Looking back now Edwina Mountbatten is most positive that always she knew in her bones that her triumphantly lucky husband would survive the war. Nevertheless, she must have shivered slightly when she heard that he had been given the command of another ship with equally bitter battle scars—*The Illustrious*.

At that moment this aircraft carrier was being refitted in the Navy yards of Norfolk, Virginia. So together the Mountbattens flew across the Atlantic, though on separate missions, he to take over his latest command, she to give exact details of the Red Cross supplies that were most urgently needed, and to give thanks at the same time for all that had already been sent, most generously, in gifts.

It was another important milestone in her career, for in the end, what might have been a dull, official mission was transformed into a royal progress of spontaneous goodwill. On her tour of all the leading American cities the former socialite figure produced a professional technique in her public oratory that was to develop into her becoming, with Lady Violet Bonham Carter and the head of the W.V.S., that very remarkable woman, Stella, Lady Reading, one of the three best women speakers in her own country.

The legend says that at this period her husband coached her in her speeches and that is so. Her gift for always making every member of any audience, large or small, feel that she is speaking to them alone: that flair was always there. However, it blossomed like so many other talents in the war, through necessity.

One evening, soon after her return from that mission, the St. John's Superintendent invited me to accompany her, and her opposite number, Lady Limerick of the Red Cross, round the East End shelters and first-aid posts, during a raid. Such memories, like parties, have on the surface a familiar pattern. But this one has stayed in my mind most vividly ever since for one particular reason. Not for the weight of the attack, or our answering barrage, but for the way that my companion spoke to every nurse by name in each post and shelter that we visited. Yet they were all volunteers, all drawn from other parts of the country to reinforce London personnel, doing two weeks' service in the Metropolis. Nevertheless their superior officer seemed to have as much knowledge of their home background as though they had been on her personal staff for months.

When I expressed my surprise and admiration, she answered crisply, "Surely that was the least I could do under the circumstances."

Outside her temporary home in Chester Street, she dismissed me, in the dawn, with a friendly wave of the hand, and as I walked home wearily to bed, I had a hunch that at that moment she was turning on the taps of her bath, and an hour later would be starting a new day's work.

It was not yet the hour before the dawn, the dance was still at its height, and round the fountains and on the lawns, little groups laughed and chattered, including a girl in a beautiful white dress whose twenty-first birthday was soon to be celebrated, too, by a dance at Balmoral. Close by two men with faces equally well known sat alone at a table, talking shop. They were David Niven and Noel Coward, whose film *In Which We Serve* retold so movingly the story of the ship that our host had loved, the most of any of his commands. Its author, I noticed, had a glass of lemonade in front of him which made me conscious more than ever how very different most people are from their public façades.

At that moment I saw our host and hostess come down the steps from the drawing-room and move towards us, stopping to speak now to one, now another of their guests, like a royal garden party, and I was just deciding that I had never seen so many medal ribbons on one man's chest before and wondering at the same time if he would recall the allusion if I suggested that ginger-ale could taste on occasion far better than champagne, when I heard someone apologize that he had not put his own war medals on for the ball, although the invitation had clearly stated: 'Decorations'.

"I decided they'd look so puny compared with displays like yours, sir."

"But yours were earned, mine were given me," was the instant reply, spoken with such apparent sincerity that one could not believe one was witnessing a show of mock-modesty. However, I had a feeling that my own companion at that moment was not convinced. But then she had not heard him say, as I had in private, that he had never sought publicity for himself, but only for his forgotten armies in Burma. So, equally might he not feel, deep down, that all his medals had really been given to him to wear for the whole complement of his ships' companies like *The Kelly*? Again, for all the commandos whom, at the lowest ebb of the war, he had taught to think only in terms of attack and the future.

How very different his supper had been tonight, I thought, from the hunk of bread and the sardines picked with his fingers out of the tin which he had eaten on the bridge the evening before *The Kelly* was dive-bombed to her death. How very different, too, from the ham sand-wich, and the bottle of ginger ale I had watched him have for his lunch the day he had talked to me at his secret H.Q. in London about his aspirations for the newly formed Combined Ops.

Those mystical phrases coined in times of war. How swiftly out of date, how curiously old-fashioned they could become as soon as the State of Emergency was over. And yet although the soft, lilting music of Ambrose's band came towards us through the open windows, I was hearing another pattern of sound, in my memory.

"After every raid we hold a post-mortem. One thing we guarantee here, we never make the same mistake twice." I saw him again putting his finger in the ginger ale, making it fizz like champagne. "Here we speak only in terms of the offensive. The word 'defensive' is not included in our vocabulary." And then he had added something else that had a significance in peace, as well as in war.

"Everybody in this party at H.Q. is between thirty and fifty. Under thirty they wouldn't be experienced enough. Much over forty they wouldn't be young enough. I think our greybeard is actually fifty. Thirty to fifty that is the perfect range."

And now Time had caught up with him, too, in that he himself was a greybeard in years though both he and his wife this evening seemed at every angle as vital as their younger daughter to drink whose health we had all assembled. When the parents, themselves still sailing on a full tide, moved on across the lawn, my companion murmured: "Do you really think he meant that about the medals?" Her eyes followed his back that rolled very slightly as though he were on his favourite ground, any quarter-deck.

"Of course he really meant it," I assured her. "Just as much as he means to be First Sea Lord one day, to avenge his father's memory. Just as much as she means never to let *his* career and her sense of obligation towards it ever to overlay her own equally strong sense of duty towards *her* spheres of usefulness as a citizen of the world. Those spheres are expanding all the time. Why, do you know something fantastic," I added, "the last Vicereine has received from India's Prime Minister an invitation to be the first visitor from England, under the new régime. They've asked her to inspect all the organizations that she started under the title of the United Council of Relief and Welfare. I am sure that invitation means more to Edwina than having ever been called Your Excellency," I ended up, with considerable conviction.

"And do you think her husband minds her increasing success in Public Life, the honours that are showered upon her, as a Personage in her own right?"

"I don't think he minds any more than other husbands mind about their wives having a career of their own."

"That's not answering my question."

I had not meant to answer it. And I was just about to suggest that we should have one final dance before going home to bed, when a diversion came, happily, from another quarter. One of the attractive young women, in the bureau of Mountbatten secretaries, recognized me, as an old ally. "Oh dear," she exclaimed, "I hate leaving the party but I must. I have got to drive back to London, and Lady Louis is sure to be on the phone at nine-thirty tomorrow morning."

"You mean, *this* morning," I suggested.

"Yes, indeed, I mean *this* morning," she agreed and hurried away.

"The legend says that the secretaries all take turns of six weeks duty at a time, and then have to have a prolonged rest! But all the same, they would not work for anyone else," I whispered in my partner's ear, as we danced our way across the room, for the last time.

In the hall now, our hostess was saying goodbye to some of her neighbours. There was the local doctor, and the Mayor of Romsey and his wife; in fact, the last three mayors. One had been a Conservative, another a Liberal and the third belonged to the Labour Party. Could that be taken as a comment on her own politics?

Recently she had admitted to me with her typical candour: "There's no question of my being Right Wing or Left Wing, as some of my friends of the old days seem to think I am now. The truth is, I like meeting people and working with people and hearing every possible point of view. It is people, not politics that I am interested in and always will be now. . . ."

Souvenir
of India

COUNTESS MOUNTBATTEN OF BURMA

"It is people I am interested in,
not politics"

"By the end of the week, everyone on the camp is calling her Maggie"

I remembered that as I thanked her for another most stimulating evening in her home, deciding that she herself looked just as fresh as when the party had begun.

"I am so glad you enjoyed yourself, Godfrey," and it sounded as though she was saying it for the first time. So much so that the warmth and clarity of her voice followed me into the darkness of the drive.

Then I looked back at the floodlit colonnade and I thought: yes, they had known right from the start where they were going, all those years ago.

SIX

THE RED COAT

THAT Sunday morning in early September coincided with a welcome burst of Queen's weather. I had been on holiday in Scotland, resting in anonymous peace in the Trossachs, for I was very weary from a long stretch of engagements. So much so that as I started to drive south again, I almost regretted that I had accepted any invitations to break my journey, stopping here and there, overnight, with friends.

The first day I only reached as far as the Northumbrian coast, staying on a farm near Lowick. Having inspected the pigs, and listened to a parable which I refer to in a later chapter, I took myself off to Berwick, walking for a long time in solitary communion on the sands. Later I explored the labyrinthine paths between the beach and the lower part of the town, where hidden from the main road to Edinburgh are haphazard but nevertheless delightfully rooted terraces of houses looking out to sea, full of character and an eighteenth-century flavour. I had had a foolish notion that architecturally one visited Berwick to look at its bridges: no one had prepared me for the impact of its untouched backcloth. The sun had come out at last, enhancing the patina of everything and giving promise of a brilliant weekend ahead, while the wind had dropped to a soft sigh. I imagine that this corner of the coast can be very bleak in winter but now as I walked on the golf course, suspended above the iridescent sands, I found myself regretting that I had spent the carefree moments of my youth, trying to master a semblance of Donald Budge's backhand drive on the tennis court, which few south paws, strangely, whatever their standard of play, ever do achieve.

The next afternoon I joined the spectators of a village cricket match at Wynyard Park, where I was not expected to do anything more strenuous than applaud every boundary, indiscriminately, and commiserate with my host's son when he gave a perfect demonstration of what happens when one does not play forward with a straight bat. Alistair's sister, Jane, had been one of the train-bearers to her Sovereign, at the Coronation. Her own bearing that day in the Abbey had been impeccable; it was equally so this afternoon, sharing buns with the visiting team. The match over, and our duty done, Jane changed into dark blue slacks and we had an uproarious, very mixed doubles with a family aunt and a younger sister, Annabel. One was very conscious that the hungry generations were not treading anyone down, even at dinner, when a devoted retainer shuffled round the table. In contrast, afterwards, the youngest members of the party picked up their heels and danced varying versions of the Charleston, to the gramophone, enveloping the table where four of us struggled to play bridge. From the wall behind Jane's head, her ancestress, Alexandrina Octavia Maria Vane Tempest, painted as a child in a white dress by Lawrence, stared down at us with innocent and Timeless gaze.

It was an atmosphere which could only be savoured in England. Naturally I was sad to leave in the morning but I must keep the promise I had made to be one of the judges at the Beauty Parade that Sunday afternoon at the Butlin camp at Filey. "Why don't you all come with me?" I suggested to the group of two sisters, brother and Etonian school friend, who had made the highest score for the home side yesterday, as they gathered round the car, to see me off. Whereupon Annabel who would have won first prize in the competition without a doubt, gave an incredulous squeak. "What's it like? You don't mean you are going to stay the night there. Will you have to sleep in a tent?" "Come and see for yourself," I urged them again. "When Pamela Mountbatten spent a weekend with her mother, she enjoyed herself so much she hated leaving."

I don't know if they believed me or if they simply imagined I was trying to sell to myself one of my own public commitments but the truth is, as I drove farther south, leaving Billingham and Durham far behind and discovering the untrammelled magnificence of the run over the moors to Scarborough, I kept on wishing most vehemently that Jane, Alistair and Annabel were spending the rest of the weekend with me, doing things the Butlin way. Would it not have been at once a revelation for them, and for the six thousand other campers, too, to have this opportunity to get to know each other?

All the same I did have doubts. For myself. Even though Filey has always been my favourite among the six camps since I paid my first visit the summer of the transition from war into peace, when

some of the chalets still had messages written on the door, left
by the departing R.A.F. personnel, for five years in posssesion.
Right from the start I had fallen in love with the way that the camp
is set high above the sea, halfway between Flamborough Head and the
Edwardian boarding houses of Filey, with miles of free sands between.
The sense of imagination displayed in the brilliant array of the flags
of all nations that is the first splash of colour to greet you on your
arrival.

It would be difficult even for the most ungregarious of mortals
to deny that this post-war type of holiday camp possesses the perfect
layout for a recreation centre on a vast scale. And, moreover,
is at the opposite end of the scale from the haphazard arrangement of
leaking tents and hazy plumbing which is the visual conception that
many people still have who have never made the effort to visit one
of the Butlin camps themselves. The whole empire—for it is an
empire now—is an extraordinary achievement for a man who,
after serving as a drummer boy in the Canadian army overseas in the
First World War, set out to make a fortune with a single stall in a
Fun Fayre at Skegness. Today he provides hot and cold running
water in every chalet, beds that are as comfortable as a first-class
hotel, and roses, literally, round the door, for a floating population
of over thirty thousand guests, during the peak weeks of each summer
season. When you ask him, as I have done, for the recipe of his unchallenged success he replies in the husky, almost timid speech that
completely conceals an absolute clarity of purpose, allied to the driving
powers of a fanatic, "Well, I worked it out like this from the start.
If you want to attract more customers than the stall next door, you
must give better prizes. And never cheat. You know, with rings that
won't go over the blocks on the hoop-la stall. Our customers—they
are really our friends now—always come back a second year, and then
it becomes a habit, because they find out for themselves that all that
we say in the advertisements *is* true. It really is the best family
holiday you can get."

Yes, but after the silence of the Scottish mountains, would the
transition now seem devastatingly abrupt? Too many jolly people,
too much whipped-up gaiety, too many organized amusements seeth-
ing all round me. They say, never go back, but I was doing just that,
after a gap of three years. One grows older. One changes. Would the
set-up be the same, too much the same? A thousand couples on the

floor of the Viennese Ballroom that evening, dancing to the perennial music of Charles Amer and his Butlin Boys who have become part of the Filey scene. By then, of course, I should be acclimatized once more but first I had to face the crowds milling round the giant swimming pool after lunch and watch the gallant efforts of the Red Coats to keep the customers amused before the initial walk-round of the competitors in their bathing-dresses, who, as they passed, would entreat the judge with timid imploring smiles. Did they never guess how nervous some of us were, too?

If Norah is one of my fellow judges, it will be all right, thus and thus I reassured myself. Norah Butlin with a grown-up son in the army, who looks like her younger brother: who has the rare, un-ransomable gift of making everyone with whom she comes in contact feel after a few minutes conversation so buoyant and full of hope themselves. I suppose it is, I decided, as the car slowed down to enter the gates, because she manages to be on such good terms with herself as well as with all the world, whether she is presiding over Billy's box at one of the Albert Hall Reunions, or entertaining in their Grosvenor Square flat the officials of the National Playing Fields Association for which the camps have already raised over £30,000, or spending the majority of her summer weekends at Filey, Skegness, Pwhelli, sharing her chalet with the Boss, like any other couple on holiday, universally friendly and kind to everyone, never apparently bored or tired. Always suitably turned out, dressed up or dressed down to the occasion, always perfuming the scene with a welcoming smile that matched her own blonde colouring, equally unsynthetic. Thus, wherever she went, her lack of artifice was refreshing as it was rare. Oh, I do hope Norah is there to meet me, I said to myself.

And she was. As though I was the only visitor to Filey whom she had greeted that year. "You know you ought to be crowned the Queen of the Red Coats," I suggested, all my doubts resolved in the first five minutes while she helped me to unpack in my chalet and pinned this year's badge into my buttonhole. "Don't worry, you have a charming Red Coat to look after you," she answered in her warm voice that still has a touch of West Country burr in it. "Her name is Margaret Lemond. But everyone on the camp by the end of the week is calling her Maggie. . . ."

Just as the petty officers in a ship are the leavening mixture which makes or mars the happiness and well-being of the whole, so in any of the Butlin camps the posse of Red Coats possess a value and importance far outweighing their actual numbers. How many of these young men, so conspicuous in their scarlet blazers and white flannel trousers and their opposite numbers in pleated white skirts are apportioned to each camp and is it a permanent job? "I mean, what happens to them, Norah, in the winter time? Do they 'rest' like pantomime favourites when the season is over?"

"You'd better ask Billy or Basil. We are joining them for a drink before lunch. Yes, I *am* judging with you. Oh dear, I always want to give first prize to the very plain girl who should never have entered. . . ."

"But was dragooned in by one of the Red Coats who have to make up the numbers. Yes, I always feel the same. And what's worse, I take a blind prejudice against the entrant who imagines she is the greatest beauty of all time. She makes that only too clear in the preliminary parade. She has got all the tricks and the confidence of a professional prize winner. She is usually on the tall side, with a mass of curls, a lot of make-up, not much care and attention given to her lower limbs but an off-white bathing dress that leaves little to the imagination, in the upper reaches. I have a savage desire sometimes to mark her nought out of ten, but never have the courage in the end, because of the enthusiastic whistles from the crowd. And when I glance nervously behind me, I always spot at least three girls who look *much* prettier than those we have chosen first, second and third. Is that because they were too shy to enter, or simply because they didn't know how attractive they were?"

"Don't be silly, Godfrey. Every girl knows how attractive she is. Her trouble is making men understand."

"Or vice versa," I suggested.

The long bar, with its bright murals, its shining chromium fixtures, and beyond the open door, a glassed-in beer garden that also served as a solarium for those who wanted simply to sit and listen to the soft music emerging from a loudspeaker, had a pleasing affinity with a liner where all accommodation was one-class, for the duration of the summer cruise. In a moment you were drawn into the atmosphere. Here Time had no meaning: here, too, was a happy starting off point for shipboard acquaintanceships which before the week was over might blossom into something deeper or more lasting. 'I first met my wife at a Butlin camp'. And if not, what fun it had all been! Every member of the family was here: Grandma was having a stout, the baby sucking a coke through a straw. In two corners, there were little groups round Red Coats, who, I noticed were drinking nothing themselves. We made our way towards the bar, where two men were standing, each with the club badge in their button hole that gave them the right to be served. They were waiting their turn like everyone else. Every few minutes a small boy or girl came up with an autograph book and pushed it in front of the shorter of the two figures. He obliged with an avuncular smile as he signed 'Billy Butlin'. His suntan had a permanent look and he was wearing the same light suit that a month ago had been his uniform in Nassau. In both places, one felt, he was equally at home, though if he had to make a final and absolute choice between the two backgrounds, there would be no hesitation on his part. The camps were more than his business and his pleasure: they were his faith.

"I was telling Mr. Butlin about the cricket week we've organized which starts tomorrow. I think the sports field is new, at least, newly levelled and spruced up, since you were here last. We've got a first-class pitch—at least, the old hands, like Maurice Tate, who is here for the week tells me so—and we certainly have a first-class idea. We have asked the public schools to send us some of their best bats, and keenest youngsters, and we've asked some of the big towns in the north to do the same thing, from their schools. Then we shall mix them up, and give them coaching each morning at the nets, side by side, with a team of first-class pros., presided over by Alan Fairfax and Bill Voce. Young Robins, who captained Eton, this year, is coming down, and I am sure the idea will have far-reaching results."

"The Battle of the Peace being fought and won on the playing fields of Butlin's Camps. Why not?" I agreed. For the enthusiasm of my host's companion at the bar was infectious. I should have written 'shadow', for Colonel Basil Brown is the shadow during working hours—and that means every day and most nights of the week—of the man whose infinite capacity for getting things done he first encountered when the now legendary leave centre was opened in Brussels after the liberation. Planning side by side, their personalities, through the attraction of opposites, melded at once, the one who makes up his mind in a second and never deviates from his hunches: the other with all the charm in the world—'bags of flannel', as they call it in the Navy—and all the sophisticated graces to gloss over awkward corners and resolve the inevitable crises which occur in any undertaking on this scale. At first when I met Mr. Butlin's chief lieutenant I was deceived by his official title 'Head of Entertainment', and by his unfailing *bonhomie*. I did not appreciate that there was another side to his character. Now I know, from personal experience, that his word is his bond and I have grown to have a very great respect for the efficient staffwork behind the mask of smiling courtesy, and for his remarkable flair for handling all sorts of folk and all sorts of situations.

"I was telling Godfrey that he must ask you, Basil, about the Red Coats," Norah Butlin said with her usual tact.

"What does he want to know? How many there are altogether? It varies a little but roughly about four hundred. Half of them men, the others, girls. Some of them have been with us since the end of the war. The campers, when they write in for their reservations, often ask if Such-and-Such a Red Coat will still be at this camp or that, and book accordingly. That's heady wine for them, of course, and occasionally they can't take their oats and have to be weeded out, after a year or two. Actually, the girls seem to be more sensible about their temporary fame, than the men. In any case there is always a sprinkling of newcomers, each season. It's quite a lure, the idea of wearing a red coat all day long. What some of the applicants don't realize is how much responsibility goes with that very conspicuous emblem."

"And how much hard work, too?" I suggested.

"And how much hard work, too," the Colonel agreed.

"I suppose the duties of a Red Coat girl are very much like those of a hostess on a cruise. But, of course, on a much larger scale. But the same reason for her presence. To encourage the get-together mood, to break down barriers of aloofness, start games and introduce those who are on their own to congenial company. Always on the spot, always on the go, but not too obtrusively. A bit like a policewoman, too, in that her red coat is a symbol. Anyone can go up to her and ask for information or advice. Or say, I want to play tennis. Can you find me someone to play with? Or billiards or ping-pong, or what have you. . . ."

"Yes, that's it, exactly. She is everyone's friend. Whether it's a girl who has come on her own and doesn't know a soul, on her first evening in camp, or a large family, where the grandparents might get left out, or some fellow, who is home on leave, and at a loose end. He wants to meet some nice girls, in a legitimate way. The Red Coat will soon size him up, that he's not a wolf, but on the level, and help him all she can."

"The job seems to combine a bit of everything. She has to be a shrewd judge of human nature into the bargain. Or perhaps she acquires that knowledge, season by season?"

"Probably, but it's quite essential. Now the girl who will be looking after you this weekend has been with us since 1947. I think I'm right—but she will tell you—that she was only seventeen then. She is a splendid type. Always at ease with all the campers—but no obvious favourites among the men. Always patient with the old folk—in fact, she's in charge of the Whist Drives. Strong and willing to tackle anything and you have to be strong, in her job. And that's why Maggie Lemond holds hers down."

"Do you keep her on during the winter? Do they all stay on?"

"Not all. The best ones, always. Some of the others have only wanted to try it out for a season, anyway. Though we have briefed them well enough, they imagined their duties consisted of posing in a pretty blazer, and being surrounded by pretty girls. They're the ones that will always try anything 'amusing' once, and can usually sell themselves, once, too."

"And what do you do with the ones you do keep on?"

"We send them in teams all over the country, attending Reunion Dances, and when they are not doing that, they will be at Head Office in Oxford Street. As soon as one season ends, we have to start preparing for the next. Now what are you going to drink?"

It was typical that the general, in mufti, stood by silently while his Chief of Staff explained all the tactical points that I had raised. He prefers it that way. However, had there been the smallest slip of any sort, he would have intervened at once. Instead, the intervention came from another source. At that moment, the music, being relayed over the loudspeaker was interrupted by an anonymous voice announcing that lunch was about to be served in the four dining-halls, labelled Gloucester, Kent, York and Windsor. It was the same voice which, the evening before, at the first meal of a new week's arrivals, had suggested that everyone should turn and shake hands with their neighbours at the supper table. That is a form of mass introductions that has not yet been tried out elsewhere, but I can assure the sceptical that it is found to have extremely beneficial results in the Butlin school of Psychology.

There is a widespread illusion, supported by those who have never visited one of these camps that life there on holiday is completely regimented from dawn till midnight: that a braying, raucous voice, reminiscent of a sergeant-major, amplified to a terrifying degree through the loudspeaker, tells you what to do, at every moment of one's waking hours, or else. . . .

Or else what? Or else, you don't. It is a complete fallacy about the regimentation. Apart from the times when meals are served, there are no other restrictions at all. Guests please themselves entirely. They can either take part in the day's list of entertainments, set out in the printed magazine, or they can wander off by themselves. They can be spectators or participants. They can make an expedition by bus, or in their own cars (and first-time visitors are always astonished by the number of cars to be seen in the parking-ground) or else they relax in a deck-chair in front of their chalet, sunbathing and doing absolutely nothing. I have often come upon the brains behind the whole concern doing exactly that himself, on a Sunday morning.

Of course, if, including the staff, there are seven thousand men, women and children to be fed three times a day, you must have meals served punctually and in an orderly fashion. Otherwise there would be chaos, and the washing-up would never be done.

So our party set an example by moving from the bar the moment that the announcer's voice summoned us. We lunched ourselves in Gloucester that day. I felt a little like an A.D.C., walking, in time, behind my host. But on these occasions what might so easily become a travesty of a royal procession is kept in its right perspective by the instinctive good taste of Billy Butlin himself, on the one hand, and of his assorted array of customers, on the other. Without turning their heads, they let him settle in peace into an unobtrusive corner of the great dining-room, where we proceeded to have exactly the same meal as the campers. And why not? It would never have occurred to my host that you could have a better Sunday lunch than roast beef and two vegetables, followed by pie and ice-cream, and preceded by plates of really hot soup. "Have another helping if you like," he said to me, huskily, "All the campers can."

During lunch my Red Coat came up and introduced herself. She reminded me immediately of Judy Garland on a taller scale. She had the same generous mouth, and wide-set, hazel eyes.

"Do you sing?" I asked.

She denied it, smilingly, though some of the Red Coats are excellent performers, of a near professional standard, having their own 'spot' in the introductory theatre show on Saturday nights—'Who's Who' and crooning or clowning their way through the week, and into the hearts of the campers. Not surprisingly that part of their duties appeals to some of them most of all. They see their names in lights, on the hoardings outside the Palladium, and they become so bemused by their own glamour that the real visiting stars occasionally have difficulty in snatching the microphone back for their own 'acts'. From my own observation I would say that the girls accept the applause, for what it is worth, with more basic common sense than the men. But then they are not subjected to quite such a barrage of admiration from the youngsters of both sexes: especially for one of the four Red Coats, who has won the coveted title of 'House Captain', it must need a superhuman effort to keep his feet firmly planted on the ground, when on Friday nights, he walks forward in the ballroom to receive the silver cup that is the accolade of his House's victory, and hears the cheers of his supporters ringing in his ears.

"Have you any particular party turn?" I asked my own Red Coat, when we were having a cup of tea together, much needed after the judging of this batch of holiday princesses was over, and I was able to slip away into oblivion, leaving the crowd to concentrate on the visual pleasures of the Knobbly Knee Contest for the Lads.

Maggie—inevitably one slips into Christian name terms at once at a Butlin camp—shook her head firmly. "I'm a maid of all work now."

"Now?" I queried.

"Yes. I joined Butlin's to be trained as a frogwoman." When she saw my look of bewilderment, she went on quickly to explain how it all happened, how it all began.

First she told me about her childhood in Hammersmith, where her father worked as a civil servant, and how when war came she was nine years old, and was evacuated with her younger brother to Canada. Whereupon she settled down so happily in Toronto that she hated the idea of coming home in 1946. In fact, it wasn't home any more. Margaret Lemond talked with a Canadian accent, she wore Canadian clothes, the old country seemed desperately slow and shabby to her, at first.

"In fact, I was all mixed up. I realize it now. I didn't know what I wanted to do. I took a course at Pitman's. I tried half a dozen jobs, I hated the lot. All I wanted to do was to catch the next boat back to Canada. I was discontented, miserable, no use to anyone. And then something happened which made me sit up. My brother won a scholarship to Dulwich College from his local school at Tulse Hill. So our family plans for returning to Canada were squashed by that. Also, I began to feel ashamed that I wasn't getting anywhere in my own life."

"So you joined Butlin's?"

"I stuck it at Butlin's." And I liked the firm, crisp way that she handled that interruption. "I only joined the organization in the first place because three of my girl friends thought it would be fun to be Red Coats and suggested that I should go along to the Head Office with them and have an interview, too. When my turn came, the only job left was a spare Frogwoman. It was the year when the camps were having displays every Sunday given by an expert team of Frogmen, who had been in the war. The star attraction was Bill Fraser, V.C."

"And in each camp, I suppose they needed a couple of girls to lend glamour to the show."

"You wouldn't say that if you'd seen the costume we had to wear. What's more, I was terrified at first."

"But you stuck it?" And now all trace of irony was banished from my voice.

"Yes, I stuck it, but my friends didn't. At the end of the season they packed up. They were quite disillusioned about the joys of being a Red Coat. They said they took a size larger shoes by the end of the season! All the same, I thought I'd like to have a shot at it myself. And I was taken on the next season at Skegness. I stayed there till 1951, then I had a summer at Pwllheli, and now here I am at Filey."

"Which is your own favourite camp?"

"Oh, I think Pwllheli. I love the view of the mountains all round. And it's the newest camp of all. But Dobbie—that's Mr. Dobson—who was my Chief at Pwllheli was transferred as Entertainment Manager here this year, so I was very pleased when I heard I was coming with him. It makes all the difference if you are working for someone who understands all the complications in dealing with the customers."

"Such as?"

"Well, when you are on duty in one of the Ballrooms, and the same young man keeps on asking you to dance. It's all right once, or even twice, in the course of the evening, but some of them don't understand that you are not there as a private guest, but to keep an eye on everything, and check up that the other girls have partners. You should see the lads' faces when I introduce them to someone who is sitting out, and suggest that they should ask *her* for a dance instead! It's the same over drinks. I'm allowed to have an occasional drink, and I am trusted to use my own judgement, but it's rather tricky sometimes, having to refuse one offer, when they've caught you with a glass in your hand, half an hour before. What I try to do is to hang on to the same glass with something in it, all evening. Still, all that is easy to cope with besides a wet Saturday."

"Why a wet Saturday particularly?"

"Because Saturday is the change-over day. Six or seven thousand campers have to be got out of their chalets and packed off in time for the new occupants to take over. For some reason known only to the Almighty, however fine it's been all week, the moment the coaches start arriving, down comes the rain. And you can imagine the feelings of Mum, who has been coaxing and cajoling the kids along since the early dawn, and now their first glimpse of the camp is in a deluge. It's a bit difficult to make them believe that they are going to have the most wonderful holiday of their lives."

"What's the best treatment?"

"A free cup of tea. It works wonders."

She poured herself out another cup, and I admired, once again, the freshness of her own appearance: the spotlessly clean blouse, the skirt that looked as though it had been newly pressed that morning: the make-up that wasn't plastered on to her face, giving instead the impression that the skin beneath was able to breathe and would still look attractive on a desert island. Considering how little time she had to herself, and that the management only provided two pounds ten towards her working wardrobe of four skirts and half a dozen blouses, I decided that her turnout was a considerable achievement.

After our cup of tea together, in the Sun Lounge, Maggie looked at her watch and found she had just fifteen minutes left, before she was on duty again, for the first heats of the Golden Voice contest—'but that's easy, compared with the Whist Drives, how some of those old dears can squabble'—so she offered to show me the chalet that she shared with one of the secretarial staff, at the other end of the chalet lines from where I was sleeping myself. It seemed to me that the first five minutes of that last precious quarter of an hour were spent in walking, and I began to wonder all over again just how many miles a Red Coat did walk in the course of the day, and how many hours, too, were spent on their feet.

"Don't you long to be able to come back here, and just flop on the bed?" I suggested when we finally reached our destination.

"Don't I just. Sometimes I am so tired on the one whole day off a week that we all get that it needs a great effort of will not just to stay in bed."

"What *do* you do?" I asked, curiously.

"I usually go into Scarborough. It's very nice there."

"By yourself?"

"Yes, always by myself," she added firmly. "You don't know what a relief it is to be by myself for a few hours. Sometimes I go to a movie and sometimes I have my hair done. The time soon goes, believe me."

"Don't some of the young men here every week try to date you up?"

"Oh yes," but she sounded indifferent, and I had a feeling that her reactions were the same as those of a dance hostess in a night club, however respectable, where after a time all men seemed to wear the same suit, like a diet of the same dish for every meal.

"But you really like it now?"

"I love it." Her voice, her whole expression changed. Now she really looked like a woman in love. "You know, it's so wonderful at the end of the week when people come up to me and thank *me* for their holiday, and tell me how tired, or how out of everything they felt at the beginning and how different their mood is now. It makes me feel quite different myself, and fresh for the new lot of campers. I know I've really done some good. Of course, at first, I admit it was just a job, but I tried to make a success of it, because of my brother."

"Because of your brother?"

"Yes. He won another scholarship from Dulwich to Dartmouth, to train as a naval officer. He came out fourth in his exams from all the candidates. I felt so proud of him, I wanted him to be proud of me too."

"Has he been to one of the camps?"

"Yes, he came to Pwllheli last summer. That's before he joined *The Sheffield*, as a midshipman."

The Sheffield! 'Our two-funnelled bastard' as the ship's crew affectionately called it, in my day. I saw myself again on the screen of my mind in filthy overalls taking a minor part in the most dreaded routine in the whole life of Naval Standing Orders. De-ammunitioning ship, before an overhaul. I remember how I swore to myself, those bitter back-breaking days in Greenock Harbour, that if I ever survived the whole show—and you don't feel you are going to survive as you hoist four-inch shells on to your shoulder, don't ask me how you manage, but you do—I would never complain again, no matter how many hours I had to sit at my typewriter to satisfy the tax collector.

"Does he enjoy it? I mean, did he enjoy his visit?" I corrected myself hastily, switching my mind back to this moment of Time when I was standing in the doorway of a chalet that was as snug as any cruiser's cabin inside talking to a smart girl in a uniform consisting of a scarlet blazer, with an array of Butlin badges like a hoist of ships' flags down her lapels.

"Yes, he enjoyed it very much. . . ."

"But he decided his sister earned her salary. That's six pounds a week and your board and keep, isn't it? Do you manage to save anything before the season is over?"

"Oh yes, I usually manage to save quite a lot. Nearly fifty pounds." Maggie had already shown me the ingenious arrangement—an alternative plug to the light switch—she and her chalet mate had fixed up for ironing their clothes. They had done everything they could to turn their summer quarters into a home. They had put a pink silk shade over the reading light, between their bunks, and imported a bedside radio, and even put up extra shelves for the packets of washing flakes and tea. The final effect was friendly and feminine—with nylons soaking in the wash-basin—and as completely un-sexconscious as Maggie herself. And as clean, too. It must be a sore temptation, I thought, to leave everything in a shambles, but it wasn't so in this case, because when it was the Red Coat's turn to be housemaid, she conscientiously spent some of her afternoon period off duty, tidying up. "Of course it all goes in the winter—the money I've saved, I mean, when I have to live in digs in Town. London is terribly expensive. It would be so wonderful if. . . ."

"Yes?"

Then it came out in a rush. If only she could be chosen as one of the picked team of Red Coats, four men and four girls, who rumour said were to take up their residence that winter at the Ocean Hotel, outside Brighton. She spoke of her goal as a touring actress will dream of being engaged by the same management to play a small part in their next production at Drury Lane. And it was the same management, in this case. "Mr. Butlin has just taken it over, you know, and is going to run it like a very posh camp, without chalets, of course. Holidays like a ship's cruise. I believe the hotel is modelled like a ship inside. All windows looking out over the sea, and I might even get a cabin to myself. . . ."

At that moment over the loudspeaker a polite and cheerful voice started to announce that competitors for the Golden Voice Competition should assemble now in the Viennese Ballroom, and at once the vision was shattered. "Help, that's me," and without even waiting to re-do her face, my companion had pulled to the door of her chalet, said goodbye to her visitor, and taken to her heels.

I expected that to be the last glimpse I should have of her, during the evening, but hours later, when I slipped into The Gaiety Theatre to see The Star Gazers, who were top of the bill in the Sunday night Variety Concert, going through their act for the fourth and last time, there was Maggie, with a torch, showing latecomers to their seats, shushing anyone who was inclined to be noisy, leading children by the hand who suddenly wanted to go somewhere. In between she stood by one of the exits, as upright and tidy as though she had just come on parade. Even though in the semi-darkness her deportment could hardly be picked out by any higher authority.

Silently I gave her more marks than I had given to any of the bathing belles. Indeed, I would have given her more than that, had I the power. As I limped back to my own chalet, and sitting on the edge

East Sutton Park, near Maidstone

The Prison Governor

of the bed took off my own shoes and massaged my ageing feet, I wished the Ocean Hotel belonged to me. I wished. . . .

Miraculously, on Christmas Day my dreams came true. For spending the evening at Saltdean where the newly decorated hotel with its long golden façade dominates the whole landscape, as the guest of Norah and Billy Butlin—and what a happy party it was, my mother still on the dance floor at midnight—suddenly I came upon Maggie, assisting a fellow Red Coat to dress up for his cabaret turn. She looked just the same, her hair neatly waved, her uniform smartly pressed, the only deviation, a sprig of mistletoe in the buttonhole of her blazer.

"So you made it," I exclaimed, "I *am* glad."

"Yes, and do you know what I have just heard, I am going back to Pwllheli, next summer, as Hostess. That's promotion to Chief Girl Red Coat. Aren't I lucky?"

And the way she smiled made me feel that I had just been given my nicest Christmas present for years.

SEVEN

THE BORSTAL GIRL

THE newest intake at the Borstal Institution for Girls at Aylesbury stood in front of the Governor's desk. The woman with the grey hair neatly parted in the centre, the deceptively gentle voice, glanced up from writing her report. "What were you doing at Skegness?" she asked.

"Skegness?" echoed the girl. "Was that the name of the town where I was picked up? Why, that was where the wagon was going...."

The 'wagon', it was explained to me, is the American movie slang for 'lorry', and the girls who find themselves finally in a Borstal establishment are nearly all inhabitants of the distorted, dream world of the cinema. This particular one had sat curled up, all through the night, beside the wagon's driver. For her it was the nearest she would reach, in her imagination, to living fully and dangerously—to adventure. And if it entailed being put down in the dawn in a strange town, with no money and nowhere to wander except in the streets, while she searched for a chance, however unlawful, to eat at someone else's expense ... well, was that any worse than the existence from which she had fled?

This is a composite portrait, of course, but more often than not the fundamental reason that brings these unwanted, uncontrollable teenagers to Aylesbury is that from their earliest childhood they have never possessed any of the advantages usually understood by the expression 'a home environment'. Until, in the end, they are picked up by the police, and after an abortive attempt has been made to recondition their outlook in an Approved School, are finally sent to Borstal, because, to use the official phrase of the magistrates' courts, they are 'in need of care and protection'.

Such would be a fair generalization about the majority of the hundred and eighty girls, between the ages of sixteen and twenty-one, now under the charge of Miss Martyn and her staff. No girl can be sent to Aylesbury before she is sixteen or again after she has, in the eyes of the Law, come of age. But, of course, between the two limiting landmarks their mentalities differ as greatly as the young of any large community. Some had the unfledged contours, the expression of children still, and had, too, I was assured during my visit, a desperate need for affection and understanding. Others were already women of the world: with powdered cheeks, elaborate hair styles, again copied from their favourite cinema heroine, the bold and staring glances of those who imagine that they know all the answers and no longer care.

It is true that many of them have served prison sentences already, but by no means all. For some have no criminal record on their classifying sheet, are simply vagrants, who have been found in bad company, drifting to perdition: for whom it is felt that Borstal, which is technically not a prison but a training establishment—and the staff are rightly very jealous of that distinction—may succeed in providing the solidity of background, the continuity of environment that alone can hope to transform such mixed and dubious material into adult and responsible citizens.

One is always wary of statistics for they can be made to prove anything in the hands of a clever campaigner; however, in this case, statistics would show the system to be a success, for of those who left in a recent year, eighty per cent so far have kept out of the police's hands. Time can only prove—or disprove—the final results, but, in another way, time is on the side of the Borstal authorities. The courses in training and teaching can be stretched, by law, to a maximum of four years.

Of these years up to three can be spent, either at Aylesbury or at the 'open' Borstal, with which I was tremendously impressed, at East Sutton Park, near Maidstone. Here in this beautiful country house, with its view on a clear day right away to the Kentish coast, its atmosphere now transformed into that of a severe but first-class girls' school, another fifty pupils are taken, who have not been picked out because they have been judged to be 'better' than the other girls at Aylesbury, but for one reason alone. Because, from their records to date, if the challenge of open windows and unlocked doors is continuously, tantalizingly with them, they are the least likely to succumb and take to their heels.

Then there is the final year when the girls go back into the world, and it does not matter any more if doors are open or doors are locked. They can come and go freely, with one strict proviso.

They are still on probation, on Licence, as it is called. This means that they must not change their address without notifying the after-care authorities, or again change their jobs, without an excellent reason.

Incidentally, when I went to see the Head of the Association with its headquarters in a mews near Victoria, which looks after women prisoners when they are released, I was enthralled by something she told me. We had been discussing the difficulty that many of those who have served either a Borstal or prison sentence have in rehabilitating themselves in the outside world, and Miss Long, who possesses a rich smile and has a most uncondemning manner, and who has been a wonderfully understanding friend to so many women, remarked that there was one type that she rarely had any trouble in setting on their feet again. "They nearly always re-marry at once, and settle down most happily in a domestic way of life."

"Oh, and what type are those?" I asked.

"They are the prisoners who have been serving a long sentence for murder."

Of course, some of the Borstal girls get into the frame of mind where they begin to imagine that they are inside for a life sentence, too, and if they are fortunate enough to be at East Sutton Park, find it easy enough to run away any night they choose. Though they seldom get far, and are usually brought back by a neighbouring farmer in the morning, having been found huddled under the shelter of a hay-rick.

Sometimes they simply run away from a sense of bravado, to prove to the other girls that they have the gumption, and having proved it once, having blooded themselves, can afterwards rest on their laurels. I was allowed to spend an hour, alone, talking, to the equivalent of the school prefects at East Sutton Park, after lunch, and they confided this point of view to me themselves.

But occasionally there are deeper, much deeper reasons, an inner compulsion that is not so easily satisfied or cured. Miss Hooker, the forthright Head of the 'Open' Borstal, told me of an instance that has stayed in my memory ever since, because of its numerous corollaries in other communities.

There was one particular girl at East Sutton Park who did not seem to respond at all to the teaching, the atmosphere, to the surrounding beauty, for the sprawling gardens with their mellow brick and fruit-laden walls, do possess a traditional English grace and loveliness and one would have to be stubbornly blind not to be influenced, and the right way, it seemed to me.

However, this child wasn't. Instead, she was listless, sulky, completely uncooperative. Finally, although she appeared to be a weak little thing, and without initiative, she took to running away. Not far away. She was always brought back within a few hours. It was as though she was too hopeless to care what happened to her. Too desperate.

Miss Hooker was desperate, too. This daughter of a farmer, who has the open-faced welcoming air of the true country woman, sent for the culprit and told her that she would have to be returned ignominiously to Aylesbury, and kept at night under lock and key. That was the obvious sequel. A failure, to be crossed off her own list. But she hated such an admission and suddenly an idea came to her. "I will give you one more chance," she said. "I will put you in charge of all the fowls. They will be your sole duty, your entire life from now on. If you let me down, you will be letting *them* down, too," she reminded her. At once there was a change in the waif's expression. Her air of listlessness fell away from her. She went joyfully from the room, and from that moment, her teachers had no more trouble with her. She almost lived in the hen houses in the garden. Her whole being was transformed. At last in her life, she had something to love and cherish, something of her very own, a living possession for which to feel responsibility. And so conscientiously did she wear her new crown of trust that very early in the mornings, long before the other girls in her dormitory would be awake, she would creep downstairs and open a window, and slip out into the wispy nothingness that heralds the dawn, not, as before, to make a bid for escape and the open road, but instead to see how her beloved chickens in the incubator had fared during the night.

When I came myself one morning into the stillness and the semi-darkness of the fowl shed, with its carpet of feathers, there was a fair-haired girl, in a wind-cheater and slacks, holding a rooster protectively against her jersey. It did not need much imagination to notice how similar her unconscious posture was to the possessive adoration of a mother for the baby at her breast.

It was then that my companion told me the story of the other girl, and how at the end of her time at East Sutton Park, she had been placed most happily on a farm, where, apart altogether from her new-found, inner contentment, and its reason, there was absolutely no question about the labourer being worthy of its hire. "When she comes back to see us," Miss Hooker said, "she looks so fit and apple-cheeked, I can't recognize the lost, unhappy waif she was."

Of course, they can earn some pocket-money—if not exactly, what one would call a living wage—during their time in either of the Borstal establishments. At Aylesbury, their earnings start with a flat basic rate of sixpence to which is added a supplement, according to individual temperament, and perseverance, which can bring the weekly total up to two or even three shillings a week. I remember that I asked the leader in one workshop, given over to the dis-mantling of earphones for the Post Office, what she had earned the previous week, and the answer was half-a-crown.

It was interesting to discover how it had been spent. One and fourpence had gone on ten cigarettes (the maximum they are allowed) tenpence for a lipstick, and the other fourpence on sweets.

"As you can imagine," the Governor at Aylesbury had remarked to me earlier, "it is very difficult to persuade a girl, who frankly admits that she has been earning twenty pounds a week or more on the streets of Piccadilly, that she would be far better off working in a factory for a quarter of that sum."

I remembered her words as we walked round the sewing-room. There was a magnificent-looking young woman bending over an electric machine. We stopped and chatted for a few minutes. "How do you like this work?" I asked. "Oh, I find it easy. I have been a machinist since I was fifteen." "Off and on," gently corrected Miss Martyn with a smile that was more encouraging for the future than condemning for the past.

"The great difficulty is to persuade them to stick to *any* job," Miss Martyn continued when we reached the kitchen and another extremely handsome girl with a riot of curls over her forehead asked if she could have a change of work, preferably to be trans-ferred to the garden, or to the farm that stretches away down to the railway line.

Now of the nine attempts to escape last year from the closed Borstal (none of which finally succeeded, because the truth is, women are not very good at running away) the majority took to their heels when they were supposed to be sorting potatoes. However, my hostess did not suspect that in this particular case such an idea was

planted in the girl's mind. Rather was it one more demonstration of
the eternal restlessness, of hating to stay put, that malaise of the age
which had driven her to Aylesbury in the end.

For the first three months they live in two wings of the prison
itself, which otherwise, in its central block, houses only the 'Star'
prisoners, that is to say those who are serving a long-term sentence,
sometimes life. And that can seem more like a death sentence: a
death within life sentence, distorting completely one's angle of vision.

For instance, there was the occasion when the elderly inmate
was sent for by the Governor. It should have been a great moment.
Her date of release had come through from the Home Office.
After all these years of waiting and petitioning, it had finally come
to pass, and not surprisingly there was a note of pleasure in the
Governor's voice when she passed on the splendid, the life-changing
news.

At once the prisoner's face fell. "Is that *all*?" she said. "Why, I
thought you had sent for me to tell me something *important*."

Something important would be having an extra pillow in her
cell, or being upgraded tuppence a week for her work as a house-
painter: or, best of all, winning her official complaint, her cunning,
vexatious, eternally drawn-out argument against the woman next
door.

Such details of her prison existence had become of supreme and
overriding importance: all the rest was mirage. . . .

"Have you looked at the locks on their doors?" I was asked.
"You notice how even the keyholes are exquisitely polished. You
would never get the Borstal girls to do that. But here on this landing
what one 'Star' prisoner has started all the others have to follow suit,
or else lose social caste."

Actually, there is an enormously rigid social caste system in all
women's prisons. The abortionists, the blackmailers, and the infanti-
cides, the mothers, who, however hard pressed, have in a moment of
terror and despair killed their own babies, are regarded as utterly
beyond the pale. No one speaks to them, even in chapel, where there is
usually much note passing and conversational exchanges in hidden
harmony with the hymns.

In the chapel at Aylesbury when I visited it three women were
polishing the brass rails at the side of the altar. I could see at a swift
glance that they were no longer young, as the Borstal girls are young,

and I wondered to myself what happened when they were all together, sharing the chapel services on Sunday mornings. Did the newcomers, their veins full of the hot, disturbing sap of adolescence glance covertly at the old-timers, so many of them pale shadows in their neat, print frocks, and wonder whether one day their own fate might not be the same? If . . . if they did not reform in time? Or was youth always too resilient to look ahead, to be warned?

The chapel itself, with its figure of the Christ, His arms outstretched in the hour of crucifixion, the body very white and naked against the terra-cotta walls, was not without beauty. The pews smelt pleasantly of beeswax instead of that ruthlessly aseptic smell one learns to dread in all prisons, while, even if the temperature was as cold as charity, the interlude was a considerable relief after the atmosphere of the corridors of cells, close at hand. Here the conditions struck me as depressing in the extreme. However, I was relieved to see that the pregnant girls, of which there is always a sprinkling among each new batch of Borstal recruits, had a bell beside their bed, and a larger grille than the average cell, opening on to the corridor.

When the time comes, unlike Holloway or other women's prisons, none of them chooses to go outside for her baby's actual birth. So perhaps I am over-sensitive and to these youngsters it doesn't seem so much like prison, after all. At any rate they are sleeping in the same bed every night and have it to themselves. While as for the babies, a dozen or so in a charmed circle were lying out in their Moses cradles in the hospital wing garden. As far as an untrained male eye could tell, they seemed, one and all, extremely fine specimens.

Indeed, I was filled with frustrated paternal longings, until my mood was somewhat deflated by the clinical and admirably brisk manner of the woman doctor in charge who assured me that most of her patients, although steeped in sexual experience and ready without any encouragement to pour forth details of their love life that made the Kinsey Report seem like an out-dated Victorian novel, had, nevertheless, the haziest ideas as to how their baby would actually be born. Many of them expect it to come out of their navel, she said.

If this statement astonished me, I had not then heard the answer that the headmistress of an Approved School gave me, when in the course of my tour of her extremely well-run country home for forty girls, I dared to put the question that many parents must ask today, in regard to their own children. Her answer was at once a warning, and a signpost.

Only one per cent of the girls who had passed through her hands during the past six years had not had sex experience with a man. Often her report showed, with many men.

"Only one per cent were virgins?" I echoed.

"If that . . . yet you must understand, Mr. Winn, many of my girls are only fifteen, and none of them is more than seventeen when she comes here, because she is in need of care and protection." Then she added something which was equally a source of astonishment to me. "If I had the power," she exclaimed—and it was a cry from the heart. "I would have all milk bars shut at half past ten at night."

So, in the course of my search for the material for this portrait, I took to visiting milk-bars in whatever town I found myself. It was an illuminating experience. Now I am not suggesting—nor was that headmistress—that by any means all the young girls who frequent milk bars end up in Approved Schools, on their way to Borstal, or are not perfectly reputable customers. Again, I am very well aware that milk bars supply a very important need in the life of the community and that the proprietors are themselves completely guiltless in that they make every effort to provide a most respectable background for their clients. Moreover, they can hardly be blamed if more and more teenagers use the premises as their secret rendezvous, their dubious hunting ground for 'dates'. . . .

Yet on the surface there is nothing to cause a tremor of alarm in a parent's mind. A milk bar—not a public house. And the atmosphere so warm and friendly and clean. All the fixtures so shiningly clean. It was a new world to me, and I was greatly impressed both with the purity of the serving 'props', the politeness of the staff everywhere, and the air of gay comradeship, the ease with which someone on their own could chat to their neighbour on the next stool at the bar, or at the next table.

But did the numerous American soldiers from a nearby camp appreciate that the majority of the girls who looked at them so admiringly and who seemed to know all the wise-cracking answers were in the eyes of the Law, and by every standard of morality, still children under the age of consent? I doubt it. I doubt it very much. For they were not dressed as children. Moreover, there was make-up on their faces and they wore the masks of experienced veterans in the sport of using the appeal of their youth like a shrimping net.

Now this happened to be Kingston on Thames, but this busy town, through which the river flows, is no different from any other of our British cities where at weekends and on leave nights there is a vast and urgent influx of Americans in uniform and civilian clothes. One has only to visit a Cathedral city like Norwich, or in turn, a very different kind of background, like Blackpool, to experience exactly the same phenomenon: the impact of an ever-increasing number of youngsters, many of them not waifs, but from 'nice homes', who, however, do not behave like 'nice girls' in their search for emotional excitement.

This is a problem that is here, I am afraid, to stay. Therefore it must be faced, and without prejudice or false accusations. Indeed, it would be quite wrong to cast all the blame at the feet of these hordes of servicemen from across the ocean, who far from their own homes are desperately in need of feminine companionship. Rather should the blame be attached to our own girls, especially our very young girls, who, in too many cases, unfortunately are 'boy-mad'. Moreover, in their eyes, *any* American is automatically a superman—their film-fed dreams come true.

During their 'dangerous age'—between fifteen and seventeen—they do not hunt in gangs, like their male contemporaries—but in couples. They go everywhere with the same girl friend: to the movies two or three times a week, to the local dance hall on a Saturday night, to a milk bar almost every night. And they are still there at closing time.

Of course, there is something very innocent about a milk shake, about drinking 'Coke' through a straw, in the taste of a strawberry sundae. Nevertheless, every time that I have watched a batch of teenagers going through the motions of childish pleasure in such enchantments, while at the same time carrying on an over-animated conversation with a cluster of youths, dressed in imitation American style clothes, I have remembered again the passionate protest which that Approved School headmistress made to me. And something else, which served as a kind of postscript.

"They live in a world of fantasy," she said. "The other day I asked one of them who was leaving us on licence, what was her ultimate ambition and she replied without a moment's hesitation.

'Oh, I'd like to marry a Yank and have a pair of invisible hands to do all the work in our home.' "

"Then they do still believe in marriage?" I queried.

"Oh yes, and a white wedding in a church. But when I remind them that they are always saying that they do not believe in God . . . yet would be willing to enter His house, for their wedding . . . they look surprised and confused."

They *are* surprised and they *are* confused. Surprised that it should have happened to them: to have been taken for a ride by their lovers and then discarded at the end of the journey, sometimes, only an over-night journey: to become the concern of the authorities and sent away to an approved school, or later, Borstal. Confused, on the other hand, as to what they really want from life.

A woman probation officer, spending all her time with these problem youngsters, who come from every class of the community and all parts of the country, put it to me like this. She said:

"Because of the physiological changes that are taking place in the bodies of these adolescents their minds are completely confused about sex. We must teach them the difference between 'boy friends', and one friend. Between petting parties and proper courtship. If we can only make that difference clear to them, there is still hope, still a chance for their future. . . ."

Love. Was there any word in our vocabulary that possesses more meanings, more subtle variations of meaning, I thought, as I stood in the ward of the prison hospital at Aylesbury, and looked down at the mother so pitifully young so soon to be delivered of a fatherless child. The mother, I was assured, would be able to keep her baby with her for a year, and whenever possible, it is arranged that they go out, back into the world, together. That final decision must depend, however, on what progress the mother makes in her ordinary 'college curriculum'.

For in many ways the Borstal at Aylesbury is very much like a college, divided into four houses. After the initial sorting-out period spent inside the main prison block, the girls move on to the newer buildings, where their cells seem like bedrooms, at the other end of the walled garden. Those houses are called 'Probation' and 'Special', but the names contain no special significance. What is significant is the manner in which the girls advance, six months at a time, through the stages, of yellow, green, to red and finally, on rare occasions to white.

A white rosette denotes a very super sort of head girl, but though there are seldom more than one or two of these at a time, I came across many wearing red stars on their gingham dresses. This means special privileges; more evenings in their club room; an occasional afternoon window shopping in Aylesbury, the treat of a visit, incognito, to a youth club in the town.

On one such occasion, a young man was greatly taken with his partner. Sitting out at the end of the dance, completely unaware of her school tie, he was overheard to ask whether she would be free for a 'date' on Friday. She shook her head. Then Saturday? "Saturday won't be convenient either," she replied with absolute truth.

Saturday is the great night, inside. If the inmates have not lost a single mark at work or at evening classes during the week, they are allowed to dance in their club rooms or in the gymnasium. One of their house mistresses plays for them. None of them want to be the man, to lead, but they must take it in turn. And no jiving! That is strictly forbidden. Indeed, it is classed as 'common', the one rebuke that has the absolute, the devastating power to make a Borstal girl crumble at once. To be called wicked is often regarded as a compliment, but to be dismissed as 'common', that really is a state of shame.

For from whatever angle one approaches the nation-wide upheaval in adolescent behaviour, one must have no false illusions. There is little doubt that the majority of Borstal intakes (many of whom have already failed to respond to the civilizing influence of an Approved School) arrive in an unrepentant and intractable mood. Now they must be taught a completely new sense of values about everything. A slow process often disturbed by storms or insidious, underground propaganda. They must be wooed by habit, by imitation. Most of all by watching the other guinea pigs, who a year or two senior to them, have, for the most part, already made solid progress in achieving a sense of personal responsibility.

Imperceptibly, miraculously—considering the soil—the seed takes root, a new confidence is born through being part of a community. Of course, there are inevitable 'incidents'. Demanding to be noticed, to be the centre of attention, a girl will pretend to be in agonizing pain, will even make an abortive attempt at slashing her own throat. Sometimes, too, they will pretend that they have had a baby outside, to add to their stature, to fulfil the demands of their fantasy existence. Or in a sudden rage of frustration and uncontrollable self-pity go berserk in their cell and smash everything within sight.

I stood in such a room during my visit to the closed Borstal at Aylesbury. It looked as though a cyclone had recently passed. I had never seen so much wilful damage in so small a space. "What attitude do the other girls on this floor take about this?" I asked. "They won't speak to her," I was told. "They feel she has let the side down."

Yet in the art room, at the end of that same passage, I was shown a really brilliant group of drawings which the same girl had made in the form of elegant sketches of an extremely chic young lady of fashion. Here was the sublimation of herself, I decided: along the corridor, the reality.

And so unceasingly, sometimes beneath the surface, sometimes in strident bouts, or sulky interludes, the struggle goes on. But even victory, in the end, is not an occasion without its own sadness. For instance, there was the girl who, going out the next morning, was, on her last night in a cell, saying goodbye to her house-mistress. Suddenly she burst into tears. "But you are going home tomorrow, and you are one of the girls who really has a home," her new friend reminded her.

"Yes, I know, but don't you see, miss, I have never had a room to myself before. Now I must go back and sleep five in a room, and I hate it, I hate it."

Marriage provides the great salvation. For I was assured both by Miss Martyn at Aylesbury and Miss Hooker at East Sutton Park that from their actual knowledge Borstal girls make surprisingly good wives, good, in every sense of the word, and settle down most peacefully. Many, too, seem to grow out of the Borstal period, or mood, as other adolescents pass through their own, on the whole, more harmless stages of exaggerated behaviour, their adoring crazes, their passionate 'crushes'. It is as though it all never happened, Miss Martyn explained.

While Miss Hooker told me of the 'old girl' who had written and asked if she might bring her baby down for its christening. I should like it to be done at East Sutton Park, she wrote. "Done," in the church, just over the garden wall, where she had been taken to service on Sunday mornings, and sat beside the other villagers in that small and friendly community. The memory had lingered. She was secure and settled now. It was a kind of insurance policy for the future to bring her new baby back and show it proudly to the woman who had done so much to make that future possible.

Just how much I realized more fully when I was shown the passport book. At least, that was my name for it. Inside were pictures of each Borstal girl, the picture that she brought with her, the picture that she took away on her last day. Two passport pictures, and we are all conscious what travesties these can be of our real selves. But these were different, these had the air of absolute truth. And what a wealth of difference there was between them. The smudged features, the frizzed mop of dyed hair, the almost criminal look of the intakes: compared with the neatly brushed appearance of the young traveller just starting forth on a voyage that one feels from the confident manner in which she holds her head will, undoubtedly, be a success.

In her turn, Miss Martyn, who in her own youth, shared a home in London with Miss Hooker, when both made their first experiments in social work by visiting the children of the barge dwellers on Regent's Park Canal, produced a letter from one of her 'old girls' at Aylesbury, which had just arrived that morning. One sentence read: "My husband is very kind and understanding. He says it is the future which matters. He is hoping, like myself, that it will be a boy. . . ."

I looked past her head at the truly exquisite model of the Madonna and Child, in white clay, on the mantelpiece, fashioned and presented to her for Christmas by another of those whom she was herself moulding into a new design.

"If you had the power to change one thing in the system, what would your choice be?" I asked.

The answer, which I am sure would be echoed by the lifelong friend who shares with her all the successes and the headaches of the Borstal experiment, was immediate, if somewhat unexpected. "Conditions outside," Miss Martyn said.

And who would suggest that she was not right?

EIGHT

THE PRISON GOVERNOR

ANYONE who seeks to be a messenger from many worlds is faced by a constant shock of surprise in the course of his wanderings. The contrast between the actual and the imagined serves as an astringent injection through his veins, since so few of the portraits, that he seeks to paint in words, turn out, in their final assessment, to be in the least as he visualized them, casually, in advance.

A woman governor in a women's prison? A female of the species, but with a trained masculine mind, and equally deliberate masculine approach, wearing a severely cut dark coat and skirt, like a uniform, and a clipped, impersonal manner, with all feeling, all femininity hidden from her eyes and voice. Surely an outward façade built on such lines, or else the daily burden would soon become insupportable.

Yet neither my first nor my last impressions were at all like that on the grey February day when I came, as a messenger, to the prison without bars outside York. I must explain that this was the second of the visits in a specially privileged tour of all the women's prisons in Britain: a tour which was to last for many weeks and was to prove at once the most exhausting and the most challenging of my writing assignments since the war.

My baptism into this world that is entirely regimented by women had commenced with Holloway, which until then, for I was a stranger to that part of North London, had merely been a name to me in court proceedings reported in the newspapers. Thus the actual physical appearance of the prison was a considerable surprise to me so that a week later, I was still recovering from the sense of distaste and claustrophobia that the buildings themselves, like a mediaeval fortress, had implanted within me. Even as one approached the great, studded doors, one felt that over the portal should be enscribed these words: 'Abandon hope all ye who enter here.'

In actual fact, the Prison Commissioners themselves are the first to admit that Holloway is a hundred years out of date, and would have been discarded long ago, as a prison for women, had it

111

not been for the intensity of the bomb damage in London which still, nearly ten years after the end of hostilities, makes homes for the homeless, with absolute rightness, first priority.

It can be argued, of course, that hardened criminals can hardly expect a home. They are, after all, being housed at the taxpayers' expense. It is an argument which is usually expressed with most fervour by those who have never spent even a few hours within the four walls of any prison themselves. For my own part, there was one moment when I was incarcerated within Holloway myself, only for a day, that I find impossible to erase from my consciousness.

I was standing at the lowest level, at the very bottom of the dungeon, in the corridor—and Holloway consists entirely of corridors —that runs between the two rows of cells where the mothers who have just had their babies are kept until they are strong enough again to finish their sentence. It was nearly dusk and above my head, stretching away towards a shadowy roof which never opens to the sky were endless tiers of cells, all linked together by carpets of barbed wire, one ceiling, as it were, upon another, placed there to prevent the prisoners from throwing themselves down into the depths (whence I was gazing up), down into the well of their despair.

I must confess that it was with great difficulty that I prevented myself at that moment from shouting aloud and running headlong towards the gates that are always kept locked and barred. So that it was only later, in retrospect, that I appreciated how extremely important it was, in fairness to the prison officials themselves, not to confuse the treatment meted out to prisoners with the actual background against which they serve their time.

There can be little defence of Holloway as a 'modern' prison; it is, in truth, the epitome of that hideous phrase, 'a gloomy pile', within and without: but there can and must be every defence of the efforts that are made by the staff to reform and help the women who come under their charge, and to turn them into citizens with a future in the world beyond the gates. Indeed, beside me, as I write, there is a letter from the anonymous ghost who waited upon me at lunch that day with the governor. Did I remember her? She had not forgotten me, a male visitor from Mars. Apparently I talked to her, as though she was a fellow human being. Now she had been released from captivity, and her letter was overflowing with gratitude, not so much for that, and the taste of freedom again, as for all the kindness she received at the hands of her captors. Truly it is important that such 'unsolicited testimonials' should be placed on permanent record.

Again, there was the remark—the warning, one might almost call it—which came to me from the governor herself, the youngest in the prison service, at the end of our time together. "Remember," she said, "during the next visit on your tour, that you could not have *any* women's prisons without bars unless we also possess a Holloway somewhere in Britain."

Of course, Dr. Charity Taylor, who herself sets such an enlightened example that she allows her own small children to mix freely with the inmates, knowing just what that must mean to those who are themselves wives and mothers, was referring to Holloway as the symbol of all closed prisons for women: the kind of existence to which any prisoner must return who consistently betrays the privileges that are offered today in an open model prison, such as the one that is situated a few miles outside York and is called Askham Grange. Not surprisingly I did recall the governor's extremely objective comment when my car turned off the highway and up a side lane to the tiny village of Askham, where nestling as near-neighbour to the church and a handful of cottages is a large, rambling, late-Victorian mansion, with no gates between the pillars of its drive.

I forgot to ask whether the gates themselves were removed for convenience sake, or as a deliberate symbol, when the Prison Commissioners first rented the house, just after the war, but the inmates, I was soon to discover, are allowed to pass between those pillars on not-infrequent occasions. They will go out on unguarded walks, or to attend church on Sundays, to buy stamps in the Post Office, or to be members of a working party on a near-by farm.

And if they do not return? Or if they choose to walk out of the unlocked front door when no one is looking their way? The answer is that it has happened scarcely a dozen times since the experiment was first launched over eight years ago now. A most encouraging record, one would suggest, in a community which at the time of my first visit contained such varied types as a woman solicitor, a miner's wife, a hospital matron, a woman who had committed manslaughter, a factory girl from the Midlands, the wife of a high-ranking officer, the sister of a journalist and the usual crop of abortionists.

Women are different from men in that they are more reconciled to the vagaries of Fate. They will stay put and have to be moved by

H

some deep compulsion. Just before my own arrival at Askham Grange, a prisoner had escaped for a night to her home town. She *had* to see her husband and get things straight between them once and for always. Letters: the monthly, supervised visit, were not enough. They must meet again and talk freely within the four walls of their own home. It was as simple as that. No more, no less.

"I rang up the police and said, 'I think you will find her at home. Leave her alone if you can for a couple of hours to settle things. She will be punished enough as it is.'"

The Governor clearly felt it would be both tidier and more humane that way. Nevertheless it was the speech of a brave woman, I thought, for Mrs. Kelley had only recently then taken over the charge of Askham Grange from someone who, having spent a lifetime in the Prison Service, has now finally retired with the blessing of so many human beings whom she helped, in her memory.

Mrs. Kelley, on the other hand, only came into the service when her war work ended, and to take further Miss Size's work at Askham (to which a heart-felt tribute is paid in Miss Joan Henry's book *Who Lie in Gaol*) was a considerable challenge to anyone and I had been most curious to meet her successor.

My first impression was a surprise, even though I was by now conditioned by the humanity and sense of understanding of Dr. Taylor at Holloway. The new Governor turned out to be an extremely attractive and elegant woman, very much in the full tide of life. She wore a becoming grey wool dress, her soft, fairish hair was neatly and charmingly arranged in curls at the nape of her neck, while the short fur coat of lynx that she wears on her rounds in the winter was carelessly thrown over a chair in her office. At first sight she looked much more like the editor of a glossy magazine, or some other kind of big executive. Indeed, her aura is far removed from any association with a prison background and she received me— and I do not doubt her other, non-paying guests—as though one had been invited to stay in her own country home.

I was not, however, misled by that welcome. It was soon very apparent that my hostess believed in discipline, tempered with imagination, and above all, in work. Not simply as a means of killing time or obtrusive thoughts: or even as a means of tiring healthily the human body so that it is ready and eager for bed and sleep when the lights go out at ten. But most of all, work as a means of salvation, in the future, so that each prisoner—and each truly is regarded as an individual case—will go back into life better equipped to earn a living, to run a home, and, if necessary, to be independent of any man.

"By far the majority of people here are not really criminal types at all. They are in prison because they were muddlers outside. They just couldn't cope and ended up by getting into real trouble. We try to teach them how to cope."

Whereupon my companion instanced the case of a woman who when she came to Askham had been unable to cook even a potato. She had fed her family entirely out of tins. Or else they had gone to a fish and chip shop, and to the local public house for their Sunday dinner. An absurdly extravagant way of trying to budget, and when this mother ran hopelessly short with the housekeeping money, finally, in desperation, she stole.

Before her sentence finished, that same woman was able to write to her husband. "I have just cooked a joint. And it really looked and tasted like a proper joint." P.S. "I know now how to make your shirts."

It is such simple stories as these that conceal great truths. And I noted something else in the same instant: how the Governor never spoke of the sixty prisoners under her charge, but always of 'the people here'. She clearly thought of them, too, as real people. Moreover that attitude seemed equally strong among the seven prison officers who, owing to the vision of the Prison Commissioners, are all that are needed at Askham.

One of them, the instructress in the sewing-room, said to me. "I used to run my own dressmaking business outside. And when I applied for this job, I did not even realize that Askham Grange was a prison. But I would not want to change now."

For she has, in sober truth, urged on by the Governor, become the prisoners' friend. In the evenings she watches over their efforts to express their hopes, their regrets, their individuality, in making new clothes. Beautiful stuffs, brilliant colours are spread out for the cutting scissors. The scene is so utterly different, too, from earlier in the day. For now instead of the stereotyped shirts for men prisoners there are the costumes that one dressmaking student will be creating for another on the day of her release. Or the clothes that they are making themselves for their children. One woman showed me with pride a blue silk Sunday best frock with exquisite smocking that she had just finished for her four-year-old child. Yet when she came in, her instructress announced, she could hardly thread a needle. Across my head the two women exchanged a triumphant and friendly glance.

Another officer was chosen to play 'the funny man', in the prisoners' own pantomime which, when it was presented in the large ballroom that has been converted into a playroom, to an outside audience, was such a rip-roaring success that the cast were invited to tour the neighbouring Women's Institutes. Surely the other members of the cast would not have invited their 'gaoler' to take part, had they not also liked her face when it had to wear its official expression?

But then as another of the officers remarked to me: "When I came into the Prison Service twenty-one years ago, I believed that there was only black and white. Now I realize that most things—and people—are a mixture, making grey." At my nod of agreement, she added, with a gesture towards the mantelpiece. "I wish you'd come in time to see our Christmas cards. Most of them were from 'satisfied clients'."

Not too satisfied? The accusation has been raised in some quarters that life is over-luxurious at open prisons like Askham Grange—a second one was opened last year near Epping Forest—but I would deny that absolutely now that I have paid a personal visit myself. The dormitories were like an ice house and there were no curtained cubicles round any of the beds, which must be an added—and surely unnecessary—torment for middle-aged women, especially, to have no privacy even at night. While though it is true that a fire does burn in the grate of the panelled library where the prisoners can sit after lunch for a brief while, and at weekends, the atmosphere, in general, reminded me of a very austere boarding school for boys or girls. And that surely is the right atmosphere?

Now at Holloway many of the prisoners themselves complain that they are not given sufficient hours to work: they have too much time to brood: too much time alone. There could be no such complaints at Askham or about Askham. For the morning bell tolls at six-forty-five, and before breakfast at eight, the inmates must not only make their beds and tidy their dormitories or the smaller rooms that they may be sharing with one or two companions, they must also perform some allotted domestic chore downstairs.

Then from eight-thirty they will work for three hours till lunch time, and again, from one-thirty till four-thirty. That adds up to a minimum total of six hours to which must be added another two hours between tea and supper, consisting of classes like cooking, dressmaking, handicrafts, or lectures on current affairs, given by an outside teacher from York. He turned out to be a pleasant-faced young man whose earnest conciliatory voice rose and fell above the sound of the clicking needles of his audience. In all, a working day of eight hours, and if the length of the sentence permits, it is planned that each inmate shall spend a certain time at each job. For instance, six girls work out of doors in the garden and take care of the poultry. (Wearing green sweater and dungarees they are indistinguishable from other land girls.) Others, again take turns in the sewing-room and the laundry where the flat rate of pay for a week is one and eightpence, as opposed to two shillings, in the garden.

However, the women seem to prefer the laundry, to find pleasure in the domestic rhythm of handling an iron, in the cleanliness of everything. At least, that is how I was figuring it out myself until one of the girls there exclaimed. "I like it better in here than in the sewing-room. I have to concentrate all the time when I am using an iron. If I am working a sewing-machine, my mind can wander. . . ."

For a moment, a look of naked agony twisted her face and then the anonymous shutter had come down again, and she was bending once more over her board, ironing a dress that was the same pattern, and made of the same cotton material, as at Holloway, but which would become the property of the prisoner whom it most clearly fitted, during the length of her stay. An innovation greatly appreciated but only possible in a much smaller community such as this one.

Just occasionally, they can wear their own clothes. If they can save three shillings—and what an effort it must be—they can spend it on going into York, to a cinema. But usually their 'salary' is already mortgaged, for cigarettes, for sweets, for presents, when one of their companions has a birthday. "They are very generous to each other," I was told.

Of course, cosmetics, soap, bath-salts, even hair-dye they can have sent in from outside, with their fortnightly letter, and indeed, noting that one woman's hair was freshly touched up, I remarked on how much better that looked than dyed hair growing out in streaks such as I had noticed so many times at Holloway. To which my companion, so absolutely *soignée* herself, made a reply that was at once most sensible and most true to her own character, as I realize now that I know her better.

"Anything that renews their self-respect or their courage, I believe in their being allowed, in reason, to have."

In one of her letters to me since, the Governor added something that was like a postscript to that. A personal postscript. "It is my conviction", she wrote, "that we start with a set of potentialities like the talents in a Bible story, and one's life work is to make the most of them, and build a human being able to know and love God, 'in the image of God'. So what matters is how you cope with whatever you meet on the way, and how you develop the spark God has given you, and whether your journey through life is happy or unhappy is not the *main* point."

Of course, in a prison there is only one main point: the date of your release. I remember, at one moment during my first visit to Askham, I stopped to talk to a prisoner who looked particularly neat in her working overall. Her hair was nicely done, she wore lipstick and a little powder. Above all, she seemed *alive*, though, after a few minutes' conversation, I had a curious sensation that she was somehow, apart. Looking back now, I think it was her stillness, the impression that here was the quiet of the aftermath, after a battle has been fought and slowly won.

Asking questions inside a prison is a tricky business. One is so dreadfully afraid of uncovering old scars. However, after we had talked of this and that, including her latest-style hair 'do'—"sometimes we have a professional hairdresser with us, and that is a great help"—I did venture to ask how long she herself had been 'inside'. Since 1948, she answered in a quiet, unemotional voice.

More than five whole years. Yet only a second before she had been talking spontaneously about what she wanted to do on her release. (They never say, in March or in June, but always give you the precise date, as though the very exactitude brought it somehow nearer). No, she did not expect to take a job. "I hope to be a better housewife," she said, simply.

It is strange how a few very simple words can assume a significance that will stay in one's mind, for ever.

There were no murderesses serving their indefinite time at Askham, during my visit, though in the past there have been one or two. After all, they could be classed as 'first offenders', and Askham is intended largely for first offenders, though lately there have been a sprinkling of C.T.s, which in prison language, is the abbreviation for Corrective Trainees. And I have no doubt that the Governor welcomes them because she spent the five years, before coming to Askham, as an assistant governor at Holloway where she was in complete charge of the Corrective Training Wing. This houses the toughest element in Holloway, the young women who are fast becoming hardened criminals, many of whom have already been to Borstal, came out on licence, only to break loose and commit more and usually worse offences against Society. So the corrective training curriculum at Holloway becomes their last chance of a future, and the longer I spent in the company of Mrs. Kelley the more conscious I became of her own passionate determination that all those in her charge should have a future.

Now although the guests at Askham Grange may apply for home leave for five days half-way through their sentence, at Holloway, once the prison gates clanged behind them, that used to be their last glimpse of the outside world, until the innovation of 'cultural tours' was put into effect. "Of course, I would only take a small party at a time," the Governor told me. "Five was the ideal number. Two couples and one walking with me. That way we were inconspicuous and manageable. Clothes? Oh, I used to keep a selection of coats in my wing. They were quite sufficient camouflage."

The organizer never planned the party ahead. At least, she never told anyone. On the morning itself, she would walk along the landing and stop those whose turn it was. "Would you like to come to the Tower this afternoon?" Another time it would be Hampton Court, and then there was the occasion when one of the party pleaded that first they should go and view the outside of the Home Office. "I've addressed so many petitions there, I really would like to see what it looks like," she explained.

So off they went to Whitehall, and once they were there, it seemed a waste of opportunity not to slip round the corner into Downing Street. Outside No. 10, two of the party bent down right under the noses of the guardian policemen. "They were astonished," the Governor smiled reminiscently. "I think for one moment they imagined we were letting off a time fuse. But all that my girls wanted, of course, were some particularly fat cigarette ends. . . ."

"Dropped by members of the Cabinet?" I suggested. Now we were both smiling, though another question mark hung in the air between us. She shook her head. "No, not one of them let me down. The old school tie feeling can be very strong, you know, in a prison community. It is here, in Askham. The others resent it very deeply when someone lets down the side."

The Governor, who had clearly studied the meaning of the proverb, *tout comprendre, c'est tout pardonner*, during the years that she had lived as a young married woman in France, looked past me out of the window, and following her gaze, it was to see two girls walking towards the open space between the pillars of the gate, with someone in a fur coat between them. She did not look like a prison officer, nor they like prisoners.

No one would recognize them in the cinema queue, though, as they turned to wave towards the windows, I recognized them as two of the gardeners I had talked to in the morning, when they had shown me the hideous laurels they had uprooted along the wall. In the spring, azalea bushes would blaze in their place, and later there would be the pageant of the summer, a technicolour herbaceous border, created by themselves, at which to warm their hearts. Meanwhile, they had exclaimed to me in chorus. "We're going to see *The Road to Bali* tonight. Is it smashing?"

The Road to Bali . . . no, the road back, I thought.

I took that road myself. Later that year, driving south after a September holiday in Scotland, I stopped the night in York, and on a sudden impulse the next morning rang up the Governor to ask if I might pay my respects, in passing. To her. For this was a private and unofficial visit and I did not see or talk with any of the prisoners. Do come at once, the Governor said, in her clear-cut but always human voice.

I found her in the garden, supervising the cutting down of more unwanted laurels, casting their shadow of darkness across a scene that otherwise grew lighter under her guidance, month by month. It was a sunny day and the last of the giant dahlias were at their best. "We are going to have lots more perennials planted this autumn, and as for annuals, we are determined to have a mass of nasturtiums next summer. I know some people find them a common flower, I suppose because they grow so easily and on such poor ground, but I love their massed colours, and I am sure the families will like them, too, when on visiting-days, they picnic on the lawn. That is another innovation, since you were here, everyone seems to like it, and I've got something else to show you, indoors."

A few minutes later, my companion threw open the door of one of the dormitories with something of a gesture of triumph. Gone were the drab, institutional colourings of the walls, and in their place, clear, bright washes that the occupants had chosen for themselves, before applying with their own hands. There was a further revolution in regard to the bedspreads. These had uniformly been that revolting sage-green much favoured by the Victorians. Now, in their place, a shade which the fashion writers would describe as Schiaparelli's 'shocking pink'.

It didn't shock either myself or my companion. On the contrary, it delighted us. For was it not the symbol of so much besides? "And come and look at the dining-room, too," she added eagerly. "I would like your advice on it. Do you think a mediterranean blue ceiling would be a good idea? A big room like that with such a hopelessly high ceiling can look so cold and uninviting, in the winter."

Her own sitting-room upstairs was on the large side, too, and an uncompromising shape (though many confidences, I thought, must be exchanged here) with great, gothic windows looking out over the other side of the garden, where they were planning something else to bloom next summer, a tennis court. And surely this room could be lonely, so very lonely, I decided, as we sat and had a mid-morning cup of coffee, before the messenger was speeded once more upon his way.

Suddenly I was deeply curious as to how it had all begun, how someone who seemed so much a woman of the world, whose own clothes I had discovered from a chance allusion had sometimes been bought in Molyneux's most exclusive *salon* in the Rue Royale, should have taken this road, and should appear to be so passionately content in her isolation and with the burden of her authority.

It would help my final portrait if I could add these final touches. At once my sitter was most co-operative and explained that it had started, as so often happens with something which turns out to be a vocation and a life work, with an accident: or rather, the accidental luck of one letter arriving a couple of days ahead of another one.

At Girton, Joanna Beadon achieved a degree in Economics— "I meant to study English, but I took an instinctive and I am sure unreasonable dislike to my prospective tutor's face"—but after her marriage, when she lived for eight years in France, where her husband's work brought her in close touch with the rare and precious, though wholly inanimate, objects in various museums, she had not intended to pursue an independent career herself.

"My husband was an American from Illinois, with a passionate love of France and everything to do with France. He worked chiefly at the Musée d'Ethnographie, in the Trocadero, as it was then called. He is what is called a Prehistorian, which meant that we dealt in flint implements, cave paintings, gravel pits and the earlier beginnings of Man. We had a lovely flat in Paris, full of beautiful things, and our holidays were spent wandering through France, looking at old churches. Glancing back now, I realize without a pain, how very happy we were. Then the war came, and separated us, like so many others. . . . I returned to England at once, feeling I must do *something*. . . ."

So first of all she ran a voluntary club for youths, at their most intractable age, and when the blitz put an involuntary stop to that by shattering their premises, she went to the Admiralty, and ended up by running their welfare department at Bath.

"I suspect this would have been a greater success," she remarks candidly, "had I appreciated then, what I realize now, that it is no use battering your head against the door of those in authority above you, or of committees round you, when you want something badly. You must coax and be patient, never *demand*."

"And after the war?" I asked, noticing that there had been no further reference to her other career; and thinking at the same time that this was a good age in which to live, when any woman, whose marriage has failed, for one reason or another, to bring complete fulfilment can find consolation and peace in winning economic independence, and by harnessing herself to a cause.

"After the war, conscious that my marriage was over, and I should never go back to live in France again, I consulted the Universities Appointments Board, and they made two suggestions: I should apply to be trained as an assistant governor in the Prison Service, or I should send in my application for a job that was to be filled as Welfare Officer to a large organization in Palestine. Secretly, I favoured the idea of the latter post myself, I loved the idea of travelling again, of getting right away, for a time, while things got sorted out in my mind . . . however, the Prison Commissioners sent for me first for an interview. Later, there came a concrete offer, and that can be very comforting. I accepted it, and I had hardly posted my acceptance, before the other letter came. I should certainly have said 'Yes' to it, had it arrived first."

I found myself looking past the very candid gaze of her deep blue eyes at the cat asleep on the sofa. I wanted to ask if she never missed the comfort of having children of her own: the reassurance, the roughage of masculine company. A woman, so feminine, so much in her prime. As I searched for tactful words, the Governor said. "Let me tell you a story before you go. I will only change the name of the heroine, but I think the story itself will make you understand why I never feel like a prisoner myself, how exciting and adventurous, how infinitely rewarding this work can be. . . ."

I was only too happy for an excuse to linger on, for I found a great sense of relaxation, of rightness, in her presence. It was as though we had been friends for a long time.

"It is the story of what happened to one of my little C.T.s at Holloway. She had been a very tough case, and I wasn't over-hopeful when the time came for her release. But I said to her. 'Do try, Maisie, this time. I am afraid scrubbing floors doesn't sound a very thrilling job, but you will be living in a Salvation Army hostel, and I know they will be kind with you, and after six months, if you have stuck it, we can get you a reference, and then it will be easier about jobs.' So Maisie said she would try, and went off to her hostel, but in my heart I really expected to see her back quite soon. . . ."

The Governor poured her guest out another cup of coffee, while her guest waited, hopefully, for a sudden new note had come into the story-teller's voice.

"And then a wonderful thing happened. One evening, after Maisie had been at the hospital for a few weeks, she had done some shopping after leaving work, and when she stepped off the tram, near the hostel, she slipped and fell in the muddy roadway, with all her parcels. . . ."

"But how was that wonderful?" I interrupted.

"It was wonderful, because in the darkness, a dapper little man picked her up, dusted her down and said. 'Now then, miss, you ought to take more care of yourself than that. Where do you live?' Maisie told him, she was used to coping with strangers, and he trotted along beside her, carrying her parcels and chatting about the weather. When they reached the door of her hostel, Maisie was about to thank him, and disappear out of his life for ever, when he blurted out. 'May I ask you a question? Are you free? I mean, are you single. . . .' And when she answered, yes she was, but . . . he went on, Maisie told me afterwards, just as though he was inviting her to the pictures her next night off, 'Then will you marry me? I know I am no oil painting myself, but I have taken a great fancy to you. I really mean it, and I have got a nice little place, with a bathroom, all my own, and I never bring home less than eight pounds a week."

"And what were Maisie's reactions to that?" I asked.

"Well, you can imagine. She was absolutely dumbfounded. She tried to tell him about herself, for she was a very honest girl, 'You don't understand,' she said, 'I have been very wicked, I have done all sorts of dreadful things. I have been in PRISON. . . .' It made absolutely no difference. You see, he had made up his mind. He was over forty and it was now or never. Maisie was gay and pretty and clearly warm-hearted, and would bring life to the little house with the bathroom. Oh, I could see it all, can't you? 'Think it over, my dear,' he said, 'and I will come back in the morning, and talk to anyone you like to produce. I promise you, I am on the level'."

And now there was no mistaking the note of glory in the Governor's voice. "That was five years ago, and today Maisie is married, most happily settled, with a baby and a contented, proud and adoring spouse."

Reluctantly I got up to say goodbye. I was still curious about one fact in the story that had been omitted. What was the profession of the Sir Galahad who had pressed his suit with such precipitate conviction?

The answer I received was the final surprise. He was a rag and bone merchant.

"Oh dear, what a pity," I could not help exclaiming.

"Why do you say that?" She was the Governor again.

"Because, don't you see, I could never tell that story in a book. It is too complete a contrast, too perfect a *dénouement*. None of my readers would believe it. Couldn't you make him a bank clerk?"

However, I did not really expect or need a reply for at that second, in a flash of illumination, I had received the completely satisfying answer to all my other questions. At last I knew why her work was able to absorb her so completely that she no longer ever gave a backward glance towards that other life. For here in this prison without bars she was surrounded by the stimulus and the challenge of all the infinite vagaries of human behaviour. So many revelations, so many visions of that ultimate truth, which comes usually only to priests and doctors, and which is not only so much stranger than fiction, but also so infinitely more rewarding.

At that moment the demure little maid came in to clear away the coffee things. "She will be gone before you return again," my hostess said.

I nodded, thinking: but there would be others. A multitude of others and each one a concrete problem, sometimes baffling at first, often stubborn right up till the final surrender, but always to be solved, in human terms. Yes, I understood now completely, and most of all, why she spoke with such passionate conviction, when she said:

"I feel so dreadfully sorry for unanchored people. How can they deal with sorrow when it comes? It must need so much courage, if one is, so to speak, without a purpose, all on one's own. . . .

"For I think," she continued, "that the unity of both mankind and the universe is a sort of final aim, and that therefore all friendship, all affection, whether for stone implements, animals, or anything else is important. Obviously the highest example of this is in marriage, which is why a happy marriage is such a lovely thing. But if that doesn't come one's way, there are lots of other means to use and so increase one's powers of love. . . ."

I had not expected to leave a prison with such a message ringing compassionately in my ears.

NINE

THE YOUNG ACTRESS

I AM not really human at breakfast. But that particular morning when Mrs. Blackton, who comes from Killarney and now looks after my London home, put my tea in front of me and the glass of unsweetened lemon juice that dutifully, as an optimistic cure for fibrositis I swallow every morning with my eyes shut, I exclaimed in the tones of an eager stripling. "The most beautiful young actress on the London stage is coming to lunch!"

All through the morning my thoughts kept slipping away from the letters I was dictating—"You ask how to become a writer, and the only advice I can give you is to buy a pad and a pen, sit down and write, as though you were addressing someone far away, who is shut off from life, in a darkened room"—back to that evening when I had taken my mother to see Charles Morgan's most moving play *The River Line*, and we had both been equally astonished by the beauty of the unknown young actress who played the leading part.

She was very fair and very still on the stage and above all, so very English-looking that she reminded me of a Rossetti drawing for 'The Blessed Damozel'. She didn't seem like someone born into this century at all and I found myself wondering whether this curiously old-fashioned aura was part of her real character or something that she had assumed for the play.

I know now that it is not assumed for this girl of twenty-two with the long tulip-like neck, the wide upper lip, and the high cheek bones turned out to be the most natural, unspoilt and completely artless—in the best sense—young actress that I have ever met: moreover, that judgment stretches right back to include the days when I was a gangling youth on the stage myself and automatically, for the run of the play, used to have romantic dreams about every *ingénue*, opposite whom I played.

That first evening at the Lyric Theatre, Hammersmith, hers was just a name in the theatre programme. But when I wrote to the play's author to congratulate him, and noted particularly the performance of his heroine, he sent back high praise. "What I wanted for the part was a young Peggy Ashcroft or Jean Forbes-Robertson. By a miracle, they found me *Virginia McKenna.* . . ."

Charles Morgan is far more approachable and far less Olympian than the intellectual austerity of his writings would suggest. I have personal proof of that. Towards the end of the war, at a moment when my spirits and my health were at their lowest ebb and I was filled with a secret dread that any talent I might have possessed had burned itself out, the author of *The Fountain* took the trouble to invite me to dine alone with him at his club where throughout the evening he talked to me as though we were on equal literary terms. My final memory of the evening was of our standing on the platform at Leicester Square, waiting for the last tube, and just before the roar of the approaching train enveloped us, he found me a title for the book I had just begun about my life on the lower deck. "Call it *Home from Sea* . . . and don't forget (he had to shout now) Stevenson wrote 'Home is the sailor, home from sea . . .' not home from *the* sea. . . ."

I tried to thank him for the title, for his kindness and patient understanding, for everything that he had done for me that night. Then the next morning I sat down at my writing desk as though the red wine we had drunk together was still coursing through my veins. All my doubts had vanished. And lo and behold, so in due course did it miraculously come to pass that *Home from Sea* continued to sell out edition after edition until now it has almost reached the hundredth thousand mark. Thus it is not surprising if the name of Charles Morgan fills me with gratitude and admiration or that I should have preserved all his letters to me in their beautiful, scholarly script.

Just before lunch I asked my secretary to search out the letter which I felt would particularly interest my guest. Going up the stairs from my office I thought to myself with a sudden stab of shyness: 'It should break the ice.' Because we had never met in real life. This was to be what our American cousins describe so graphically as a 'blind date'. Was it wise? Would I not bore her with my middle-aged conversation? Might I be disillusioned when she spoke her own dialogue?

The nearest I had been to her, without the footlights between, was a few nights before when, as I came through the stage door of the

Criterion Theatre, a breath of youth had rushed past me up the stone steps, away into the night. How well I knew that particular passage-way. For had I not acted in that same theatre the part of Marie Tempest's son in Noel Coward's *The Marquise*. For eight months I wore romantic eighteenth-century clothes and a powdered wig. At that time the object of my affections had been an entrancingly pretty heroine named Eileen Sharp, who succeeded in having a most devastat-ing effect upon me in our scene together which opened the play and heralded the entrance of the star. She would give a half-suppressed giggle and at once I was completely helpless. I would dissolve into silent, tortured mirth, knowing full well that it would mean yet another reprimand from the stage manager as soon as I made my exit. But somehow it didn't matter, because when you are very young, and I was nineteen, everything is a lark.

At the end of the play's run, both the young lovers left the stage for ever. Not because we were banished for our fatal habit of giggling in front of the audience, when we should have been dreamily gazing into each other's eyes, but because we both had different ambitions and the tide took us our different ways. My stage sweetheart was married to the son of a famous surgeon while I myself, on the advice of Somerset Maugham, who had read my recently published first novel, sold my box of grease-paints and bought a Thesaurus instead.

Do I ever regret the decision? Many times I have been asked that question, and whenever I revisit the theatre where I strutted in front of the footlights for the last time, a pang touches my heart until I remind myself again that the stage is a profession for women, not for men, unless they happen to possess the talent of an Olivier or a Redgrave. And how often does that happen? For the rest it is a calling that is always precarious, sometimes humiliating, and in middle-age, often most pitiful.

I had returned to the Criterion Theatre that evening to see Virginia McKenna in her current play *The Bad Samaritan*. It was a challenge to myself, lest I should be disappointed, the second time. However, greatly to my relief, I wasn't. The same golden aura surrounded her, though the part, on this occasion, lacking the distinction of Charles Morgan's art, turned out to be that stock character, the transparently good girl, who, because of her very innocence, is the easier victim of suddenly awakened passion, with the inevitable consequence of a Victorian melodrama.

Suschitsky

MISS VIRGINIA McKENNA

"What a precious combination real youth and real beauty can make"

Afterwards I went back-stage ostensibly to congratulate that very under-rated actor, Michael Denison, who suffers in the critics' eyes through being a film star: all the evening I had been nursing the secret hope that he would introduce me to the girl whom he quixotically married, baby and all, at the end of the play. Alas, even as she fled past me up the steps, I knew that my plan to play the stage-door johnny had failed.

Did I give up? Not at all. Let it be a lesson in perseverance to other, younger men. I sat down and wrote a fan letter. It came from my heart. I pointed out that I had met her mother years ago, when I was her age. That was true, too. Her mother, whose professional name is Anne de Nys, is a brilliant cabaret performer, who sits at the piano in a restaurant, and sings lilting, sophisticated songs. Half-French, she has a Parisian charm, and with her piquant, *gamin* looks is a complete and utter contrast to the Grecian profile of her daughter. "Won't you come to lunch," I wrote, "and bring your mother as a chaperon. . . ."

In 1953? Yes, in 1953. It was a compliment to her aura. However, in the end the daughter came alone. Her mother was away on a holiday, she explained. As I entered the living-room of my flat, and found her already seated quietly in one of the high-backed, gold chairs, her beauty struck me with a fresh sense of surprise. I shall always remember how she looked at that moment.

It was one of the few really hot days of a capricious summer and my guest had seized the chance to put on a cotton frock bought off the peg and made by Horrockses, she told me later. With it she wore no jewelry, her bare neck and arms were golden brown, and her untouched, *cendré* hair was knotted very simply at the nape of her neck.

With the letter in my hand, like a passport at a frontier, I found no difficulty in chatting away at once about the other link between us. Did I once upon a time occupy the same dressing-room as she did now? Mine was on the left as you started down the passage. Hers, I discovered, was on the right. Anyway, I used to rush up the steps and away, after the performance, just as she had done the other night. "You were so quickly out of the theatre, I believe you went home in your stage make-up," I suggested.

My companion denied that at once. "But I don't have to waste time, re-doing my face. I don't use any make-up off the stage," she confessed without the least trace of coyness.

I

It is rather disconcerting when everything you have ever read or believed about the feminine art of being glamorous is suddenly discounted and contradicted flat by someone who is the living proof of her thesis. For as the young lady—and I use the term in its original sense—who is regarded as one of the three most glittering new stars in the theatrical firmament sat beside me at lunch with the brilliant canvases by Mathew Smith and Graham Sutherland on the grey walls behind her, her own unadorned loveliness was in no way eclipsed, but rather did she keep on reminding me herself of a picture by Renoir. It was the luminous quality of her skin. Yes, that was where the likeness lay I decided, as Mrs. Blackton, who has such glowing Irish colouring herself, came into the room with the next course.

I was delighted to notice that there was nothing ethereal about my guest's appetite. Too many young women today are inclined to eat too little and to drink too much alcohol. I have watched girls young enough to be my daughter swallow three or four cocktails straight off at a party. This used to be the prerogative of American *débutantes*, fighting their way through the jungle of a London season. Now it is a habit that has been copied not only by their English counterparts, but by all classes of the community. Bars have become respectable places for both sexes and all ages. I shudder to think what these 'lovelies' of today will look like at my mother's age, if they survive the pickling process.

A pompous diatribe? I apologize, but I am not often given to censoriousness since tolerance has always seemed to me to be the ultimate Christian virtue. Nevertheless, I stick to my guns. A drunk man is a bore, a woman who drinks is a blasphemy. It may take more courage at a party to ask for tomato juice than to accept the dry martini that is offered but . . . well, I was very glad to hear my guest at lunch ask firmly for a glass of water.

I was equally glad to discover that she had no poses about how a young actress should present herself to the world. No publicity agent had been allowed to get busy on building her the sort of false façade that only publicity agents imagine the public expect and welcome. Clearly my goddess was a happy, healthy girl with no inhibitions and affectations, who loved bathing and playing tennis at Ranalagh and supping in small restaurants in the King's Road, Chelsea, preferring that infinitely to being taken to the more usual meeting places of the successful members of her profession, The Caprice or the Savoy Grill.

"To be quite truthful, I don't possess a really grand evening-dress," she said. And I was conscious even as she spoke, that it was a statement not so much of fact, as of an attitude of mind.

"You mean the sort of elaborate affair that young starlets no one has ever heard of, think up for film *premières* in the hope of being photographed and having their picture next morning in *The Daily Mirror*. Not because of their talent which is practically non-existent but because of their plunging neckline which is only too apparent."

"I loathe making a public appearance myself, like I had to do when our play was at Portsmouth, before coming to London, and the last film in which I played *The Cruel Sea* was showing at the local cinema. They asked me to make a speech. I was simply terrified. However, the Navy was in charge and you know how undefeatable they are. They produced some naval rum and after that I couldn't stop talking. I still haven't the vaguest idea what I said. But on the whole," she added, as we got up from the table, "I think actors and actresses should only be seen on the screen or from the other side of the footlights. As they were in the old days. Besides, we live such ordinary lives. At least, I do."

"What do you do?" I asked. "I mean when it rains and you can't play tennis or swim."

"What other hobbies have I got? Let me think. Well, I read an awful lot. Plays and poetry and books about the theatre. Anything that I feel will teach me something and make me a better actress. And I collect Bohemian glass . . . and friends," she added, in a charmingly serious voice. "You see, I think meeting new people is always exciting."

More exciting than the curtain going up and down at the end of a first night, to an accompaniment of thunderous applause? More lasting, perhaps, I thought, while, aloud, I asked if there was any part that she was particularly ambitious to play.

"Oh yes, there is," she answered at once, "Bernard Shaw's *St. Joan*."

I did not like to tell her that I had been one of the pages in the original production. Or that her leading man in *The Cruel Sea*, Jack Hawkins, had been the other. It would surely make me seem too old in her eyes: too old almost to be alive.

"You'd make a wonderful Peter Pan," I suggested, thinking wryly, of the boy who never had to grow up.

"Oh do you think so? I'd love to play that, too. I wish you'd suggest it," she exclaimed.

I was touched by her naïve belief in the power of my pen. But I was even more touched by something else: her utter candidness. No, she had never, as a child, wanted to be an actress or believed that she could act. All through the war, when she was evacuated with her mother to South Africa, she had lived the life of a tomboy and never gone through the phase of posing in front of a mirror and reciting Ophelia's lines. . . . *There's Rosemary, that's for remembrance . . . pray, love, remember.* . . .

"Surely you must have been conscious you were growing into a beauty?" I interrupted.

She shook her head emphatically. "I didn't think I was. Then or now."

Then there was the first silence between us. For a moment her utter truthfulness defeated me. One wasn't used to such modest self-appraisal in the world of theatrical make-believe: of false eye-lashes and false illusions.

"How did it all start then? Your first job? After all, it's the closest trade union in the world."

"Well, Mother decided that I ought to take a course of stage training. Not in the hopes of a career, but to get rid of my coltishness. So that I would learn to speak and walk properly, and not look like a rag-bag. And I was very lucky. I went to the Central School of Speech and Drama. It is not so well know as the R.A.D.A., but Peggy Ashcroft went there, and so did Larry Olivier, and I think it is absolutely wonderful. Do you know about it?"

As a matter of fact, I had visited the school only a few weeks before in the Dome of the Albert Hall, where, for nearly fifty years now, a complete and flourishing entity on its own has been in existence whose only bridge with the life below in the auditorium, and upon the stage where stands the waiting grand-piano is that it, too, is concerned with the vital art of self-presentation.

Here are classrooms: rehearsal rooms: wardrobe rooms: a complete little theatre: and an atmosphere of enormous enthusiasm engendered by the students who come from all over the world to take a three-year course, divided into terms, like school, that cost the very reasonable sum of twenty-five pounds each. Some of the youngsters exist in hostels, others live with their families or friends: nearly all take a job like washing-up in an hotel or helping with the harvest, during the long summer vacation, to build towards next year's fees. There is little hard cash to spare, but a fortune of dreams that can come true.

Founded by that great teacher, Elsie Fogerty, the tradition is carried on today by the present principal, Miss Thurburn, who stressed to me the vital importance of complete co-ordination between what comes out of the mouth in the way of speech, and what accompanies it, in the way of bodily movement. I looked at her guiltily, remembering my own clumsiness on the stage, and how Marie Tempest's husband, producing *The Marquise*, had suggested to me that my best hope—he meant, I rather suspect, my only hope—would be to spend my first week's salary on having some fencing lessons.

I never did, the sacred fire was never lit in my breast, but as I walked round the Central School I came across the classroom where the fencing lessons were held and there was a youth who took off his mask to be presented to me, and told me that he had journeyed all the way from Iceland. His name was Benedikt Arnason and he had been chosen to come here on a grant from his State Theatre. Three years of concentrated endeavour, of devoted preparation and practice and still more practice, until the moment comes for the public matinée held in a London theatre, in front of an audience; not of adoring friends and relations, but of critical managers, fully fledged members of the professional Theatre and agents looking wearily for that rare something which is so much more important than good looks, call it personality, call it the power of sustained attack, call it what you will, that sets a performer apart from the crowd.

It was after her first appearance in public that Virginia McKenna was given the chance of serving her apprenticeship at the Dundee Repertory Theatre. At once she took that chance, though she still had no inkling, in her own mind, no flowery hopes as to where this first opening night might lead. She was engaged for one play, and then greatly to her surprise, was asked to stay on.

"It was the happiest time I have ever had. I often wish I was still there now. There wasn't anyone in the company who wasn't nice, I got six pounds a week, and I was always broke, but somehow it never mattered. It was all such fun, even the panic of remembering one's lines on each successive first night, and I can't understand why they say Scottish folk are dour. Perhaps it's because I've got some Scottish blood in my veins, but certainly they were lovely to me."

It was during this time that Miss Daphne Rye, the casting director for the powerful Tennant Management decided to make a tour of all the British Repertories in search of new talent for the London stage. Before the curtain came down upon the current play at Dundee, she knew that whatever other discoveries she might make her journey had not been in vain. Immediately the company's *ingénue* was put under contract and brought south to play in the first play of a very promising young writer, John Whiting, at the Haymarket Theatre. Ironically, the play failed, but the other success story did not falter. Here was authentic star quality.

Today a third of all that Virginia McKenna earns is automatically placed in a special account, for tax purposes, at the suggestion of a very wise 'aunt', who is one of the principals of an organization that takes care of the affairs of many American and English stars. Olive Harding possesses a warm if authoritative manner and might at a first meeting be mistaken for the headmistress of a better-class girls' school rather than for the shrewd, tenacious theatrical agent she is. It must be a source of considerable pride to her that three of her protégées have been nicknamed The Three Graces. They are Dorothy Tutin, with an electrifying power for playing tragedy in so slight a body, Claire Bloom, whose Juliet is already a legend, and the third name I need not mention again.

Of course, I do not know if Miss Harding is equally firm with her other pupils under her charge, but my guest at lunch told me that at last she had been allowed to buy herself a very small green car, which is the pride and joy of her life, to go with the equally small flat, where (until her recent marriage) she lived all by herself in a square, off Knightsbridge. Tucked away behind a garage, you climb up to it by some picturesque iron steps, but it is all very different from the imagined splendour with which actresses always surround themselves in romantic novels.

We went to see her bachelor domain after lunch. "I used to share a flat with my mother," she explained, on the way, "but that meant we could never entertain our friends at the same time, as we had only one sitting-room. So now I live on my own, and Mummy and I seem to see more of each other, not less. *And* understand each other better, too. I am sure being independent is a good thing, for both sides of the family. Don't laugh when you see my kitchen," she added.

I did not feel like laughing, just then, because as we turned the corner into Trevor Place, I caught a glimpse of the street where I had once lived, in digs, at the same time as I had been acting in *The Marquise*, and earning ten pounds a week. No. 12 Charles Street. Now the name had been changed to Trevor Street, and this seemed like yet another link between us, on this halcyon day, though noticing that change made me feel for a moment that I had never existed as a person at all. A young person, that is to say, who was acting by night and writing his first novel by day, seated behind the lace curtains of the first-floor front room, hiding away on just such a blazing summer's afternoon, when my co-sharer of the sitting-room, another actor by profession, would urge me strongly to come to Richmond and take a punt on the river.

Bobbie Harris had a charming light baritone voice and sometimes he would sit down at the piano and sing my favourite song out of *The Young Mozart*—'*Depuis ton départ, mon amour*'—with which Yvonne Printemps was enchanting London. But after a few minutes he would shut the lid down, and want to be out of doors. You work too hard, you are too ambitious, he used to chide me. You may get all that you want *one* day, but what's the use of that? You will be middle-aged, and the slave of your career. It is *now* that matters.

He was right, of course. No amount of success is worth that degree of self-abnegation. I realize that now. In a way, I never had any youth. I squandered it, not in riotous living, but in striving too hard for what lay eternally round the bend of the river. Too greedy. Too eager. Too single-hearted. It must not be like that for her. She must keep the ultimate burden of success at bay long enough to enjoy this summertime of her youth, I thought, as we climbed the iron balustrade to her flat door, and she bent down to stroke the kitten, like a stand-in for a watch-dog, sunning itself on the top step.

"Not afraid of burglars?"

"No."

'Not afraid of anything . . . not even of growing old?'

I did not ask that question aloud because it was not a day even for thinking such thoughts. "Don't laugh at me when you see the kitchen," she said, again.

The kitchen was certainly minute, a slit in the wall, and on the miniature side, too, were the sitting-room, with its cabinet filled with blue glass, and its row of books heaped upon the table, and the bedroom, which had one photograph of a very handsome man, beside her bed. I recognized that the picture was of her father, Terry McKenna, because I had known him, at the time this photograph was taken, when he had had an executive job at Christie's, in Bond Street and his daughter was still a small girl. There could not be any later picture because Terry had died before the war, and his loss had left a gap in her life which had not, upon that summer's afternoon, been filled with the protective tenderness of any other man.

It is easy to ask any American film star who has been married four times and is always crossing the border into Mexico for another divorce, about her love life but I had no intention of prying into the private affairs of this blessed damosel until she volunteered of her own accord. "As a matter of fact, I have lots of men friends, like I have lots of girl friends, but no special one. I believe that I shall know at once when it happens, but it has not happened yet."

I remembered her words when one morning last winter I opened the paper and saw the announcement of her engagement to a fellow player of great quality, an actor of many sensitive performances, Denholm Elliot. The moment that I saw the name I thought: he is the perfect complement for her, and what a wonderful-looking couple they will make on their wedding day. And I remembered, too, how when she had come to visit me again, this time on my birthday, young men of her own era had surrounded her in an admiring phalanx at the supper table, and one of them, whose name had been romantically coupled by the gossip-writers with that of Royalty, had rung me up, still in a dream, the next morning, to ask my advice. Did I think it would advance his suit if he dispatched a single white gardenia in a box all by itself?

He was right in his gesture, but wrong in his pursuit. She was not for him. He was at once too rich, too worldly, and too capricious in his affections for someone so very special. And even as my last night guest chattered on the telephone, I saw myself that July afternoon, leaving Trevor Place, and becoming lost in the surface bustle of Knightsbridge. I could not tell him, for he would have laughed at me, but I had had the strange and overwhelming sensation that I was a young actor again, with the whole future ahead of me, unexplored.

Would I still call my first novel, *Dreams Fade*?

At least let them not fade for her, and if my whispered prayer was drowned by the traffic and wafted away upon the summer air, I can repeat it now, as I did upon her wedding day, for here surely is the proper ending to this chapter, which set out to record once again what a holy and precious combination real youth and real beauty can make.

Yes, and how intoxicating an experience it is to chance upon that combination, untainted by vanity, self-consciousness or false illusions of grandeur.

TEN

PORTRAIT IN OILS

AFTER the war was over, I signed the peace by starting to keep a visitors' book again. Sometimes I am laggard in chevying my guests, but sometimes, again, I do remember that there is a very special reason why I am eager for someone to sign his name on a fresh page. It was so the winter afternoon that a young man, with a contemporary hair style, a vaguely broken nose, and wearing a dark red polo jumper under the jacket of his city-grey suit came to visit me in my London home.

Two hours must have passed like a moment for suddenly there was no light left in the room until I stood up to reach a lamp's switch. Then the spell was broken, for I had been listening to one of the most extraordinary true-life stories that had ever come my way. An artist of twenty-four had just confessed to me that he could neither read nor write. It did not matter. His only desire, his only need was to be able to pour himself out on his canvases that were being acclaimed in art circles as the work of a second Rousseau. So powerful was the passion that consumed him, so complete his absorption that he was able to produce a new picture every week. For his work there was now a queue of the celebrated and the rich waiting to buy, at the Redfern Gallery, off Bond Street, which, having believed in him and encouraged him, from the start, were now his exclusive patrons.

"Would you like to see the rest of my own collection of pictures before you go?" I suggested. "The Mathew Smiths and the Sutherlands are in the dining-room."

Politely he got up from the green sofa on which he had sat, like a small boy, at a grown-up's party, and followed me through the little library, not glancing, I noticed, at the striking Chirico on one wall. I turned on all the lights, with rather a flourish. It is a moment that never ceases to give me an absolute sense of pleasure. I waited for his appraisal, his appreciative comments: but nothing happened. He gazed at the array of contemporary work with blank, myopic eyes: the eyes of a sleep-walker. Then it was that I realized with a

stab of astonishment that the walls might just as well have been un-
covered, that these examples of the work of his fellow artists had no
message for him at all. It was as though a woman in an exquisitely
beautiful evening dress had attended a ball where there were many
other equally elaborate toilettes, but she was completely unaware
of any of them: all her vision was concentrated inwards, she could only
see one figure walking towards her and it was herself.

"Have you been to the Tate?" I asked.

My companion shook his head.

"Would you like to go? There are examples of Rousseau's work
there." Again the complete lack of interest. I was nonplussed, though
I knew by now that there was no trace of arrogance in his isolation.
So that it was not to try and pierce his armour that made me, as we
returned to the library, invite my guest to sign his name in the book.

He picked up the pen and hesitated, standing beside the Regency
desk. "Probably that pen doesn't suit you. Don't worry. You must
do it another time," I went on quickly. "It's a pity you haven't got
one of your home-made paint brushes in your pocket and then you
could do it with that."

I watched him, with his tongue stuck out of the corner of his
mouth, slowly and laboriously, trace the letters of his name. JACK
TAYLOR. The unfledged, slanting signature reminded me of the first
epistle I had written home from school, though it was not myself I saw
but another small boy hauled up in front of the class and ordered by the
mistress to spell the word 'A'. At the time it was a huge joke for
the rest of the pupils at Brockley Turnham Road School. With the
instinctive cruelty of children of that age they relished every detail
of the crucifixion. But for the victim it has been a recurring nightmare
ever since and deliberately from that moment he absented his senses
from all efforts to make him either read or write. Dumbly he went on
playing with his crayons and his paints, whenever he could come by a
drawing book. For the rest, he shut himself away in the world of his
own imagination. No teacher would ever find the key, or possess the
power either to reach or hurt him again.

"I print my signature on my paintings," he was saying in the
soft voice with its trace of East End accent and which seldom rises
above a lilting whisper, "I learnt to do that right at the beginning."

The beginning and the recognition was only two years ago, and for myself even less than that, I thought, remembering the afternoon when I had dropped in to the Redfern Gallery in Cork Street to look at the first exhibition in England of a contemporary of Monet. One of the paintings was of Monet's garden and I was drawn to stand in front of it for a long time. Indeed, I was much struck by all the examples of the work of Paul Dumont, though the name was completely unknown to me. Again and again, his pictures reminded me of another impressionist, Van Gogh. The same eagerness to spill paint across the canvas, as though the artist had a premonition that already there was a shadow waiting behind him to obliterate the sunshine for ever.

"What is Paul Dumont's history?" I asked Mr. Millar, one of the directors of the gallery. I was curious for without doubt here was the authentic flame.

"At a comparatively early age, he went mad. There were violent scenes, he would start threatening people in a café, with a knife, he had to be put away for everyone's sake. He died in a lunatic asylum."

Now the pattern was clearer, and with it his affinity with Van Gogh who in his lifetime had only been able to sell one single canvas, and that to his own brother-in-law. "Yet when you look at the examples of his work in the Tate, you simply can't understand why he was not appreciated in his lifetime," I exclaimed.

"It is not only the public who are like sheep. The art critics gang up, too. You need some brave voice to start the ball rolling. Once the impetus has begun, the rest of the journey is comparatively easy. Many artists have found that." My companion broke off from the contemplation of the landscape by Dumont that his client had just bought and said, abruptly. "Look, there are some other pictures that I would like to show you. They are in the basement. A bit dusty but I think you will feel it is worth while."

I was led into a little back storeroom which I had never been privileged to explore before. Here were canvases piled high to the ceiling. An Aladdin's cave for those with eyes to see. "What do you think of that?" my guide inquired.

Immediately I was reminded of the words of Blake. 'He who does not imagine in stronger and better lineaments and in stronger and better light than his perishing and mortal eye can see does not imagine at all.'

Here was a city in a dream, built turret upon turret against the hill-side, in which the human beings were dwarfed beside the splendour of the most original setting. For it had something of the Orient in its evocation and its brilliant colours: or rather what a child might imagine the eastern world to be. And yet the more I examined the unframed canvases propped up in front of me—here was a flight of strange birds across a stranger sky, here were toy ships in the city's harbour, protected from all winds that blow upon the mortal scene—the more conscious I became that I was having my introduction to a talent that owed no allegiances though it could be roughly classified as a product of the School of Primitives.

For the second time that afternoon, I asked for a painter's history. This time only the first few chapters of the story had been written and astonishing they were.

"One day at lunch time, the winter before last, a great navvy came into the Gallery and asked to see the Boss. He was carrying a couple of small canvases under his arm. He said, 'Look here, chum, you sell pictures. Are these any good?' 'Who painted them?' we asked. 'My mate did, but he was too scared to come in with me. You see, we've been doing a haulage job round the corner on a site in Bond Street. Dumping stuff, and taking it away. Sometimes we have a walk round in our dinner break, and we see your place. There you are, Jack, why don't you go and chance your luck? You're always belly-aching about wanting to pack up and be a bleeding artist. Well, go and ask them what they think. But he wouldn't so I said, bring up a couple of your latest, and I'll pop in myself. And here I am. Of course, I can't make nothing of them myself, but you're the experts, so take a dekko. . . .' "

It was fortunate that Rex Nan Kivell the Head of the Gallery was on the premises that day, since there is no shrewder judge of potential talent in the London art world. Although immensely successful across the years, he is still never too busy to take trouble, on an unknown quest. At once he asked the navvy to leave the pictures with him and to bring his mate in with him to collect them himself on the morrow.

"And did he buy them?" I asked.

"No doubt he would have done, in a book," my companion replied drily. "But, in actual fact, my partner couldn't be absolutely certain from the two small pictures. However, he did talk to the boy, most encouragingly, urging him to persevere with his painting in every possible spare moment and to bring us everything he had accomplished in six months' time. Then he would be able to make an exact assessment."

"That was fair enough," I agreed.

"Yes, and when the boy did return in six months' time, he had a dozen canvases to show, and each one an improvement on the previous one. Our encouragement had really set the spark alight, and now we ourselves were certain that here was a wonderful new talent. Rex told him at once to quit his manual job, so that he could devote himself entirely to painting from now on and that we would pay him each week exactly what he was getting and subtract that from the percentage of what we hoped to sell. However, in actual fact, a few months back we were able to raise his weekly sum on account, to eight pounds. We also promised him a one-man show in the Gallery as soon as he had produced sufficient pictures."

"And most of the work he does produce you really have been able to sell?"

"Every picture. In fact, we've a waiting list at the moment. The price? Oh, it varies between fifteen and thirty pounds. It's best not to fly too high too soon. What we want is to get his work hung and admired and talked about. Stephen Spender had one of the earliest pictures, the Leicester Education Authorities were so impressed that they bought half a dozen to display in their schools, even the Gallery next door have been buyers. Then one day Ninette de Valois came into the Gallery, with John Piper, and asked to see not the current exhibition, but, instead, any examples of Jack Taylor's work we had. They came down into the basement just as you have done, and they were so impressed that they demanded at once to meet the artist in person. When they did, on this very spot, they commissioned him to do the costumes and the back-cloth for a new ballet by Rodrigues. Jack had never been to Sadler's Wells till he was taken to see Rodrigues' other ballet, *Blood Wedding*."

"What's the theme of this one?" I asked.

"A seven-day bicycle race in Paris."

"But will he be able to create all that entirely out of his own imagination, too, and get the sketches in the right perspective, and his back-cloth for the stage? And you say he has never had a painting lesson in his life. . . ."

"He has already finished the commission and his sponsors are absolutely delighted with the result."

"Yet he has never been to Paris, or seen one of the races?"

"Good heavens, no. Except when he was evacuated in the war, or in the army for a short time, he has hardly left the East End where he was born. He's married, he told us, and he has two children. That is all we know about his private life. He comes to the Gallery once a week to draw his money, his interim dividends, and brings us each new picture as soon as it is finished. We trust him and he trusts us."

"And his wife?"

"We have never seen his wife, he always comes alone," Mr. Millar said.

A sudden overwhelming desire possessed me. "I would like to meet his wife. I would like to paint her portrait, in my own way. It must have been an extraordinary metamorphosis for her. How do you think she reacted when he came home that night and burst out about his meeting with a real picture-dealer at last? Do you imagine she is conscious yet that she is cooking for a genius every day?"

"I have no idea. You had better ask her. If her husband will let you." I could see that my companion had lost interest in that side of the conversation. But I hadn't.

Fortunately, the husband did let me. First, however, he came to my flat to inspect me, not my pictures which I realize now did not interest him. No pictures interested him except his own: nothing in the world except his own inward vision, which was all light, all transforming beauty, shutting out the drabness and the cruelty of the London streets where as a boy he had walked, cap in hand, a supplicant.

None of the colour that shone so gloriously on his canvases was reflected in his own exterior. He had the wide, curved generous lips of a poet but the overall look of an underground worker, someone who did not often see the sun.

"Would you like to go abroad and paint?" I asked him that afternoon.

"There's one place I would like to go to. Italy."

I agreed that Rome had always been a Mecca for painters. There was supposed to be some special texture of refracted light. "At least, all my painting friends tell me so."

But I was on the wrong tack. It was not that. "I want to visit the Colosseum and stand quite alone in the centre."

"And afterwards will you paint what you see?"

He shook his head. That landscape would not fit into the boundaries of his own private city. Even when last Christmas they took him to see the Circus at Olympia, and afterwards, from memory, he painted his portrait of one of the clowns, he did not place him against the sawdust and the tiers of faces, but shut away inside a small room, within the castle walls.

"When did you first realize that you *had* to be a painter?"

"I am not sure." He sat in the middle of the sofa, balancing his cup of tea, searching back in his mind. He saw himself leaving school at fourteen, and then one job after another, and each one more loathsome to him, dead-end, dead. Twenty-five shillings a week the first one was fitting tin caps on to bottles as the implacable stream passed him on the conveyor belt, mopping up the floors of Guy's Hospital was another, and in between there were twenty or thirty others that he cannot even remember now. Except that he hated every moment of every one.

If he had any money left over at the end of the week, which was seldom enough, he'd buy Swedish hardboard, which is cheaper than canvas, and treat it himself and try to paint. And when there wasn't any money left over, he'd join a local gang of tomorrow's spivs and lay-abouts. He fell in with them one evening outside the local 'caif'—as they call it—which was their meeting-ground, and he heard one say, "Let's whip a drag." Translated that means, pinch a car, just for an evening's joy ride. He admits candidly that he enjoyed the sensation: the wildness called to something in his own suppressed being. At the time he thought perhaps that was what he was looking for, it could be the antidote to his restlessness. And then one day he found himself standing in the local magistrate's court, accused of trespass on other people's premises, and it was the end of that dream. He was put on probation. The act of generosity and understanding was like a cold draught of water splashed across his face. The need would never happen again and it hasn't. Henceforth the search to assuage his inner restlessness would lead elsewhere.

It did not lead him into the army. He found himself there, by law. And strangely enough, at first he felt happier than he had been for a long time. It was a challenge: he accepted it: he turned himself into the smartest recruit in his platoon, he was promoted to be a corporal. And then gradually the flavour faded from the new life of

The Bird Man in the Magic
City

The artist: Jack Taylor

Alec Murray

"A push-cart for the
children"

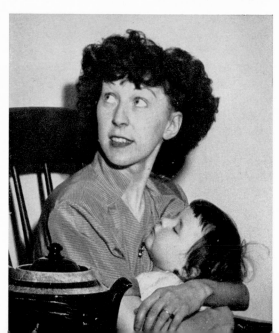

disciplined non-thinking, of keeping his boots clean, and complete submission. Try as he did, he could not blot out the colours and the figures that persisted in taking shape upon the canvas of his mind, coming between him and the fixed and normal routine of army life.

So he started running away, and being brought back to the barracks of the Queen's Own Royal West Kents. And running away again, and fetched back once more on charge, until one evening, he could not stand it any longer, and tried to escape for ever into his own world, stringing up his mortal body, in one of the wash-houses, deserted at midnight. Fortunately a guard found him, before any final harm had been done, and he was taken to the Royal Albert Hospital, at Woolwich. There, like the wise magistrate, he found an equally wise physician, who passed his patient, lost in the solitude of his own despair, on in turn to a colleague dealing, as far as any human being can deal, with the unexplored territories of the mind.

"There *must* be something you want to do in life."

"I want to paint. I want to be a painter."

Over and over again, the same words poured out. It was at once a plea in mitigation and a lament. In the end they sent him home and crossed his name off their army books. To them he was a misfit, nevertheless there was a place for him somewhere. "If you care enough about your painting," the good man who healed minds said to him, in farewell. "You will find fulfilment in the end."

In the end? But how could he be sure that as a painter he was travelling along the right road. He had no one to teach him, to advise him. No one who cared the price of a piece of Swedish hardboard. His family's attitude was that he was simply wasting his time and theirs with these fantastic creations which had no connexion with anything to be glimpsed within their own horizons and one can hardly be censorious or even surprised when one remembers the reception that Van Gogh received throughout his tortured, painting life. While the artist's wife became so exasperated at his indifference to the need for being a bread-winner, that at one moment she went home to her father. It was, indeed, a strange new version of the eternal triangle. She was not jealous of another woman, but of the hours her husband wasted every evening and at weekends at his 'daubs'. Unless you give that up, I'll never come back to you, she swore.

So he promised and failed to keep his promise. It was, after all, the sort of vow that a man, moved by such a compulsion as possessed

K

him, could hardly be expected to keep. For six weeks he put aside his paint brushes as a chain smoker will shun cigarettes. Then the urge became once more overwhelming. However, on that momentous day in his career, that immense step forward when he sold his first picture to the head of the Redfern Gallery for ten pounds, he divided the spoils equally between the two utterly separate sides to his life. Half the ten pounds he put in one pocket, half in the other. Then leaving Bond Street, he drove home on his bicycle, through the dusk, via Catford. Here was the shop, owned by John F. White, where so often he had pressed his nose longingly against the window filled with all that a professional artist's heart could desire. This evening he could swagger inside and spend five pounds like a millionaire, on paints, the best and most expensive tubes, on brushes to replace his home-made ones, on proper canvases at last. The other five pounds was sacred. That was for his wife and children.

Did his wife resent that the whole of the prize did not find itself in her lap? Some women were like that, though I had to acknowledge to myself that I had moved on to dangerous ground. I had not yet met the artist's wife. I must not judge. Aloud I said. "That was the day when you really knew you *were* a painter. It was proved at last and from now everything else had to give way. . . ."

"Yes, and if. . . ."

When he paused, I tried to feel my way cautiously, to finish the sentence for him. "If you had known for certain earlier, you would not have tied yourself down, in marriage?" I hazarded. "At least, not so young."

He nodded. "Mind you, I love the kids, and my wife is a very good mother to them, she hasn't been out at night for months, and I mean to do my best for them, too, always. But I must get a studio of my own, where I can shut myself up all day and night, if I choose, and not worry about meals or anything else. My wife's given up getting me my food at regular times. She says it's just waste and I can see her point. Sometimes I work all night and then the next day I am fagged out and I want to sleep, at least I would if the babies would let me. Leigh John is two-and-a-half, Nina is fourteen months. We called him Leigh so that it would be all right if he was a girl. I really believe he's going to be a painter, too. He comes and watches me in my room for hours and scribbles on the wall."

"Your room?" I interrupted. "Then you have got a room for yourself to work in?"

"It's not a room. It's a cubby-hole. It's just big enough for me to stand up in, and the baby at my feet. You couldn't put a bed into it, or even a couple of chairs." He looked away towards the windows. "When I got married, I was twenty. I thought I'd escape that way."

"Escape?" His voice was so light, so little more than a whisper, that I had to be sure that was the word he had used.

"Yes, I was living with my family, trying one job after another, and nothing any good. And all the time I had this feeling bottled up inside me. I worked it out that what I wanted was to be married and live on my own, even if it was only in two furnished rooms, just like once I had wanted to be one of the wide boys, whipping a drag, and then I found that wasn't it, either."

I could understand now, completely. His side of the story. This pent-up longing like the weight of sexual desire that had to be assuaged, but could only be assuaged by one thing: the recognition of his promise as a painter. Still, that had happened at last. "So isn't your wife pleased about the ballet designs that have been commissioned and about your selling every picture that you paint?" I suggested.

"Oh yes, she says she thinks the pictures are good *now*. She never use to say anything before. She just ignored them. And it's the same with my family. As soon as they heard I'd sold my first pictures, they told me we could come and have the top rooms of the house they share at Sydenham. I suppose they reckon that if I can pay the twenty-five bob a week rent, out of the sale of my pictures, they *must* be good."

I said. "When my first novel was published I was the same age as you got married. My family thought my book was good, too. They didn't however, when I was writing it. They more than hinted then that I was wasting my time. It is the same with all families, where there's an embryo artist. We are the cuckoos in the nest. May I come and visit you at home?" I meant, of course: may I come and judge for myself.

"If you want to. It's not like this." The very quietness of his voice made everything seem doubly fraught with meaning. In the fading light, he glanced for the first time round the living-room of my flat. Up till that moment his eyes had always seemed to be looking past me, through the walls. Now the paleness of his face was merging fast into the encroaching, shadowy dusk. For an instant of time, I wondered if everything he had told me was part of some waking dream, that we were both figures in a limbo of nothingness, waiting, pleading to be born. It was then that I got up abruptly, reaching for the switch.

The actual house in which they lived was a surprise. It was one of those relics of a bygone age that had been left behind by the tide, standing by itself on its own small plot of land, down a lane where my car could not turn. This might have been far out in the country, had it not been for the colony of pre-fabs, built where the land-mine had dropped, I was told. The foundations of the house must have been strong to resist that, I thought, but they looked strong. And the roots of the giant pear tree in the front garden, just blossoming into life, which again wasn't in the least like the front gardens in Forest Hill, through which we had just passed.

"One evening not long ago we had a caller. It was one of my lorry driver mates from round about here. 'Is it true,' he said, 'you've sold one of your paintings, Jack!' I told him, yes it was true all right and this was the one I was working on now. 'Will you sell that, too?' he went on. I said: Yes, it was already sold. 'Strike me pink,' he said, 'I'm off to buy a box of paints myself. And tell my mates . . . we'll all be at it. We couldn't do worse!' "

"Well, that was frank enough, anyway. Perhaps you have founded a new sect. The Forest Hill artists' colony of lorry drivers. I hope they'll ask you to be the official opener of their first show."

Jack had come to fetch me and show me the way. Once when my car came to a standstill for a long time, caught in the rush hour, hemmed in by the scabious, peeling façades of the south-east London tenements, I intercepted a look of disgust on my companion's face. "It's never got any colour," he said. From the permanence of that projection he had fled and closed behind him the jewelled gates of his own city, where everything grew by magic and was beautiful to behold.

A sudden train of thought occurred to me. "When you were evacuated, didn't that give you a glimpse of something different? Green fields, a bright sky."

I found myself shouting above the traffic, my words suspended, fatuously, in mid-air, while his own quiet voice seemed to reach me on another wave-length.

"The first place I was evacuated to was near Paignton. I lived on a farm. There was another boy and myself. He was different from me, better class, I mean, and when the weather wasn't nice, he was allowed to stay indoors and play with his toys, but I had to clean out the sties, and if I hadn't done it to satisfy the farmer, when he went to look at the pigs, at night, with a hurricane lamp, I had to go out there and then and do it all over again."

At that moment, we had reached Camberwell Green, where we had to turn off to the right. "I should never have found the way by myself," I said, because I had no other answer to this latest instalment. For it seemed like that to me, one long, continuous story, emerging in small pieces, to be put together like a jigsaw puzzle.

Buses were converging on us at the roundabout from all sides. That gave me another idea. How did he manage not to be confused himself, unable to read their destination boards? Or was it sufficient just to know the numbers?

He said, with a sudden smile, that was very rare and made his face look many years younger. "I don't make many mistakes now. I know which bus goes to Westminster, and Victoria, and which to Piccadilly. The numbers, I mean. And Doris—she's one of my sisters—writes my letters for me. Of course, it was different when I was a vac, in the war. I came back to London from Paignton and then when things got a bit hot again, they sent me away, this time to a place near Northampton. I was lodged with a very old lady who kept cats. Fourteen of them. How the place stank. There were messes everywhere, under the chairs. I was fair sick of it, so I ran away. But in the wrong direction! I walked thirty miles north, instead of south."

"What happened then?"

"Oh, I gave up, and went to the police station. I've never been able to bear the sight of a cat since."

"I've seen dogs in one or two of your pictures."

"Yes, but never a cat. And you won't find one at home, either." The perpetually anxious look came back to his face. "The wife is very nervous about your coming. It isn't much of a place, you know. I told her you would understand."

I did understand, so that was why the house itself turned out to be rather a surprise. Built of grey stucco, it had a pleasing square look, and when you climbed the stairs to the garrets at the top where the Taylor family were squatting, you didn't feel enclosed, but instead, you had a sense of freedom at once: if it hadn't been for the pre-fab mushrooms spoiling the view, this might be anywhere, I thought. Or nowhere.

The artist's wife was a surprise, too. I don't quite know what I had expected, but certainly not someone as elegant as this. She wore black in the way that an Italian woman will wear black: there were small paste diamond earrings in her ears that were very delicate and fine: her hair was cut in bubble curls, copied, one felt, from a film star like her namesake, Elizabeth Taylor. She had put on almost a stage make-up in honour of her visitor. With her dark vividness she did not seem English at all until she spoke and then at once you could place her standing at the bench of the toy factory where she had worked before her marriage. Her younger child, clinging to her wide skirt, its nose dribbling, had a wax-like paleness in comparison. "I brought her cot in, Jack, so that she could have a sleep this afternoon. But she's just wetted her nappy, and I haven't got a dry one." The voice of Nina's mother had the fretfulness of a child herself. One felt that its nervous edge was only part of a larger, all-embracing malaise of the spirit. I tried to comfort her by drawing attention to the bonny condition of her son. Leigh John had bright scarlet cheeks, like a Mabel Lucie Atwell drawing, and his summer-blue woollen rompers provided a reassuring splash of colour in the otherwise very bare room that was strangely negative in atmosphere. In fact, it was like a waiting-room, at a frontier, I thought, not a home, where children play with toys upon the floor.

Most obligingly Leigh John caused a diversion at once which helped to lessen the tension and to put us all at our ease. Recite the names of the painters, his father commanded, expanding visibly in parental stature, as he spoke. I noticed, too, how candidly pleased he was to be reunited with his offspring, even after such a short absence. "Go on . . . Leigh . . . Rousseau. . . ."

"Rousseau. Picasso . . . Van Gogh . . . Van Dyk . . . Constable."

The child stumbled at the last fence and had to be helped. Otherwise his delivery was immaculate. He had a sweet, piping little voice, the air and tone of a young aristocrat. Nor was there any apparent shyness in front of the stranger, though in his ecstasy at being invited to show off his one trick, he started to bite the oilskin covering to the table in the window, where the artist's wife had set the teacups before our arrival.

"Now stop that . . . or what will Daddy do? He will spank your
. . . ."

"Posterior."

Again, the lisping, angelic accent that transported one far away
to another realm, where once upon a time there would be a nursery at
the top of almost every house of this size, with a starched nanny on
guard beside the fire, waiting for the magic ritual when she would
read her charges a bedside story. Once upon a time. No nanny would
survive twenty-four hours today, I thought, when every drop of water
had to be fetched from the parents' flat many stairs below, and all
cooking and washing facilities shared, too. No wonder the artist's
wife looked to be stones thinner, I decided, than in the picture of
her taken on her wedding day when, plump and confidently beaming
in her bridal finery, she gave the impression of overlaying the immature,
slight youth at her side.

The picture hung in his cubby-hole, where the artist took me now
and which was exactly as he described it. It reminded me, in size,
of the closet where my mother had kept her shoes, in my childhood, and where I would be locked in, for an hour, when I had been
particularly obstreperous. I used to pass the time arranging the shoes.
It had no window as far as I could now remember. But this one had—
there was the difference—one narrow wall was almost all window,
looking out on to the mushroom-growth of pre-fabs, and just below,
the neatly kept front patch of garden, dominated by the foaming
pear tree that seemed part of another, immemorial landscape. What a
glowing picture that would make, I thought, before I remembered
that he never painted from life, that he would not even see the pink
and white foam when he glanced out of the window.

I examined the contents of his four-foot square retreat. There
was a huntin'-shootin'-fishin' jacket, with leather supports to the
elbows hanging up on a peg. A present from one of his patrons, and
he used it for work, as in *La Vie Bohème*, a young artist would wear
a smock. "I don't hold with trying to look and dress like an artist,"
he confessed. "I don't believe those—and he meant those with straggling
beards and sandals—are the *real* ones." "I didn't, either," I agreed.
Then he showed me the virgin hardboard that he would treat with
zinc oxide and French chalk, and the paints that he could now afford.
"I give my wife five pounds every week, and keep the other three.
It works out better that way because by Tuesday, when her purse is

usually empty, I've always got something left of my pocket money for her to draw on." "Do you go to your local cinema or local pub, in the evenings?" I asked. He shook his head. "If I'm not painting, I'm usually trying out a drawing. (I used to paint direct out of my head, but now I generally try mapping it out first, in crayon.) And if I've finished a picture that day, then I usually spend the evening trying to read a bit of this."

This was a small black book, stacked in the corner of the bench-table on which was strewn his paints, his palette, his cleaning rags. There was a little group of half a dozen books, altogether. I was curious to look at their titles. *The Canadian Front, Princess Mary's Gift Book, King Albert's Book, Art in Modern Ballet.* The last was on loan from Sadler's Wells, the other three had been a present from a friend. Rather out of date these relics of the First World War, I thought, and then I remembered that he would not be able to read the text, anyway. And that brought me, with a sharpening of curiosity, to the small black book.

It was a copy of The Salvation Testament. You could put it in your pocket, conveniently and easily. On the fly-leaf the inscription ran. 'To Jack with Christian love from Pat and Les.' And underneath in the same hand. 'The blessing of the Lord, it maketh rich, and he addith no sorrow with it.'

"Pat is one of my sisters and Les is her husband. No, she's not the sister who writes my letters. That's Doris. There are eleven of us altogether, mostly girls. I am the eldest son. My mother swears that my grandfather was a painter called Samuel Nethercock. But we've never been able to find out anything about him. Some of the family are very dark. Like foreigners."

I thought: it is you who are the foreigner to them. I picked up the Testament again, so light in my hand, compared with the family Bibles that once upon a time would have all the names of the children and the great-grandchildren inscribed upon the fly-leaf, stretching back to Samuel Nethercock and beyond. Now there was this instead, a gift of belonging, between a sister and her brother. The opening of a door that had before seemed irretrievably to be closed.

"But you can't really read it?" I suggested.

He agreed that he couldn't At least, not properly "If I stick at one bit each night, I can sometimes sort of manage the sense. Anyway, I like just looking at the pages. It makes me feel quiet inside."

From the other side of his cubby-hole's door there was a continuous stream of brittle clamour from his offspring. I shuddered, as I visualized trying to work and concentrate, with that as a perpetual accompaniment, like a never-ceasing dentist's drill. However, was it not equally torturing for the other partner?

A few minutes later, when we re-emerged into the larger garret, the baby was on the bare floor, its damp bottom showing, the boy had just banged his head against the corner of the table and had resolved into tears. I found myself wishing that I had had the sense to bring a piece of chocolate in my pocket. Say the names of the painters, Leigh. It was no use.

"What do you do when your husband joins in and moans, too?" I asked.

She could not smile at the jest. It was too much like a belly blow. In that instant, an overwhelming sense of pity struck me, too, like a pain. Suddenly, I was acutely aware of all the occasions when the husband called out for silence, for creative peace, and by his protests only added to the general uproar, the hopeless, endless confusion that was nobody's special fault, and least of all that of the mother, who, having in swift succession, produced two healthy children, naturally sought the security of a weekly wage packet and the normal background of any other working man's wife.

"Go on," said the husband in his usual zephyr-quiet voice.

"Well, you *have* got a bad temper sometimes, haven't you, Jack?" It was not an accusation but a plea for justice.

"I is right."

I? Oh, short for Iris. There was the final irony. His pet name for his wife. 'I'. Couple that to the all-embracing egotism of every artist. The great I am. A satirical writer would have made much of that, I thought. But I did not see things that way. Or rather, the more one scratched beneath the surface, dug right down, the more genuine points of view emerged. One could try to hold the balance, to be fair all round. Even to the father, who had to pay the bills for the electric light.

"That's when I get most mad, with everyone," the artist was saying. "You see, I made a bargain with my family, twenty-five bob a week for the rent, to include the light, too. Well, my father doesn't like us using two lights, at night." He jerked his head towards the privacy of his cubby-hole. "That means, I have to try and paint in here, though I've got a light in there. Otherwise, it means another shilling in the meter, down below. That's when I get mad with everyone," he repeated.

It was an endless repetition, the perpetual succession of irritating, frustrating pinpricks. Up and down the stairs, up and down the stairs, all day long, having to plead for every concession. No free time for the wife, ever. Or for the husband, either, for that matter. Bound together by bonds of economic steel. I saw it all. I felt it all. I understood now exactly why the artist always came alone to the gallery. It gave him a sense of temporary, spurious freedom.

"Aren't you thrilled about his having a whole Show by himself?" And even as I spoke, I realized that the boundaries of her world did not reach that far, and I went on quickly to ask what she would like to buy, if the Exhibition was such a success there was something left over, in the pool.

She knew at once. She did not hesitate. "Oh, a push cart for the children." Immediately, she saw herself going out shopping with a push-cart as other women, in other circumstances, might dream of driving to the opera, with a coronet of diamonds upon their hair.

"A push-cart? Nothing more?"

Now she was silent, unable to visualize anything beyond the concrete image of that mingled relief and splendour. And when I left her, she was still musing upon the vision that her chance visitor had aroused in her dying imagination. I looked back as we started to walk up the lane. She had not come to the window but Leigh John was peering over the sill. He did not wave. Years later, would any echo of the visit remain in his consciousness, I wondered. Rousseau, Picasso, Van Dyk, Van Gogh, Constable. The names would have a new evocation for me, henceforth.

The artist had offered to show me the return route, as far as Camberwell Green. On the way, the car was brought to a complete standstill by a great concourse of Salvation Army men and women, in their dark blue uniforms, marching six abreast, across the road. On this occasion, there was no band, no banners unfurled. For themselves, there was no need, to keep in step.

All the same, my first reaction was one of acute irritation that our progress should be completely suspended in this way. I was itching to be at my own easel before I forgot a single vital blob of paint. And then as we waited, in an increasing, impotent line of traffic, I remembered how, on Sunday nights, in the East End, The Salvation Army lasses would come quietly through the doors of the noisiest pubs and go from customer to customer, asking them to buy copies of *The War Cry*. What courage that must take. What faith.

Yet the artist's wife had courage, too, I thought. And now above the echoes of the marching feet, and the sound of the buses' engines behind me, I heard her calling to me. A push-cart. A push-cart for the children, she said.

ELEVEN

'THIS IS WOMAN'S HOUR'

THE routine when you appear on the programme is always the same. You have sent in your script four days ahead, and on the morning you are requested to be there at half past eleven, so that the producer to whom you are assigned can give you half an hour's private rehearsal, tactfully blue-pencil any phrases that could, by the remotest possibility, offend anyone, and time you—the most important item of all—before you join the general run-through in Studio 4A, on the fourth floor at midday. From then on the tension increases, sometimes markedly so, until zero hour at two.

For my own part, I have never been able to conquer my initial nerves, which induce a woeful sense of instability, not to say, inadequacy the moment that I reach the entrance to Broadcasting House at the top of Portland Place. It may be that I am only calling for a friend, to keep a luncheon date. The recurring terror remains. I have fought, with serious determination, this personal reaction, this permeation of impending doom. I have reminded myself again and again what a pleasant façade the entrance hall does, in fact, present. Many of the commissionaires in their blue uniforms are familiar faces now and acknowledge my arrival with an informal salute. Again, the ladies behind the desk are the most welcoming team I have encountered in any public bureau. Waiting one's turn, one overhears them taking enormous trouble about the queries and inquiries, sometimes exceedingly bizarre, that assail them all day long. While behind their heads is a freshly arranged urn of expensively matched flowers. It should please one's aesthetic sense, especially in winter, but somehow, it always reminds me, whatever the season, of a funeral urn.

"Mr. Derville is waiting for you in B.X. You know your way by now, don't you?" I thank her, with excessive gratitude, for those few polite words, because her smile is so very human, and it stays with me until I reach the lift, and the doors swing open, and start to close again with such inexorable speed that if it had not been for the intervention of a fellow passenger, who pulls me towards him through the dangerously diminishing gap, I should have had no breath or stomach left for the rehearsal. "These lifts take a bit of getting used to, I am afraid." The tone of his voice, inoffensive though it is, makes it abundantly clear to me that he suspects this to be my first term at school. I give a covert glance at his thick brown tweed suit, his green shirt and red tie and decide that I am in the momentary presence of someone high up on the Third Programme. This does nothing to diminish my lack of self-confidence and when the doors slide silently open at the second floor, I dart through the gap, as though bent on escaping from the Beak.

"I do hope I'm not late, Anthony," I begin nervously, as soon as I reach B.X. and find the lights on in the small, cell-like studio and my producer already ensconced at the control panel, on the other side of the glass wall. We are old friends now, and even meet off-duty sometimes, on the front at Brighton, at weekends where, like myself, he likes to watch and study the influx of visitors. Antony Derville had been my producer on scores of occasions. His judgment has been proved right again and again, and yet on every occasion that I rejoin him in a B.B.C. studio, it is for me as though we are meeting for the first time. And it is quite apparent to me that he is not unaware himself of the strained atmosphere. Instinctively, he assumes a professional manner, at once soothing and yet impersonal.

"Janet likes your script very much, but she thinks the first part of your week's diary so original and so thrilling, that it makes the last page an anticlimax, and, as on my timing, we shall have to cut forty lines, I wondered if you would care to consider stopping at the end of the story about the artist and his wife."

"And have nothing about the new council school, on the housing estate, and the family where the mother is a German and all the children play happily together? Oh, Antony. . . ."

"Then shall we just go through the script before we rehearse and see if there is another forty lines that you could cut?"

"But why must we take out forty lines at all?"

"Well, I am afraid we have got rather a heavy programme today, and you won't be able to run over eight minutes."

"You know I usually have nine or ten."

Each time my protest becomes weaker in volume, because I know that it is no use. I walk through dejectedly into the studio itself.

Here there is just space for a small, modern-wood table, a microphone
in the centre and two chairs. The air-conditioning plant has, with
complete efficiency, squeezed the air dry of all living quality. When
my producer takes the other chair opposite me I am reminded of the
day when I was shown the inanimate props for a prison visit in a
room about the same size as this, and the same kind of furniture.
However, any microphones *there* were concealed. And there is another
difference now, too, I tell myself. I have become the prisoner and
opposite me is my solicitor concealing his pity behind his glasses as he
explains in a soft, deprecatory voice that he is afraid that he cannot
hold out any hope for a reprieve.

"And there are just one or two other small points I wanted to
raise," he continued gently, "before we begin. You speak about them
living in Sydenham in one passage, and then a little later on—halfway
down page 2—you explain that he has never left the East End. Don't
you feel that all the other families who also live in Sydenham might
be upset at being referred to as 'The East End'? Oh, you'll change
that? Thank you so much. And then there's just one final point. If
we transpose the last paragraph of all, having omitted all the part
in between about the school, and personally I like it very much, you
are sure about cutting off the heads of daffodils when they are dead,
in the garden, to increase their flowering next year. And also about
not picking the leaves as well if you want plenty of blooms."

"Quite sure," I reply, on firmer ground this time.

"Good. We don't want any *experts* writing in, do we, as they have
a fatal habit of doing with the B.B.C. Shall we start the rehearsal
then?"

My producer disappears again behind the glass wall, the red light
on the desk flickers, I begin. "As a matter of fact, I do keep a diary,
though not a very expansive one." What a damn silly opening,
how stilted and wooden my voice sounds, everyone will switch off, I
tell myself, I shall get another postcard like the one I received that was
printed in capitals for every member of the staff to read: CAN'T
YOU PUT A SOCK IN IT, YOU MISERABLE TWERP. Why did
I ever imagine that I could conquer this infernal medium, why am I not
at home in the country, cutting my own dead heads off the daffodils.
Surely a more satisfying occupation than this. . . .

I stumble over a word. Instinctively I slow down, something
begins to happen. I am no longer self-conscious, uncertain, my

thoughts elsewhere. I am absorbed, utterly absorbed in the sweep of the story that I am telling: I am speaking to one elderly widow, whom I have never met, who told me in her last letter that she keeps a budgerigar, and looks forward every day to 'Woman's Hour'.

The preliminary, private rehearsal is over. My solicitor comes back into my cell, but now we are on Christian name terms once more. Before he can speak, I blurt out my confession. "I know I went too fast at the beginning, Antony, and didn't think enough about the real meaning of what I was saying. I always do. But I *will* remember when I go on the air. And Janet is quite right. The description of the new school would have been an anticlimax. It looked all right on paper, but it always sounds so different when you read your script aloud. I never *quite* get used to the difference. But I am sorry I argued, Antony."

My breathless *apologia* is most graciously received. We go over the pages side by side. The corrections are mostly matters of intona-tion, a pause here, a quickening of pace there. "And don't you think you could use a starting-again voice when you come to visit them in their own home?" I agree at once and practise it. I begin to feel a little more relaxed, my producer is smiling behind his glasses. "We *all* thought it one of your best scripts and I am sure everyone who hears it, is going to like it," he says kindly. "Shall we go upstairs now and join the others?"

The studio, 4A, whence 'Woman's Hour' goes out over the ether every afternoon, from Monday to Friday, is a very grand affair compared with the cell I have just vacated. It is like a suite in a hotel, with a passage joining the two main rooms, one of which, instead of bedroom furniture, is equipped with all the paraphernalia of the control panels. Here are the engineers, a young man in a tweed jacket, a girl, looking, in her cotton frock, like a university student, some of today's speakers and some of the permanent staff for this programme. I shake hands with everyone, hopefully. I can tell at once who is staff, and who is a stranger, like myself. It is not so much that we are palpably shy, as that the others have a universal pallor, a grey look, as though this great building that has been likened, architecturally, to the prow of a ship is, in reality, a colossal dungeon, built below the ground, like the Maginot Line. With no windows in the studio, no visual contact with the world outside, and the walls giving the impression of being padded to make an acoustic paradise, even after an hour or two one begins to feel as though one is locked away for the rest of one's life. And will never see the blue sky again or lead once more an ordinary sort of existence, waiting at the corner of the street for a bus, or trying to secure a bargain, in the summer sales.

Today, the assistant editor of the programme, Miss Scott Moncrieff, is taking the final run-through. She is a tall, slim woman, with fine bone structure, and the delicate, unusual looks of a Borzoi. At a first glance, she seems such a bad colour one wonders if she ought not to be in bed. I try to reassure myself by remembering that the fluorescent lighting takes all the warmth out of any woman's make-up, turning lipstick into a purple gash. I stand up and offer the assistant editor my chair. She looks at me with some surprise. Obviously, she is much too busy to sit down and does not feel in the least like fainting.

Each producer conducts their own speaker through to the other room, the other side of the glass wall when their cue approaches and hands us over to the *compère* who appears to be considerably more healthy than the representatives of the internal staff. But then she has a different status: although she is constantly inside the building, she is a free-lance, like myself. And what a splendid buffer Jean Metcalfe makes, I decide gratefully, when my turn comes to sit opposite her at the table and work out our introductory remarks together. She greets me as if I were the only speaker she has to announce that day, and for the first time, since I entered the marble-studded hall, I feel almost at ease. Certainly not on guard, any more, though when originally I met Jean Metcalfe, at a rehearsal of 'Woman's Hour', I was instinctively suspicious of her compelling charm of manner. It seemed too good to be true. She had brought her microphone technique to such perfection that she could not turn it off, even between the run-through and the performance itself. That is what I suspected. But I was completely wrong to react like that, and I am extremely ashamed now that I did, even at a first encounter. For I should have known better. I should have remembered one of the fundamental laws of broadcasting which is that the least sign of insincerity is at once damningly apparent over the air.

Today there is a mother who will tell an audience of millions—sometimes as many as four million—what it is like to make the dis-covery that through no fault of your own or of your husband, one of your children has been born a Mongol baby. Although it is clear at the final rehearsal that the speaker has been carefully and patiently

MISS JANET QUIGLEY

MISS JEAN METCALFE

rehearsed, it is equally obvious that she remains an amateur at the microphone. If you close your eyes, you can sense at once that she has a script in front of her. There is little variety in her voice, less pace and attack. It does not matter. She is reading with her eyes, but she is speaking from her heart. Most important of all, there is nothing second-hand about this story, it is personal history, so personal and so blazingly sincere that this unknown voice will go over the air stamped with the authority and the urgency of universal truth.

"I was so terribly glad when she said at the end, that her next child was quite all right. Oh what a relief it must have been for her, even though the doctors swear that it never happens twice."

"Yes, and what a vision on Janet's part to choose that script out of all the hundreds that are sent in every month. After all, it was quite a tricky decision to make. I'm sure it wouldn't have been in the programme in the early days of 'Woman's Hour'. By the way, is Janet coming to lunch today?"

Now the scene has changed and I am sitting next to Jean Metcalfe, who is wearing a comfortable adaptation of a dark blue fisherman's jersey, at a long table in another closed-in room which is used for committees and staff meetings. It has been turned into a temporary dining-room. Twelve places have been laid, and in front of each a plate has been set on which there is one small portion of pork pie, surrounded by lettuce. In the centre of the table are two larger plates of chocolate biscuits, and two others of bread and butter. On a side table coffee, and bottles of beer.

I find that I have eaten my ration in a flash, and drunk my cup of coffee, too. So when Jean, who is acting as hostess, asks me whether I wouldn't rather have had a bottle of beer, I hear myself answering that, yes I will have one after all, though it would appear a dangerous, if not suicidal combination just before a broadcast. However, it is free and on the Corporation, and what an instinctive attraction that is. Indeed, although I am quite aware that I have had my quota, at a moment when there is a diversion at the door, I reach out for another chocolate biscuit. Most tantalizing of all is the empty place opposite me, and its unclaimed piece of pie. What would happen if I asked if I might have it? Would it be like a Bateman drawing? *The broadcaster who asked for a second helping, inside the B.B.C.* To try and remove my thoughts to a loftier plane, I turn to my other neighbour, Antony Derville, and inquire if this is the same boardroom where every Tuesday morning, all

L

the 'Woman's Hour' team hold their weekly post-mortem. Everyone's pets are criticized or approved with equal objectivity, new ideas eagerly canvassed, there is a general free-for-all which never becomes too hot under the collar because of the cool, aseptic personality of the editor in chief, Janet Quigley, whose influence and whose strength of mind and character have transformed the programme from the blancmange it originally was into the unsentimental, imaginative forum it is generally acknowledged to be today. To make the listeners laugh, cry, and above all, think, is her precise formula, her own explanation for this metamorphosis, and remembering it again, I momentarily forgot about my unappeased hunger. It must be a form of broadcasting nerves, I think.

"Why did you ask about Janet?" my neighbour is saying, his eyes fixed on the place opposite, too. "Did you particularly want to see her about something?"

"No, nothing special, Antony, it's just. . . ."

Of course, I always wanted to see Janet, ever since she had first taken me generously under her wing, for my own broadcasting baptism, in the early part of the war. At that time I was suddenly offered the freedom of the air to give half a dozen afternoon talks under the shy-making title of 'A Cup of Tea with Godfrey Winn' about the messages I had received from the troops I had visited on various battle-fronts. The series was intended to raise the morale of the women-folk left at home, and it was an admirable idea, but, alas, I had not yet discovered the difference between the images of the written and the spoken word. My scripts were soggy, my broadcasting technique non-existent. I talked down the microphone as though I was addressing a public meeting, and I talked myself off the air. For ever, perhaps, if it had not been for the stubborn faith of the woman who was my sponsor. Through her influence I was given another chance, broadcasting this time not on the home front but to America and Canada, in the small hours of the morning. Often these talks had to be recorded, ahead of time, and I was able to hear my voice and what I had to say played back to me. It was a shock from which I have scarcely recovered yet. Far worse than any blitz I had to face on leave. A form of self-revelation so devastating that in a way it was a merciful release to disappear into the anonymous ranks of the Navy myself and know that my broadcasting apprenticeship was suspended for the duration of hostilities.

And when the war was over and we all dribbled back into Civvy

Street, my friend and ally inside this frightening building decided to get married and go to live peacefully in Dublin, and I had to fend for myself as best I could in my passionate eagerness to learn some more about the art of broadcasting. But I never forgot my debt to my first teacher, and it was a joyful day for me when she returned, three years ago, to take over the running of the only programme entirely designed by the B.B.C. for women.

"I don't think Janet can be coming."

"No, it certainly looks as though she is giving lunch a miss today."

"Then . . . do you think . . . what about . . . I don't see why someone shouldn't. . . ."

We were all gazing towards that indifferent piece of pork pie that has assumed the magnificence of a feast in the Kremlin, and my mouth is watering. But, alas, it is too late. Jean Metcalfe is looking at her watch and shepherding her flock towards the door. Still it does not matter. A few minutes later, as I hurry down the corridor of the fourth floor, with all my old fears crowding in upon me again, I see a slight figure, in a grey coat and skirt, limping a little, as she comes towards me.

"Janet, I am so glad." If it hadn't been a B.B.C. corridor, I would have embraced her. But how white she looks, how absolutely exhausted. "I have been doing my weekend shopping and only just got back in time to hear the broadcast. But I wanted to catch you for a moment."

"Not another date?"

"No, nothing as exciting as that. Kevin wondered if you would care to spend a weekend with us at our cottage in Oxfordshire. It's always such a rush here, we can never have a proper talk, I scarcely feel human. And if we plan it for the end of May, we *should* be able to sit out in the garden."

There is just time to tell her that there is nothing that I would like better before she has become an impersonal referee behind a glass wall once again, and I am sitting in my shirt sleeves, opposite Jean, and minus my tie, waiting for her to give me my cue, and getting ready with my right hand to beat out a rhythm, like a conductor, as I always do when I am broadcasting. I don't know why, but it seems to help.

Half an hour later, I am going down in the lift with my producer. There is a courteous custom in the B.B.C. that you are always shown off the premises. Having been educated at Eton and Balliol, my companion on this occasion performs this ceremonial act with particular grace.

"Antony, do you really enjoy producing talks for 'Woman's Hour'?" I ask on a sudden impulse.

"Enormously. When I was fourteen at Eton, I used to read women's magazines. And when I first got into the B.B.C. I was on the News side, and I didn't like that at all. I leapt at the chance of a transfer. That was when the programme had only been running a very short time, at the beginning of '47. And I have been there ever since, though I produce quite a lot of other talks, too. Of course, it is particularly pleasant working with Janet. She inspires loyalty from everyone."

"Why is that do you think?"

"It is because she has got all the best qualities of a man."

"But you enjoy so much working with women on a woman's programme."

"Yes I do." His voice has lost its usual smooth gentleness. It is emphatic, vibrant. "You see, I have always been fascinated by the vanities of women."

Then he has gone, and I am thinking how he would never have made that comment in one of those remote, monastic cells. But most of all I am conscious that there is a sky above my head once more, and trees burgeoning into green close by in Regent's Park, and that I am a living, breathing creature in a free world.

The horizons still seemed free enough the weekend that I drove down to Oxfordshire. Past High Wycombe I left the familiar road that I knew so well, which would have brought me soon to Oxford, and turned off to the right, climbing higher and higher on to a ridge that was crowned with superb beeches, in their freshest verdure. At last I came to the cross roads that my hostess had warned me to wait for and the steep descent, leading me down to the village of Chinnor which long ago Prince Rupert had ravished, scotching out a nest of Roundheads.

Just before I reached the first houses I came upon a policeman, pushing his bicycle up the hill towards me. I put on my brakes and leant out of the window, holding my letter of instructions in my hand. "Can you tell me where a house called Crossways is?" I was just

about to add 'where Miss Janet Quigley lives' and then I remembered
that here she was her other self, her married self.

"Ah, you want Mrs. FitzGerald's house." Unconsciously his
country voice reproved me, in the impression that it gave that the
boundaries of the world were the boundaries of this village in the
valley. "Now keep straight on till you come to the Bird in Hand
and then take the lane opposite. Mr. and Mrs. FitzGerald live in the
first house on the left. The thatched house."

I found it easily and I discovered, too, that it had its back to
the lane, as if to point that here, above all things, weekend peace
was sought. So I wandered round the side, thinking, it's only right
that the front door should be at the back, in an Irishman's house.
And there was my host, tidying up the last of the tulips, against a
delightful background of deep purple lilacs, a lawn leading to a wide
herbaceous border, and the trees of an orchard beyond.

Kevin straightened himself to welcome his guest, looking so
exactly like the portrait of a countryman, in a book, even down to the
leather patches on the elbows of his gardening jacket, that for a
moment it was difficult to realize that he did, in actual fact, hold
an important position in Industry, and that we had always previously
met wearing dark clothes at a London cocktail party.

"Janet's inside trying to get warm. We've put all the central
heating on again, in your honour. You'll be wanting a drink. What
about your car? I can get half of it into the garage. Will it mind its
posterior being exposed to your English summer?"

"Well, it does rain sometimes, even in Ireland, I have been told."

"Dear boy, you have been misinformed."

My spirits, despite the dampness in the air, rose as I followed my
host's huge, ambling frame indoors. In a few seconds he had succeeded
in making me feel as completely at home, as unreasonably I always
felt out of place when I had to meet his wife on her official territory.
Janet was crouching over the fire, her bad leg stretched out stiffly
towards the blaze. This had been a burden for her to bear ever since
her childhood, for she had been born with one leg slightly shorter than
the other. However, by the time that I had come into her orbit myself,
she was so completely equipped as an adult human being that one was
quite unconscious of what must be, for her, especially at the end of a
tiring day, a considerable physical strain. The overwhelming impression
I had now—and not for the first time—was that no climate in the world

would be too hot to thaw out her eternally cold bones. Some people, I knew, mistook that chronic condition of external coldness for a lack of internal warmth, but then they had not worked with her, as I had worked. It is always the acid test.

Today she was dressed again in grey, but not in the casual, loafing clothes that one associates with the country. She might have come straight from the office. The sitting-room was charming, and not in the least austere, with dusty-pink covers for the high, wing-back chair standing beside the wide windows and two sophisticated canvases by the rising young Irish painters, Daniel O'Neill and Colin Middleton. In consequence I had no impression that this was the interior of an Oxfordshire cottage: instead, had I been blindfolded and placed with my back to the window I would have sworn that I was in a flat in Eaton Square. Was it that the urban roots of the editor of 'Woman's Hour' were so strong?

"All the same, you must find it a tremendous relief to have your weekends down here," I suggested, noticing that though her dungeon pallor remained, it had now assumed, in a kinder light, a more becoming, matt tint and that her eyes, set flatly in her face and their most characteristic feature, seemed rested and tranquil. But then her whole personality suggested reserves of tranquillity: one could not imagine her raising her voice, even in an intellectual argument.

"We do love our weekends, even in this weather—what has happened to our summers, or is it simply that we are all getting older and notice the cold so much more?—all the same we do wish, don't we, Kevin, that we could persuade Mrs. Munday to come on Sunday mornings."

"I seem to have heard that conversation before, in the homes of others of my friends who commute and have a local lady who obliges for them."

"As far as this?"

"What do you mean, as far as this?" I echoed.

"Well, we have to get up at six o'clock every morning, to catch a train soon after eight from Princes Risborough. That means, in the winter, from Monday to Friday, we never see the house in daylight. Thank goodness, Mrs. Munday does have supper ready for us, and a fire lit in here. And, of course, I can get through a pile of work in the train. I make a point of reading every letter that the programme receives: they are sorted out in batches for me under different headings, and I assure you they make the train journeys go very quickly. To me, the correspondence is the life-blood of the programme, and so many of the listeners write such extraordinarily good letters, though I have discovered that over a period they are inclined to cancel each other out. I mean, if we have a succession complaining that we have too much, for instance, about children, considering how many of our listeners aren't married, then that is swiftly followed by a number of pleas for more practical talks about children's ailments, or child psychology. One thing they *all* agree about: they love hearing about other people's lives, and other countries, holidays, travel, adventures. Just as much as men do. Perhaps more. Because so many of our audience wear domestic chains." She broke off suddenly, and offered her guest another glass of sherry, as if in apology for talking shop. Actually, it was my own shop, too. Did I not take the same passionate interest in my own weekly spate of letters, too, and hadn't my secretary strict orders to place all critical letters on top? For I had learnt across the years that the reading and listening public are extraordinarily acute in their assessments. Nothing phoney or second-rate, nothing written or spoken, with one's tongue in one's cheek, could deceive them for long. And a most excellent thing, too.

"I drive the car to the station each morning, and leave it there," my host was saying. "Then we both catch the five fifty-nine home again from Marylebone. Whoever gets there first bags the seats. Of course, sometimes we stay up for a theatre or a party, and then I have a room at my club, the Athenaeum, and Janet stays with her assistant editor."

"What we'd really like is to have a little *pied-à-terre*, in town, and use it for two or three nights in the week," his wife broke in.

"Or import a maid from Ireland, to live in down here, who would make the weekends more comfortable for Janet."

I could see that the advantages and the disadvantages of the two compromises had been discussed to the point of exhaustion. Both were tantalizingly attractive, and both would have doubtless been possible were it not for the monstrously unfair law that lumped the earnings of husband and wife together for income tax assessment.

"What happens if one of you misses the evening train?" I asked.

"It's quite simple. The other waits on the platform, and we take the next train down."

"Does it occur often?"

"Only twice, hasn't it, Kevin?"

"Yes, once it was my fault, once yours."

"That was tactful of you both. Do you try to divide up everything equally?"

"Do we, Kevin? Not consciously, I think. Kevin always cooks our Sunday joint. Fortunately he likes cooking, and is a good cook, into the bargain. I cope with supper tonight, and the washing up afterwards. And we all come down to breakfast, guests included, just as we are, on Sunday mornings, and dress and bath, in lazy relays, afterwards."

"But we have to be down punctually for breakfast, at nine," Kevin added, "to get served before we all listen to Janet's programme, at nine-ten. We have a portable set in the dining-room. 'Home for the Day'. You know, the Sunday supplement to 'Woman's Hour'.

"Of course he knows, Kevin. Godfrey is in it tomorrow."

"Are you? What splendid timing. I shall enjoy listening to that." And he seemed to speak with such genuine enthusiasm, my heart was warmed. What exquisite manners the Southern Irish have, I thought, and the impression stayed with me throughout the weekend, especially at breakfast the next morning, when my host emerged from behind his *Observer* as soon as my name was announced, and appeared to be listening with rapt attention. At the end, he said: "Does it worry you to listen to yourself, in a recording?"

"I don't dread it as much as I used to," I admitted. "But it still never sounds good enough. Quite right. I always feel at the end disappointed and am left wondering if everyone else notices the bad spots, too."

"I think the whole programme sounded a little thin this morning. Not in material, but in volume. I must check up about that tomorrow. Recordings can differ quite a bit, in tone." My hostess was an editor again, a clear-brained professional woman, dressed, as in a dream, in a blue house-coat to the floor, and clearing away the breakfast dishes, at the very moment when she should be entering her office. The contrast should have seemed incongruous: it was incongruous and yet so strongly did she control any scene, in which she played a part by the kind of magnetism that has nothing to do with age or looks, or clothes, that helping her to wash up while her husband took first turn in the bathroom, I was able to go through the motions automatically while my whole mind concentrated on the discussion that we were having about joint careers.

"When I married Kevin I imagined that I was giving up my job for ever. I said goodbye to all my colleagues in the Talks Department at the B.B.C. quite happily."

"Quite happily?"

"Yes, indeed. I am not one of those career women, who have so tied themselves up into working knots, that they cannot enjoy leisure when it unexpectedly comes their way. I was delighted with the prospect of settling down in Dublin, one of my favourite cities in the world, I rejoiced in the opportunities I now had to catch up with my reading, to go to art exhibitions, most of all, I must confess, to be able to ring a bell with any confidence that anyone would answer. (I don't mean a secretary, I mean a smiling maid.) I enjoyed enormously acting as hostess for Kevin, who had taken up a five years' appointment as the General Manager. (Oh, the bliss of having all day to prepare for that evening's party.) What I hadn't calculated for was Kevin being so Irish."

"Surely you knew that when you married him. After all, Kevin FitzGerald is a very Irish name."

"It certainly is, but I had forgotten that many Irishmen prefer being Irish in England. At the end of the five years, though he had been a success at his job, Kevin asked to be recalled to London, and that meant, temporarily, since there wasn't a comparative executive post vacant, taking a lower salary. So I went back to work. Or rather when the B.B.C. asked me if I would return to the fold in charge of 'Woman's Hour', I accepted with alacrity. It was a programme that I had always wanted to get my teeth into, though when Kevin did get back to his old level of salary, I did offer to resign."

"And what did Kevin say to that?"

"He insisted on my staying. He said that I was a much more pleasant person to live with, when we were working, in double harness. Didn't you, Kevin?" Looking more than ever like the prototype of every weekend gardener in an even older tweed jacket, bursting at the seams, her husband had appeared in the doorway to announce that the bathroom was waiting impatiently for its next occupant. So I left the drying and went away to wash myself, thinking that my host was quite a character actor, and not in the least cast true to type. A member of a very old Tipperary family, yet preferred to work in a London office, and, instead of using up his spare time and energy, in endless Irish anecdotes, wrote thrillers, in secret, that were an immense success, and though as masculine as John Bull himself, was happily content to pretend to friends and visitors that his wife possessed the only career in the family.

"I don't believe you *were* really convinced," my hostess began again, when a couple of hours later, we resumed the conversation, out of doors.

"Well, I was, in your case, because Kevin arrived at the crucial moment to give supporting evidence. But you must admit, Janet, that most husbands don't hold that view about their wives having a career of their own. They tolerate it sometimes as an economic necessity and they do their best to hide their jealousy and sense of chagrin. But, all the same, it leads more often to the divorce court than a silver wedding celebration."

"I wonder if you are right. In our own case, let me tell you something rather significant that may apply to many other couples, too. Now that I am back at the B.B.C., Kevin likes me to tell him all my troubles at the end of the day. He says it takes his mind off his own! I think it flatters and pleases him when I consult him, and use him as a safety valve. And because of my own working problems, I am more sympathetic when he is tired and in a bad mood. I can put myself in his place. I know *why*."

I had to admit that she certainly made out a very good case. But then weren't they two rather special people? Enormously civilized, tolerant, no longer green in judgment. "I have often wondered," I said curiously, "that you did not marry a long time ago."

"There was someone else a long time ago. But he was too impossibly possessive. And possessiveness in any form is something I cannot endure. Are you sure you are not too cold?"

I shook my head but what I wasn't sure about was whether my companion had merely wanted to change the subject. She was sitting in a chair in the summer-house in the orchard, a rug tucked round her feet shrouded against the vagaries of May. We had brought the bright summer cushions out in a wistful wave of optimism when the sun had momentarily appeared. This should have been a scene of enchantment with a summer blue sky above the young green of the apple trees, and dappled shadows on the grass. We had the world to ourselves at that moment but we could not command the weather.

"I believe you are thinking of the drawing-room fire," I exclaimed. "Not really, though it would be nice to move in a moment, before it actually starts to rain. What I was thinking was how strange it was that I should live in the country now, when all my adult life has really been conditioned by my overwhelming love of London."

"But you weren't born in London were you?"

"No, in Belfast, of a Southern Irish father, from the west coast, and a Scottish mother."

"Those who don't like Belfast swear that the Ulsterman possesses all the faults of the Southern Irish plus those of the Scots and none of their virtues."

"What a brutal suggestion. I wonder if it applies in my case?" she added, not asking for reassurance, but assessing the conflicting evidence coolly in her own mind.

"I think in your case the Scottish blood came out on top. Except for your English accent I would have thought you were pure Scot. With all the virtues thrown in."

"Thank you. As a matter of fact, when I was quite a little girl, we moved back to my mother's part of Scotland. But later, I wanted to go very much to Dublin, and study medicine."

"How very strange, because I can see you very clearly, in a white coat moving round the wards."

"Don't you mean limping? My parents thought that, with my leg, I wouldn't have the physical strength to make the grade. So they sent me to Oxford instead, where I took English Literature, and when I came down from L.M.H. . . . but are you sure all this is not boring you?" When I simply went on looking at her she understood and took up the thread again. "I heard that I could be apprenticed to something called Women's Publishers Ltd., and as I longed to get into publishing, I persuaded my father to make one more investment in his daughter and put up the money. I lived in digs in Bloomsbury. In the basement. The rooms, the bathroom, everything was quite awful, but it was absolute bliss for me. And when a year later, Women's Publishers Ltd. went into voluntary liquidation, I was determined to stay on in London, somehow or other. I remember my last chore with them was to sit all by myself in a kiosk at Wembley Exhibition, handing out brochures to anyone who stopped out of curiosity. And all the time, I could hear someone calling outside, 'Any more for the water, any more for the water.' It is strange what one does remember years later."

"And what happened after that?"

"Well, I persuaded a store to start a bookshop, and they sent me first for six months to an established firm in the Strand to get experience in actual selling, in studying the customers' reactions, which is what I am still trying to do, in a different way today. Then later when there was a crisis in the book department and I resigned, I got taken on by the Empire Marketing Board. But I hated that."

"Why? Too many civil servants?"

"No, too little work to do."

"You really mean that?"

"Yes, I really do love work. I have never worried about what I was paid, so long as I could get along. When I left the Empire Marketing Board to go to the B.B.C. in '30, it meant quite a drop in salary, at first. But I didn't mind in the slightest. I was so busy, there were so many possibilities in this new medium for bringing the world closer together, and breaking down barriers."

"And you still feel like that?"

"Yes, I do, though some people take the view: why have a whole broadcasting hour set aside exclusively for women? Why treat women as something different from the rest of the listeners? But they *are* different after all: those who are our responsibility are tied to their homes in the middle of the day, sometimes all day. They need all the windows that we can open for them."

"It's rather remarkable, in a way, to hear you talking like that considering that for all except five years of your grown up life, you have gone out to work yourself."

"Well, I suppose when you have reached the fifty mark, as I have, life should have taught you how to stand in the other person's place."

I could appreciate with some feeling the situation with which she was faced: to satisfy her intellectual conscience, on one front, the public at large on the other. In a minor degree, it was the same for myself when my turn came round to *compère* the perennially popular programme 'Housewives' Choice'. A few weeks back I had been spending an evening in an East End youth club, when a typical Teddy Boy, aged about sixteen, with drain-pipe trousers and hair as long and carefully waved as the girl with whom he was having a Be Bop session, broke off his gyrations, for a moment, to tell me that he hadn't thought much of my last selection of records. Couldn't I hot-up my next session?

"And what did you reply to that?"

"I said: 'are *you* a housewife?' "

"No, I am the housewife today." Kevin, looking quite unruffled by his kitchen activities had come silently through the gap in the hedge, behind me. "Janet, you are shivering. Come inside at once and have a glass of sherry. Lunch won't be ready for another quarter of an hour, I am afraid. I made a slight miscalculation at the start. When I was preparing the joint for the oven, I was quite certain it was beef, and then I happened to glance at our butcher's bill, which clearly stated Mutton."

"So that means that we shall have neither horseradish sauce, nor red currant sauce."

"I am afraid it will, my dear."

A glance passed between them of amused tenderness, of absolute understanding. He helped her up from her chair, and fussed round her, like a deck steward. "Never mind, Godfrey will be spared our efforts at supper. He has to go back, after tea, because he has an early broadcast." Her self-deprecatory manner was part of her armour, it sprung unconsciously from the days when she was convinced that no one at college dances would want her as a partner, because of her halting leg. But they had, of course, just as I had seen her at a party in London surrounded, like the picture in the advertisements, by an amused, masculine quartet. Equally, the creature comforts of the weekend had been overflowingly generous. Their life together, I decided, as we walked back together towards the house, was the sublimation of the understatement.

Underneath the windows of the sitting-room, some lilies of the valley were flowering among the roses. Kevin paused and looked down at them with a mingled look of love and doubt. "They shouldn't really have established themselves there, but they are Janet's favourite flower. Still, I think I can manage a small bunch for our guest," he added, with his Irish charm.

My hostess had moved on instinctively towards the fire. Joining her, I was struck suddenly how little she had changed in the twelve years I had known her, how little she would change again, in the years to come. Because she had never been able to run and jump about like other children, because she had never been really young, now she would never be really old. It was the one law of life, the law of compensation, that never failed.

"I think you had better sign the visitors' book now," my hostess said in her eternally unruffled voice. "Most of our guests are inclined to forget in the slight upheaval of our Monday morning start."

It is my Monday morning start. Hurriedly at eight o'clock I scurry into the entrance hall in Portland Place. In my hand, I carry a small bunch of lilies of the valley. I mustn't make a bad impression by being late on my first day of office. As it is, my producer is already standing beside the desk. I hand her the flowers, with the clumsy silent gesture of a kindergarten child and his teacher. The flowers are more powerful, I hope, than words. Certainly the mask in front of her face changes. "Oh, lilies of the valley," she exclaims, immediately her other-self. "They always remind me of my childhood. We had a huge bed of them in our garden at home. Have you brought them up from the country?" The ice barrier has cracked, the marble coldness of the hall has vanished. Even the lift, as though only half awake, stays open long enough for us both to pass through without fear of injury. Broadcasting at this hour has its compensations, too, I think.

At the fourth floor, like a sleep-walker, I follow my producer down the familiar corridor towards studio 4A. The engineers are already in possession of the control room, sorting out the gramophone records, testing all their mysterious apparatus. How ill they look, how tired. The cruel fluorescent light beats down upon us all. Only the lilies are alive. At this moment, I think, is Janet standing on the platform at Princes Risborough with a similar bunch in her hand, which, to please Kevin, she is taking up to place upon her office desk?

It seems so strange to have this large studio all to ourselves. But this is not 'Woman's Hour'. This is the hour of clearing away the breakfast things and making the beds, getting the children off to school, and standing strap-hanging in the Tube that will deposit its hordes in the City. Then what am I doing here in my shirt sleeves in front of a microphone, announcing that I am about to knock on someone's door in Doncaster? My producer comes through from the other room. "You have been taking the names and addresses rather fast. I know it's only the run-through, but remember how much it means to the house-wives who have asked for the records, whose day of glory this will be." And I am remembering, too, once again what my hostess at the week-end, the wisest woman in broadcasting whom I have personally met, has created as her own coat of arms: "To make the listeners laugh, and cry, and think."

My producer has returned to her side of the glass wall. She gives me an encouraging smile. Through the amplifier at the side of my desk I can hear the announcer coming to the end of the News. He has reached the weather reports. How confident and Olympian his voice sounds. I shall never achieve that proficiency in a hundred years, I tell myself, as I wait for him to say: 'And now it is ten past nine and time for. . . .' I take a gulp of water, I moisten my lips, I seek to stop the wild beating of my heart. It may be only one more session of a stereotyped gramophone record programme, but for me it is a challenge and a trust.

TWELVE

THE POWER BEHIND THE LOOMS

THAT Sunday afternoon the winter cold struck deep as I walked down the platform at King's Cross towards the train which was to take me, an unwilling prisoner, into the frozen hinterland of the north. It would be late, of course. All trains on Sundays were late. That was as much part of the English time-table as families taking their holidays in August even though the weather had been proved again and again to be so much better in July. Still, the worst August day would be welcome now, and how different even the station looked on a Sunday, as though some dread epidemic had decimated the traffic in passengers and atrophied the limbs of the porters, who were only able to conjure up a spark of interest when asked to put their fares near the tea car. "No restaurant car on a Sunday," they cried with melancholy relish.

I began to feel positive that I was sickening for something myself and thought longingly of my own fireside at home, which because of the cryptic entry 'Dewsbury, Mathew C' scribbled weeks ago in my diary, I now had had to relinquish for yet another expedition into the unknown, armed only with a Parker fountain pen. A mood of rebellion momentarily warmed my mind so that waiting for the last door to slam (and the heating system to start circulating in harmony with the motion of the wheels) I chided myself that my enthusiasm, unflagging for so long, for learning at first hand about other people's lives, wasn't really a virtue at all: it was fast becoming overweening, quixotic folly. What did I know about blankets, and their manufacture? What did I truthfully care about blankets and their makers, except as coverings and creators of warmth? It is true that even a discarded army blanket would have been welcome round my shoulders just then, nevertheless I was in no frame of mind to be quizzed by my travelling companion, as to how when and why blankets were so named. Of course, I had no expert knowledge—to be honest, I had never given the matter a single thought—and he was delighted, as we all are with facts and figures that have become part of our conscious life, to be able to lessen my ignorance before we settled down in conventional silence to the Sunday papers.

"Once upon a time," Mathew began pontifically, "in the city of Bristol there lived a weaver named Thomas Blanket, who was credited with having produced, through his own initiative, a fabric with a very definite nap on it, that was not surprisingly used as a bed covering. Mr. Blanket was considered such a benefactor to the community at large that he was encouraged by the local magistrates to set up his own loom, in 1339."

I could not help smiling at the triumphant way in which my companion produced that concrete date; moreover, he had not finished with me yet. There were a plethora of dates to follow. How in 1367 Edward II prohibited the export of wool from the kingdom, and special permission by charter was granted to Mr. Blanket for the manufacture of his newly created household boon.

However, rather surprisingly, the blanket industry did not really get moving until a whole century later, when it was embarked upon both in Witney, and in Yorkshire.

"I have been to Witney," I said.

"It is only the Yorkshire product that we are concerned with," Mathew continued firmly, "and you will see tomorrow that its outstanding characteristic is its fleeciness. The weft is thick and the warp fine, while the fibre in the weft is. . . ." My companion had not stood as a Parliamentary candidate in the Liberal cause for nothing. Noticing that I was flagging, as always, at the first reference to technicalities, he recognized that it was the moment to switch the attack. Now he sought to rouse my imagination by a description of all the various kinds of blankets that I would find tomorrow in the largest factory for their manufacture in the world.

"We will show you the striped red and black blankets that go to Basutoland, and the Spitfire blankets, covered with emblems of the R.A.F. that the West African natives delight to drape about their shoulders, happy warriors at their feasts, and the warmest blankets that you have ever touched which are made exclusively for the trappers of the Hudson Bay Company, in the really frozen reaches of the north. And then there are the Chinese wedding blankets. . . ."

Skilfully he had kept his trump card until the last, and when he saw how instinctively I leant forward in my seat, he felt he could pause a moment, and make a few other points on the way. "You will

M

be surprised to see how differently blankets are packaged these days. At least the 'Dormy' ones are. All done up in Cellophane, like something from a flower shop. Pink, blue and green, and I am told that just now, green is the most fashionable shade, especially when brides are buying their trousseau. Oh, yes, they have special bridal blankets, and babies' blankets. . . ."

"I am sure they have, but tell me about the Chinese wedding blanket," I interrupted.

"Yorkshire has been enjoying a steady blanket trade with China for over two hundred years, and even today with so many commercial and political complications, Chinese parents will do everything in their power to smuggle a pair of these blankets from Hong Kong to the mainland, when a nuptial feast is about to be celebrated in the family. You see, they incorporate in their colour and design the Confucian symbol for Love and Protection."

"And are they very beautiful?" I asked.

"You must decide that for yourself." For having sensed that the ice was broken, the student's interest strongly aroused, Mathew retreated with some satisfaction behind his copy of *The Observer*.

His strategy was admirable. For thus it was left to me to try and describe their beauty, their very special beauty; on the one side of the blanket, a blazing heliotrope to signify the male element of love, and on the other side, a gentler shade of chrome, to represent most suitably the female element.

"And what is that?" I was to ask in due course, when the moment came for me to examine the ten-bar black stripe knotched at the end of each blanket. That, it was explained to me the next day by my guide, Mrs. Calder, represented the Ten Heavenly Stems: for stretching back into antiquity the Chinese have always believed that the Heavens were divided into Ten Celestial Houses. Thus these ten 'houses'—or 'stems' of the Heavenly Tree—became the domestic symbol for protection at night, so that even the humblest citizens, drawing up their blankets round their throats, would feel that they could fall asleep without fear, and would be utterly safe during the hours when they believed their souls were absent.

Had I once thought of blankets as utilitarian objects, dull necessities, nothing more? Even when we were decanted on to Wakefield Station, inevitably half an hour late, and a blast that seemed to come straight from the Russian steppes beat against us, I did not shiver.

No longer had I cold feet about the adventure, and I was delighted with the welcoming remark of one of our hosts who had come to meet us in his car.

"Well done, Mathew, you've brought a splendid cold wind with you. Just what we want. It really feels at last as though there's snow in the air tonight. I do hope it's the same in the south."

It was winter sports talk. No, it was the hymn of the blanket world. Praise God for cold weather. Never on earth could it be cold enough for the Sales Director—what an autumn it has been, more like summer, he complained, why people haven't been wearing overcoats, let alone wanting to buy blankets—as we drove the few miles to Dewsbury, while I secretly prayed that there would be blankets to spare in the guest house, where my body was to rest, a hundred yards away from the gates of the main factory.

Disembarking at the gate I was startled to see a brilliant coronet of light, shining through the darkness, like the control tower of an aerodrome. In huge glittering letters the word 'DORMY' proclaimed its message to the world. A great deal more effectively, too, I decided, than the garish panorama of Piccadilly Circus. How far away already I felt from the night life of the capital, especially when my host exclaimed. "If you feel like turning out tonight at ten o'clock, we can lay on something that is quite unique. You can watch our night watchman take down an ancient blunderbuss from the wall, and pointing it to the sky, press the trigger. That's to show all is well. You know, watchman, what of the night, sort of stuff. Actually, it's a custom dating back to the days of the Luddite rioters. I wonder what they'd say if they could see the mass of machinery we've got today. Come on inside, you'll need a drink."

I need have had no qualms for my welcome. The sort of fire you only seem to get in the north, in the sitting-room, roast venison for supper, an electrically heated blanket on my bed. How many other unsung housekeepers can I honour at the same time, who like Mrs. Shepherd, are up, winter and summer alike, at six in the morning, and refuse ever to think of retiring?

It was nearly midnight before we went to bed ourselves. Such good talk, from my two hosts, Mr. P. J. Walker, the Chairman, and Mr. Billy Wormald, who up till that moment had been simply names to me on a letter heading. I should have had far fewer last minute doubts on King's Cross Station had I been conscious that I was about to make two new friends, who, delightful companions in themselves, clearly had a great deal more to them than their charm of manner, and that. was their crusading belief in the strength and national importance of all long-established family businesses. The kind where any man can go and speak to the boss forthwith, without first putting in for half a dozen interviews with Trade Union intermediaries.

One snatch of conversation remains most vividly from that first meeting. It was after supper. P. J.—as I was soon to hear him affectionately called by everyone inside the mills—was standing by the fireside. He reminded me of a brigadier, in mufti, talking of the men who had fought with him on many campaigns and whom he loved more than anyone else on earth. Though he could curse them sometimes, and they him.

The male operatives, I gathered, were much more stubborn than the female of their species. The latter worked, with patience and resignation, lip-reading each other's chatter above the unceasing uproar of the looms, asking few questions of their bosses. A man rose to be a foreman and then he was a little god in his own shed.

"There was one shed," P. J. was saying, "where things kept on going wrong. It didn't seem to be anyone's fault, but I had one theory, and the foreman in question had another. One day I sent for him, and said, 'Look here, I've got to go and look at some new machinery in Switzerland and Italy. The very latest thing in looms. Might do for us. I thought of taking the car and having a bit of a holiday in between. Like to come with me?'

"He accepted at once. I was pleased about that, I don't think it was just the thought of touring Europe in my Bentley. It was when we got to Rome that things came right for always. We were looking at some machinery together, I was letting him ask the questions, through the interpreter, and suddenly their head man turned to me, with an amused smile. 'There is no need for me to explain the merits of this loom to your colleague,' he said. 'He quite clearly knows more about the job than I do myself.'

"I felt so proud of him at that moment, and when I explained what the Itie had said, well, I think it did something to him, too. It made all the arguments and the worrying ourselves blue about keeping up to scratch really worth while. In short, we were in it together. Everything has been as smooth as silk in his shed since. Of course, I always knew he was a good man, but. . . ."

There was no need to explain. Here was the kind of comradeship that you attain in war, between all ranks, but so often fail to preserve in the uneasy peace. I had another vivid reminder of it early the next morning. Perhaps to break me in gently they introduced me to the prettiest young lady in the place. Inside an office where, maybe, they thought I'd feel more at ease than in one of the sheds. She looked at me with a special kind of sales-talk smile and I could understand why in the year of the Festival of Britain they had crowned her their Queen. That was the year when P. J. had decided it would be a rewarding idea to take the whole works with their wives and children up to London to show southern folk how northerners can enjoy themselves when there is something worth enjoying, and they had done the Festival by day and the Battersea Fun Fair by night and returned home in the dawn, without a single body being left by the wayside, and a very good time was had by all, including Miss Dormy, 1951.

Shirely Young was a twenty-year-old wages clerk then: today she is the star member of a travelling team that goes up and down Britain, meeting customers in the big stores, and embroidering their personal initials on their blankets, while they wait.

"I expect you enjoy all the new places?" I suggested.

"Yes, that's exciting, of course . . . but what I like most of all is talking about Dewsbury and our wonderful mills. I tell people there is no other place like it in the whole of the country."

I did not know what to answer. There were no shining aluminium fittings: no modern rest rooms for the workers, done up in pastel shades. They couldn't even have 'Music While you Work' played over the loudspeakers because the implacable din of the machinery would have drowned it. The sales-talk smile was still upon her lips, as though she was gazing into an invisible camera, and yet I sensed that she was speaking from her heart. Here was her space: other kingdoms were clay. It was a strangely moving evocation. Such passionate loyalty was worth all the beauty crowns, I thought.

Again, how attractive it was, against that dour, unchanging background of buildings whose bricks were darkened by the smoke of countless chimneys, countless years, to come across a young girl, Dorine Thompson, with brilliant Titian hair, carrying a basketful of fresh spindles across the yard, or to be made conscious of the etched character and engrained wisdom that shone, like a beauty pack for older women, upon the face of Mrs. Musgrave in the Spinning Department: indeed, upon the countenances, too, of all the veteran workers in the vast spinning shed, many of whom have spent thirty years or more, at their looms.

So it is not surprising that they should have a possessive affection for their looms, as though, in fact, those unwieldy intricate contraptions were as much a piece of private property as a kitchen dresser. Precious and even beautiful to look upon. Indeed, I was very struck by the spontaneous and revealing remark made by one of this group of spinners, when, because it was impossible for us to talk together above the clamour of the machinery, their foreman had gathered them together in his office. There it was explained, much to their surprise, that a picture was to be take of them.

What? For the PRESS. Here was high drama, indeed. A clucking of excitement broke forth, enveloping the males, so much in a minority, in its backwash, until suddenly, like a clarion call, above the murmuring host, the judgment of Mrs. Nelly Richardson imposed a momentary silence upon the company.

"If any picture's going to be taken, I reckon, I ought to be in front of *my* loom," she exclaimed.

Whereupon, I was reminded of an occasion, years ago, when I had visited the new *Mauretania*, in the Liverpool docks, being made ready for its relaunching. "And how soon will that be?" I asked a riveter, working over the side. "*My* ship will be afloat in a fortnight," he answered instantly and with some emphasis, as though the whole board of directors, architects and crew had been rolled into the shape of one man in a pair of dirty blue dungarees, an inconspicuous dot against the ship's stern.

Until I visited the Dewsbury mills, I had always imagined that men took a far more personal pride in their trade, and the tools of their trade, than women to whom the wage packet at the end of the week, and what it represented in household necessities, was the main, if not the sole motivating point. However, that theory had now been exploded for me for ever by a tall, thin woman in glasses, who looked as though she had worked every ounce of flesh off her bones, and will, doubtless, be astonished to find her picture in a book, standing next to its author.

Duff Cooper in his autobiography *Old Men Forget*, so tragically timed as to become his own obituary notice, confesses that when at the commencement of his Parliamentary career he became the Member for Oldham, he was wont to feel most uneasy each time he was conducted round yet another Works because he knew less than nothing about machines and suspected that every question he asked only laid more bare his utter ignorance.

Along this path I am content to follow in the footsteps of a man who at his death left behind a far greater and more varied concourse of genuine mourners than most politicians are able to collect in the course of their journey through life. I have no desire to dabble in politics myself and when I visit a factory, in whatever constituency it may lie, there is no suggestion of vote-catching in my mind. The first sight of the machines often induces in me the same sense of memory-stricken nausea as the impact of the sea upon queasy travellers. Yet, however much I have to steel myself to leave the safe and silent shore, the voyage always proves rewarding in the end because of the people who work the machines, the power behind the looms.

For instance, there was that giant in the dark blue jersey, standing in the Pulling Department. How could one have guessed that the previous Saturday afternoon, he had played the part of hooker in a Rugby League match against Wales? Now it was Monday morning again and Harry Bradshaw was back at work, but as his hands mechanically went about their usual tasks, all his thoughts were concentrated on the possibilities of being awarded his cap for England and chosen for the team that was booked to tour Australia in a few months' time.

In contrast, there was the short, thickset man, whose accent was so different from the rest, and whose dreams all lay behind him. Borleslawi Opawski came to Dewsbury in 1946. Today he prays that he may be allowed to stay there for the duration of his working life. It is peace for him of a sort. "No, I have not married. I live in a boarding house in the town. They look after me very nice," he told me.

"It's a pity. . . ." I began, and then as though he sensed what I was about to say, he broke in quickly. "I have argued much. I do not think it would be fair to her. My life has been so troubled. I do not know about the future."

Later I discovered that he had learnt the weaving trade originally in the Polish textile town of Lodz, expecting to spend the rest of his days there, inconspicuously, with his family. Then came the war, overnight, the invasion from the west and from the east, and he had lost a year in prisoner of war camps, first in Poland, then in the Ukraine. When permission was given for the Polish Army to be reformed inside Russia, he joined a tank regiment and fought under General Ander's command in Irak, Palestine, Egypt and Italy, with the bitter, tragic onslaught on Monte Cassino as his most vivid memory of any campaign.

Nineteen forty-five found him in England, demobilized with the rank of Warrant Officer. On the one hand, he was a brave ally: on the other, he was an alien in a foreign country, exiled from his own people, now lost to him behind an iron curtain. What must have been his thoughts on that Monday morning in 1946, when he clocked in for the first time at the mills at Dewsbury? What were his inner feelings this Monday morning as he stood in front of me, a polite and patient animal, trying to answer my questions in his stumbling English, not understanding very well all the reasons for my presence?

Was I, perhaps, some official come to catch him out and hound him, now that at last he had found asylum and acceptance among his fellow weavers? I saw the suspicion cloud his very blue eyes. Until I reminded him—and my companions—of what Sikorski had said in that long ago of 1940, to Winston Churchill. "I hand over to you Poland's fairest flower—her army." How magnificently they had fought everywhere and now here was one of their survivors absorbed with resignation into the anonymous ranks of another kind of army. To meet him was a reminder of so many things. How fortunate it was to be permitted by Providence to live out one's life in the country of one's birth, and how important it was to try and understand the feelings —the sudden moods of blind, unendurable despair—of those who, through force of circumstances, are compelled to be exiles for the remainder of their span on earth.

"We have quite a number of them, all mixed nationalities, who settled in with us, soon after the war ended, and when we were short of labour. They are all excellent workers, and I think we have done our best to make them feel at home."

It wasn't the chairman speaking, to be taken down in short-hand, at the Annual General Meeting; it was any human being who loved his fellow men and believed that he had a duty towards them and that to be given authority over them was to inherit a sacred trust.

The Scots have a splendid saying—Jock's as good as his master— meaning that all men are equal who are labourers worthy of their

MRS. MUSGRAVE

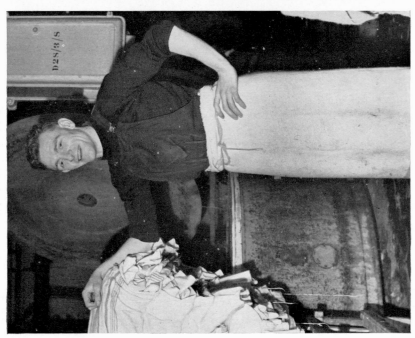

MR. HARRY BRADSHAW

MISS DORINE THOMPSCN

MR. GEORGE MORRIS

MISS SHIRLEY YOUNG

"Such passionate loyalty was worth all the beauty crowns"

"The Dormy blankets
are packed in Cello-
phane, but Mrs. Key
refuses to retire in
cotton-wool"

hire. Indeed, I was very conscious of that when in the Warping Department, I met, standing against the barricade of spindles, another quiet, unobtrusive, middle-aged employee, in blue overalls, whom I should probably have passed by had not someone, as we approached, whispered in my ear—"Ask him about his family."

And what an uplifting story Mr. George Morris had to tell me; how he and his wife living all their married years together in the same little house in Dewsbury, had brought up a family of five children, of whom four today are teachers, and the fifth possesses the added distinction of having carried off, in open competition, one of the most coveted plums in the academic world, entrance into the Foreign Service.

Mr. Morris was ticking them off one by one on his hand.

"Vera, she's thirty-nine, teaches at Belvedere Secondary School, near Bexley in Kent; George, who is thirty-seven, went to Leeds University and now has a good job in Exeter. Jack, who's thirty-five, and Clifford, who's thirty-one, both teach in their home town, while Willie, after getting eight distinctions in his Matric, won a scholarship for St. John's at Oxford. . . .

"And, then, in his last year there, competing with the best brains of his age in the country, he gained one of the very few, very coveted vacancies in the Foreign Service."

Finishing the list of citations for him, I could sense the pride, which being by nature a taciturn man he tried to disguise, swelling in him, overflowing and warming the whole shed with its inanimate web of spindles behind his head. What a record: what a family: and how proud their mother must be. In a way, she was the real heroine of this chapter I decided later, and alas, I hadn't a picture, either of Mrs. Morris or of Mrs. Parkinson of Castle Street, Skipton, whom I had to thank indirectly for my expedition into the heart of the blanket world. For, after reading a previous book of mine,[1] Mrs. Parkinson had reproached me because she could find no mention there of the West Riding.

Now Dewsbury, with its houses of yellowish Yorkshire stone, wind-slashed, smoke-grained, where even the Town Hall is built on a steep slope, and every other building seems to be a chapel of some sort, is utterly typical of the West Riding, and after spending two crowded, rewarding days visiting the Wormald and Walker Mills

[1] *This Fair Country.*

which *are* Dewsbury I can truthfully put on record that her people
are very fair people: fair in their dealings with each other, from
t'boss downwards, fair in their greetings to strangers—though rightly
they give one a canny glance or two of cautious appraisal—and
fair enough to look at, though one could not help noticing how
many of the older operatives, among the women, wore glasses, like
a badge of office.

More than ever today, with the cost of living at a nightmarish
level, human beings brood and worry about what is to happen to
them when they are too old to work long hours. Their State pension
seems woefully inadequate to support them, however modest their
needs, while all classes of the community find it increasingly difficult
to save any appreciable capital sum. Therefore I was very impressed
to learn that the Chairman of the Dewsbury Mills has made a special
study of this problem, which in the past has been such a scar upon the
face of industry, and has recently inaugurated a scheme that is not
only very enlightened in itself but may well serve as a signpost for
other commercial undertakings.

In a group of pleasantly furnished huts, beside the recreation
grounds, which once housed the exile Poles, he has organized a unit of
pensioners, starting with three men and three women, all congenial
companions, who have taught each other how to make delightful
soft toys and such useful and decorative articles as childrens' dressing
gowns out of blanket remnants from across the road. The scheme
had got off to a flying start and now gradually they hope to elect to
this most original club more and more operatives of pensionable age.

I could appreciate the toys, unlike the machines, but still it was
the human element that meant most to me. Like Mrs. Key, who
widowed in the First World War in the first year of her marriage,
now after forty-two years service in the mills, has found a new
outlet, four days a week, for her as yet unquenched energy and
imagination. With this time-table she doesn't become too tired, yet
it is sufficient to keep boredom and a sense of emptiness at bay.
The extra pocket money helps her to feel more independent: but most
of all it is the consciousness of being still useful, even in retirement,
that made it easy for Mrs. Key to smile at the camera.

She left her sewing machine for a little while and poured me
out a cup of tea. "I have often heard your voice over the wireless
but I never expected to meet you." She looked at me with a frank

and open smile, and I found myself wondering if she was disappointed in the reality, since secretly I always expected that reaction. "Of course," she continued, "your life must be very thrilling, but don't you also find it very tiring, always being on the move, always meeting strangers?"

Her question startled me by its perceptiveness. For a moment, I did not answer. Then I replied, truthfully, that though I sometimes dreaded the starting out on each new expedition, I nearly always enjoyed the end.

"Because it *is* the end?" she persisted, "and you can go back to your own home?"

"No, because I feel I have made new friends, and learnt some more about how other people work and live." I hope my answer did not sound like the platitudinous response of a politician.

"You couldn't expect to learn anything from someone like me," she persisted and I could sense that her comment was without irony.

Couldn't I? To have been widowed at such an early age, yet never to have lost faith, across the childless years, or allowed that cruel mischance to turn her into a monument of self-pity. Still to be grateful for the eternal bounty of living. She had such a happy face. Why had she never married again? That I could not ask her. But one thing was certain. No one could present such a façade to the world if their heart had long since been consumed by worms of envy for other women's husbands.

"Years ago. . . ." Mrs. Key began again, with a warm upward rush of feeling and then broke off, shyly.

"Yes?" I echoed encouragingly.

"Years ago . . . I went for a holiday to Peacehaven, where Gracie Fields used to live. She is a great favourite of mine and I bought a plot of land near Fryer's Avenue. You see, I hoped to retire there one day, and build a bungalow. Things didn't turn out quite as I hoped . . . but I don't like the idea of giving up the land . . . even now."

Such are the dreams we all dream, such are the secret thoughts that sing above the strong, harsh music of the looms, the impersonal beat of the machines, everywhere.

On the journey back, the heating had failed in the express from the north. We sat, huddled in our coats in the dining-car, a woe-begone lot. The stranger opposite me tried, at least, to break the conversational ice. "I do think it's a disgrace, don't you?" she complained. "I can't think why the railways aren't denationalized like steel. No one works these days. My husband says. . . ."

"But it's wonderful blanket weather," I broke in soothingly. She looked at me as though I were mad and huddled closer into the collar of her mink coat.

THIRTEEN

'SEPTEMBER SONG'

MANY times in the course of my writing assignments I have had to be a spectator at a *cause célèbre*. It always gives me a trickly sensation down the spine. For I have never been able to grow accustomed to the muffled and sterilized atmosphere as others have whose work makes them frequent visitors to the Old Bailey or the Law Courts in the Strand. Guiltily I try to check an instinctive feeling of sympathy surging up in me for the defendant in the dock, however wicked their crime, however guilty they are clearly about to be proved. I suppose it is because everything seems so smug, so implacable, so shut away from life. And the court itself is conducive to claustrophobia, for it is usually little larger than a classroom in a school, where the headmaster, seated on his isolated throne chooses for some odd reason to wear a grey wig, while the witness on show in the box, being interrogated in front of the whole class, tries not to stumble too stupidly or to be caught out over his answers.

It is no fun being a witness, even in the Chancery Division, where one hasn't to face the scrutiny of a jury, and the general atmosphere is considerably less tense than in a criminal court. All the same, however altruistic one's reason for being there, it is not a pleasant experience, as I know now, since not long ago it happened to me for the first and, I should like to think, the last time in my life.

I was asked by the Corporation of Eastbourne if I would give evidence in regard to a test case they were fighting as to when a concert is no longer a concert in the eyes of the tax collector, whose arm, it would seem, is even longer than that of the Law. There was an all-star cast on this occasion, for the defendants, resenting bitterly the suggestion that their sedate Winter Gardens at the Devonshire Park ever put on an entertainment that could be labelled 'Music Hall', had assembled such theatrical names as Mr. 'Stinker' Murdoch and the Mayor of Muddlescombe (Mr. Robb Wilton) to dazzle the court with their performance in the witness box so that laughter was universal and prolonged.

Then suddenly it was my turn and I am no comedian. Instead, with dry mouth and shaking knees I soon was made to feel like a criminal as I faced the cross-examination of Lord Hailsham, who that afternoon, seemed to belong to the school of advocacy which believe in thunder in court. Yet the poor witness's only crime was that he had been present at one of the five controversial concerts, an ordinary member of the audience.

"And what were you doing there?" I was suspiciously asked.

"I had been invited by Miss Gracie Fields. I was planning a portrait of her in my next book. I wanted to see her, performing as she does today, in concerts."

"And what makes you think it was a concert?"

"Because. . . ." Hypnotized like a rabbit, I tried to break the spell, and turned towards the Judge. "My Lord, when I was a schoolboy in Eastbourne thirty years ago, we were sometimes allowed to go to concerts at the Devonshire Park, when some famous musician like Pachmann was performing. To return now was for me an extraordinarily nostalgic experience. The piano on the stage, the potted ferns, the old-fashioned drape curtains, the mixture of starry-eyed schoolchildren and the smudged, middle-aged faces of retired folk, everything was exactly the same as I remembered it. Pachmann used to talk to us between items and explain what he was going to play next, and sometimes made us laugh with his funny, exaggerated gestures, and foreign English . . . while Gracie told us Lancashire stories between her songs, and made us laugh, too.

"But the atmosphere, My Lord, hadn't changed in its essentials in thirty years. It was completely and absolutely that of the Concert Hall. How does that compare with the Music Hall? Well, the atmosphere of the latter is so much brassier: noisy and gregarious and beating at you with its unflagging gaiety: and the performers are so much broader in their effects: they attack and attack again because they know that they have so little time in which to capture the attention of their audience: and they dress up in funny clothes, or undress as the case may be. Everything is out-size, and there is no place for subtlety. . . .

"But Gracie just wore an ordinary evening dress, My Lord, and she used no props except a scarf that she picked up off the piano and tied round her head, like Ruth Draper does when she is playing the part of an emigrant. In this case Gracie was about to sing the lament of a Neapolitan fisher-girl and she sang it with the same artistry as she brought to a special setting of the Lord's Prayer when the silence and the belief of the audience were complete. Only a very great artist could do that, and not make it seem like a cheap and embarrassing trick, to gain the sympathy and milk the applause of the audience. But then Gracie Fields is a very great artist whose stature has matured across the years and who has wisely changed her style to suit her years. So that now she no longer turns cartwheels on the stage and has allowed her hair to grow grey, though it still stands up off her forehead in the same triumphant waves and without noticing it, until one comes to paint her portrait, one discovers that she has become an autumn beauty. . . ."

Did I say all that, did I produce such a monologue in the witness box? Of course not. One only remembers afterwards all the things one meant to say. Walking away down Fleet Street, after the Court had risen for the day, once more any black-coated traveller at the rush hour, I remembered something else, too. The words of another song she had sung that night. 'The September Song.'[1]

"And the days grow short when you reach September,
And the autumn weather turns the leaves to flame,
And I haven't time for the waiting game . . ."

Not exactly a masterpiece and yet the packed seats had been utterly still. She had succeeded in turning an ordinary ballad into a work of art, making the words sound as though they had been written by Keats. There had been something very special in the communion between the artist and her audience at that moment.

Later that evening, driving across the Downs, to Peacehaven, that bungalow town near Brighton, where Gracie had invited me to be the guest of her family for the night, she had said.

"You see, I always think of the words that I am saying and what they *really* mean. When I used to do films with Monty[2] directing me, I was always messing things up, getting my back to the camera having the scenes pinched from me, because all my mind was on what the words really meant. Monty used to get mad with me some-times. But I can't do things by tricks. I have to feel it or nowt happens."

[1]September Song: Kurt Weill and Maxwell Anderson. Chappell & Co., Ltd.
[2]Monty: Miss Fields' second husband: Monty Banks.

I watched her at our midnight supper party, surrounded by her family who had all been at the concert, sitting in front of the huge log fire in the sitting-room that was as large as a stage set, but a great deal more comfortable, or indefatigably playing duets at the grand piano with her mother, and the relaxed, all-embracing happiness of the scene was a revelation to me. So utterly different from the last time we had sat together, just after her second husband's death. At that time Gracie had seemed almost an old woman, panting as she climbed the stairs to the flat in Harley Street where she was hiding from the reporters.

Now she was a woman in her prime once more, her skin glowing, her voice full of resilience, clearly in complete command of herself, her audiences and her future. And when she confessed, as you do confess to an old friend, "Why, lad, I believe I am in love, really and truly in love for the first time in my life," despite the slight Lancashire intonation which still creeps into her voice when she is strongly moved, and the so utterly English seaside setting that was our backcloth at that moment, I found myself instinctively thinking of Capri, as it is in the high noon of summer, when the houses on the hill-side are dazzling white in the sun, and the sea is the colour of crushed butterflies' wings, and there is much music in the piazza every evening.

Moreover, in that same instant I became urgently curious to meet this stranger who could possess the power to make her feel as though she was still in the high noon of summer herself. To fall in love, in the fifties, really in love, is something of an achievement on both sides.

Nevertheless it had happened. Not in a book, not in a film built round the pictorial attractions of this island that has attracted those in search of escape and asylum for countless centuries now, but in real life. Yes, but how had it happened? I slept that night in a guest room, where the ash-tray beside the bed was a piece of Italian pottery, and driving back to London, my mind full of the fascinating contradictions in the career of this Lancashire woman whose heart was now lost to and in Capri, I came to a sudden decision. I had soon to go to Rome on business and afterwards I would spend a week-end in Capri, to have the chance of meeting her third husband. Only in that way could I be certain whether there must be a place made for him on the canvas of my portrait.   *   *   *   *   *

However, in my enthusiasm, I had forgotten something. It was now no longer September but November and November is hardly the right time of the year to visit the Blue Grotto. I appreciated that nautical truth the moment that the absurd little paddle-steamer, more suitable for a musical comedy, pulled out into the Bay of Naples. Soon it was very rough going, indeed, and the last batch of American tourists were succumbing all round me.

Take me back to Sorrento, one woman in a mink coat, was moaning an hour later but she did not make it sound as inviting as Gracie had done, when she sang that number from her repertoire in her Eastbourne concert. Full of mutual sympathy and sorrow, hanging on to the deck-rail, I peered through a mist of rain at the silhouette of the island ahead of us, so near and yet so far, which at that moment resembled nothing so much as the half-submerged head of a very wicked-looking crocodile. Then I began to wonder whether perhaps after all I hadn't made a mistake to come.

It was still raining when I took the bus the next morning from the Piazza, down the narrow curving road to the Marina Piccola, and my doubts were much with me, but the driver smiled when I asked to be put off at the gate of Gracie's villa. *Canzone del Mare. Song of the Sea.* Perhaps he was only smiling at my accent, though I had the feeling that he was really smiling at his own memories of this English-woman who walks about the island with a scarf tied, mill-fashion, round her head, and sings to the passers-by when she feels in the mood the Neapolitan love songs she has made her own.

"You friend of Gracie?" he asked me. And now I was sure why he was smiling, now I could tell that the whole island looked upon her as their friend, and in a way, too, their mascot, for had she not opened a bathing pool, and a restaurant down here by the water's edge that might make the ghosts of Tiberius and the characters of Norman Douglas's *South Wind* shiver and shake their heads, but nevertheless brought a considerable influx of English tourists during the summer.

Hadn't Gracie given me many stories of these visitors, I reminded myself, as I opened the high garden gate with the one warning word written on it in huge letters. PRIVATE. And in English, pointedly in English. Not that that made any difference. Not that that kept her admirers at bay. All very flattering and necessary, of course, and Gracie was entirely philosophical about belonging most of all

o

to her public: nevertheless, there must be times . . . and now I was smiling to myself, as I recalled the story of the two ladies from Oldham, who seated on a rock the previous summer, dangling their feet, had lost one of their shoes to the tide. Whereupon, Gracie had taken her compatriot up to her villa, and had fitted her out with a pair of her own shoes.

On her return home this lady was so proud and delighted that she had given an interview to her local paper, speaking with imaginative enthusiasm about her benefactress's large selection of footgear, "and now next summer I shall have charabancs full of applicants, bless me," Gracie had finished up her tale.

Actually this possibility clearly worried her far less than the memory of the party from Yorkshire in the restaurant that had ended not in pools of Chianti but in floods of tears. One of the guests cried loudly that she had been 'cheated' if not 'insulted' because Gracie was not there in person to sit down at the table and make her 'fans' welcome to her new island home.

So in the end word was sent up to the villa, on the terrace above, and at once Gracie left her own private guests to come down and comfort the visitors. "They seem to think I go with the place, thrown in with the cruet," she said.

But that sort of example of possessive encroachment in regard to her property in Capri was nothing beside the real problem. The paying out and the paying out and the paying out. Up till last year, everything had been run at a loss. There was so much constructional work to be done, so many leakages, so many estimates that somehow doubled themselves before the work was finished. And finished so slowly.

Now with the advent of Boris into her life, for the first time there was money going into the bank just off the Piazza, instead of Gracie having to liquidate more and more of her savings in America to settle the bills that were beginning to make her dreams of ending her days peacefully in Capri, impossibly, nightmarishly expensive.

"I call him Honest Boris," she said to me that evening at Peacehaven, "and you will see why when you meet him."

Indeed, I did see why the moment that he opened the door of the villa because he at once gave the impression of being a shaggy sheep dog standing there beside the Alsatian, Spender, who in some ways is rather more articulate. Except that with Boris you feel that every word counts, nothing is said for effect.

At our first meeting he was wearing a comfortable pair of dark blue corduroys, a black jersey, and a blue and white shirt open at the throat. A powerful frame, with the shoulders of a boxer, and he possesses striking, deep-blue eyes under a thatch of dark hair, duplicated on his chest. You would know at once that he is a Slav.

When he shook hands his grip was like that of a boxer, too, though there was nothing in the least clumsy about his gait as I followed him down the freshly polished hall with the attractive green tiles, past the dismantled radio set, standing there in the corner, I decided, where one would expect to find a bag of golf clubs in an equivalent English home.

It was as though the wireless set was deliberately there as a reminder of the fact that it had been a faulty set of radio valves which had in the first place created the spark to touch off their romance. I had much to ask him about that: meanwhile, we had reached the lounge that leads through an archway from the wide-windowed dining-room with its superb view of the sea and the legendary Faraglioni Rocks, and there on the equivalent of a bridge table were stacked, not packs of cards, but all the mysterious bits and pieces of an inventor's tool box.

"Not permitted when Gracie is here," my host volunteered with an engaging, schoolboy's grin.

It certainly introduced a new note into a room full of luxurious chairs and sofas—all very 'posh' its owner would have described it once upon a time—where the one really homely touch was a protective cover for a magazine lying on top of the piano. This had been worked over in wool, with the words, *Gracie's Radio Times*, as the highlight of the pattern.

"I heard Gracie on the radio last night, from England, but she did not sing our song," Boris was saying.

"And what song is that?" I asked.

" 'The September Song'. You know it?" he replied in his very quiet, rather gentle voice.

Yes, I knew it. To me it had sounded like a prophecy and a promise, when I had heard his wife sing it. However, I did not know my host well enough yet to tell him that, I reminded myself, as I watched him pour me out a glass of Cinzano. He apologized because there was so little drink in the house from which to choose an *aperitif*, and that he could not offer me lunch because he only had a sandwich when he was alone in the villa.

In contrast, I found myself recalling some of the other husbands of famous theatrical stars whom I had met in the course of my work, and how lavish and idly spendthrift they were prepared to be with their wives' possessions, liquor, money. The wife went off to work at the studio, or in the theatre, the husband stayed at home and played the rôle of the rich inheritor.

Not this one. Here was the exception. The star's husband who remained at home and worked. At his inventions, the dreams of his youth to become a great inventor, still unquenched. At all the improvements, below the terrace, of the swimming pool and the restaurant, all the tidying and checking over for next season. When his bride had left for England, to fulfil the contract for her concert tour, they had sensibly decided that it would be a complete waste for him to follow her round from one provincial hotel to another. They would be reunited for Christmas. Meanwhile, he had her tour list, and wrote to her every day.

"Yesterday I wrote to her at Dundy," he explained.

"Dundy?" I queried and then the next moment, the mystery was solved. He meant 'Dundee', where last time Gracie had had such a success she had had to give a repeat performance for the overflow. All her triumphs past and present that were as yet an unknown, alien world to him. Moreover she meant to keep it that way as far as possible, always, she had assured me with passionate emphasis.

"Boris fell in love with me for myself. I wasn't famous in his eyes. I was just another resident on the island."

With what pride she had stated that, and now there was a question that I must ask him. "Boris, what *did* make you marry Gracie?" I asked.

He thought for a moment, and then he said, simply. "It was her charm." He made it sound as though one was hearing the word for the first time. "You see, she is so natural, so, how do you say, relaxed. She is not one person when she is alone, and another person when there are other people present. She is always so. She makes you feel relaxed, too. When other persons come here, I watch them on the sofa where you sit. In a moment or two, they are at ease. No longer strangers. Close, good friends. She made me feel like that, too. So much at peace."

Then suddenly I was very conscious of all the years when he had been without roots, a man without a country, without a family.

"Don't you feel lonely without her now?" I asked.

"So very very lonely and at first I was afraid."

"Afraid she would not come back? Oh surely not?"

"No, not that. But you see I had grown used to being alone. For twenty years I had lived in my own small apartment, quite content. Then in a moment it was all changed. There was Gracie. Gracie to talk to. Gracie to laugh with. Gracie to ask questions, to make plans for the future. So now she has gone, it is very quiet. But I have good fortune. There is much work to be done."

He took me out on to the terrace overlooking the sea. The rain had stopped and there was no need for the mackintosh that Gracie had given him on his last birthday. The panorama had the forlorn, out of season air that all such places have, though it was not difficult to imagine the scene in the summer, with a band playing in the evenings, and the colonnade of luxury shops doing a brisk trade with the tourists, and in the courtyard beside the swimming pool, the orchid tree in flower, so very rare an addition to the spectacle, because there are only eight such trees in Europe. At least so my companion assured me, and somehow everything that he said had a convincing ring.

Here, too, were the *cabinas*, the changing rooms copied from the luxury of the Lido, one of which King Farouk had hired in exile, each day for seven thousand liras. And why not? He was a customer like all the other customers. "And the kids were sweet kids," Gracie had said to me.

Always, I noticed, her voice changes when she speaks of children. For it is the one deep regret of her life that she could never have any of her own. So as we went from *cabina* to *cabina*, furnished in a manner that was so far removed from Blackpool, it was not surprising that I had a sudden vision of a small girl aged twelve, hand in hand with a child from the same theatrical troupe, walking through the streets of another Lancashire town, in search of her birthplace.

Gracie herself had given me this revealing glimpse into her childhood. How, when they were away on tour, she had boasted to the

O*

rest of the troupe of performing Tots, of having been born over a fish and chips shop. "But I didn't say it was what we call a one up and one down house, and when we got to the end of Molesworth Street in Rochdale and I saw it ahead of me, I suddenly panicked and walked past it with my nose in the air. 'Was that where you were born, Grace?' my little chum asked me. 'Oh no . . .' I replied, 'it was a *much* bigger fish and chips shop than *that*.' After which we went on walking round the town for an hour, till I found something suitably grand."

She relates the story now because there is not an ounce of snobbery in her disposition. Never has been, never will be. Yet how far she has progressed along the highway, until this meeting at the final cross-roads with the man who himself was born in Bessarabia and came to Capri for a chance weekend over twenty years ago: but has stayed on ever since, captured by the timeless sense of security the island provides for the wanderers and the homeless.

"Was it here that it happened?" I asked as we returned to the terrace outside the house.

"What happened?" Boris echoed.

"When Gracie proposed to you?" When he did not reply, I added. "It's all right. Gracie confessed that to me herself."

Then he spoke, pointing with his arm, away to the left, to the hill-side, guarded with sentinel cypresses, jutting over the Faraglioni Rocks. "No, it was there, in the gardens of my own home. I will take you there tomorrow."

Capri is celebrated for its flowering vistas yet the garden to which Boris took me is one that none of the casual visitors ever chance upon, although it is only a few minutes walk from the over-public Piazza. Hidden behind a wall, and masked by cypresses, it is part of the large estate of the Cerio family whose menfolk, for nearly a century now, have been regarded as the uncrowned kings of the island.

The garden itself is something of a surprise, too. You have no impression of its size at a first appraisal. It is only when you start to explore and find at each new twist and turn of the path some fresh impact of loveliness, a fountain playing against a background of brilliant bougainvillaea, a group of stone jars filled with marguerites, the freezias on the terraces that slip away down the hill-side, that you become increasingly conscious of the atmosphere, at once welcoming and at the same time, so still, so withdrawn from life.

"Here it is like an island within an island," my companion exclaimed softly, showing me the small white house he had inhabited for twenty years, in the heart of the garden, with its workshop remote and secluded, too. "Yes, that is how Gracie described it, too. When we walked here, outside my workshop, it was as though we were truly the only two persons in *our* island. That is until the photographers and the reporters came and banged on the door."

"Did you never think of marriage before with someone else?" I could not help asking, curiously, for it was very clear that he must have been very handsome, indeed, when he first came to the island. But he shook his head at the suggestion and the sudden look on his face, sad and troubled, served as a mirror for his words, most of all, for his memories.

"I was too much afraid, you see. Not for myself, but for the other one. The world was so angry. Even here on the island, we heard the rumbles, like Vesuvius. Always there was war somewhere. First in Abyssinia, then in Spain, then in Europe. . . ."

Afraid that the holocaust would catch up with him, the stateless exile from Bessarabia. When one speaks to Gracie's third husband of his exact nationality, he shrugs his shoulders and reminds one of the status of Trieste. There is a considerable parallel. For the corner of Roumania where he was born was shortly afterwards trespassed upon by the Russians, so that, by the time he was a youth, Abraham Boris Alberovitch was glad enough to escape from his birthplace and journey to Rome, there to become a student, first in architecture, then in engineering. That, he discovered was his real bent.

And when he discovered Capri a year or two later, it seemed like Paradise set in an eternal summer sea. The asylum from persecution that subconsciously he had been seeking. Nevertheless, in the end, the strife of nations did catch up with him, though not as he had expected, as he had feared in his youth. *Persona ingrata* with the Fascists because he did not possess the passport of an Italian national, he seized the first chance he had to throw in his lot with the British, and fought at their side, from the landing in Salerno to the end of the campaign. For his services as an engineer, he was given the rank of sergeant, and looking back now, he sees those three years as the happiest of his life until his marriage. He had a niche.

He belonged. He was accepted as one of the team. "And I learnt my English. Is it good?" he says with an unexpected grin.

For even today he is not much given to laughing out aloud, except when he tells the story of the first time he saw Gracie on the stage of an E.N.S.A. concert, at Naples, when the fighting in Italy was over at last and the Opera House was packed from roof to ceiling on a Sunday night.

Fate plays ironic tricks. Gracie had just returned from a long tour of the Far East, and this was to be her first appearance in front of her countrymen on the mainland of Europe. A gala occasion for everyone . . . until a storm blew up that completely isolated Capri from Naples. That wretched little paddle steamer, whose vagaries I have already described, could not possibly put forth. No aeroplane could land upon the island. What was to happen?

What had happened already was that the star of the show had caught a vile cold and when the afternoon wore on and still there was no sign of any rescue launch from the mainland, almost thankfully, she made up the fire in the lounge of the *Canzone del Mare* and swallowed a large dose of lemon and rum, as a suitable remedy for her ague.

So she was dozing in front of the fire when above the storm she seemed to hear her name being shouted from the direction of the beach. Putting on sea boots and a sou'wester she hurried forth with a lantern and there to her amazement below, close to the rocks, was a magical launch that somehow had penetrated the blanket of the storm. It was the British Navy to the rescue of their favourite star.

Later, lying on the deck, tossed from side to side she says she remembers nothing of the voyage until the moment that someone removed her sea boots and coat in the wings and pushed her on, just in time, to wind up the evening with 'Land of Hope and Glory'.

"I felt so weak after the nightmare of the trip, and so hazy from my anti-cold nightcap that I had to grab the microphone to hold myself up. How I sang I shall never know."

However, she did sing, encore after encore, for she is that sort of trouper and then the whole audience rose to their feet to acclaim her, and among that roaring, cheering throng, out there in the darkness, stood the man who, unknown to both of them, was destined to become one day her husband.

Gracie and Boris, on the terrace of their Capri home

"John and Amanda went forth to greet their new destiny"

It was here, in the garden, that Boris took up the threads of the story.

"All my friends in the sergeants' Mess, they say to me, 'Boris, you come from Capri, too. Of course you know Gracie.' I do not like to answer that I do not know Gracie, except seeing her, now and then, in the Piazza. So I think for a moment and then I say, 'Of course, *everyone* in Capri knows Gracie.' And it is true, because everyone does. . . ."

Nevertheless, he did not get to know her any better himself on his return from the wars. He became a recluse once more, spending every day in his workshop, seeing few people outside the immediate circle of the Cerio family who had by now adopted him as one of their own. Until one afternoon there was a tap on the window. Boris went to the door and opened it to find a young man standing there. It was Gracie Fields' nephew, Tony, and he explained quite frankly that he had jumped over the wall.

"There is something wrong with our wireless set down at the villa. We can't get England, and it's driving my aunt crazy. Do you think you could spare the time? Everyone on the island says what a clever radio engineer you are. . . ."

Two days after he had visited the *Villa Canzone del Mare* for the first time, to perform a neighbourly act, there was a knock on his window again. This time the nephew was accompanied by the aunt. "It was raining," Boris explained. "So, of course, I asked them to come in and shelter."

"They did not explain what they were doing in the Cerio garden?" I asked.

"No, but Gracie ask if I will come to tea the next afternoon, so I tell her that I am busy, so she say, what about the next day, and I say, busy, too. Always busy when I am working, and always working at something."

"Was she disappointed? Did she not think, perhaps, that you were giving her the brush-off?"

"The how?" Suddenly he understood my meaning and there was a twinkle in his dark blue eyes. "No, I do not think so, because you see, at the same time, I said she would be very welcome if she would like to come again, when it was not raining, and I would show her the garden, as I have shown it to you."

"And she came?"

"Yes, many times she came. Almost every day. And I would leave my work and we would sit here sometimes beside the pool, and sometimes we would walk right to the far end, to the Belvedere, at the edge of the cliff, where no one goes. And we would talk, or rather, she would talk and I would listen. And sometimes she would sing snatches of one of her songs, and I would ask. Which is that one? And she would tell me when first she had sung it. There were so many things she had to tell me about her life, and yet she is so modest, she never talks about herself as a great star. Indeed, I do not think of her as that. Either then or now. Instead, she was just someone who came into my life at the right moment, as I into hers. All the same I do not think either of us knew what was happening to us, until it happened. . . . "

I looked down over the cliff's edge to where, away to the right, one could catch a glimpse of the roofs of Gracie's own home. And Boris's now. In his shyness it must have been a wrench, a tremendous upheaval, to leave the privacy of this retreat, but there was no air of regret in his manner as we turned back towards the garden.

"Of course, I think sometimes of the years when I did not know her," he was saying, "but I cannot believe that she was ever such a fine person as she is now. I remember one day she say to me: 'I'll make my hair blonde again for you, Boris,' and I say: 'You are to do no such business. Anyone can be blonde out of a bottle. Few can afford to be as natural as you.' I love the grey in her hair. And I love, too, her shoulders. She has magnificent shoulders. . . .

"Mind you," he continued, as we started to retrace our steps up through the terraces of cypresses, "When she came to see me here, she never dress up. She wore anything that made her comfortable. We are very much alike there. But when she went to England to take part in a special concert. . . ."

"For the Lynmouth Disaster Fund, at the Coliseum?"

"Yes, that was it . . . I sat in a box with her family, and when Gracie came on to the stage, it was someone I had never seen before. This was another Gracie. The one that can never belong to me or to any other man, but always to her public. I had not understood how vast was that public or what a truly great star she was, before I came with her to England. She was so wonderful that night, I could not believe it afterwards when she told me she had never had a singing

lesson in her life. I wish she would have her voice trained, properly trained, but she says it is too late now."

"But not too late to fall in love," I reminded him. "Don't you wish that you could have met when you both first came to the island? To have lived so close to each other all these years. And only now...."

"We were not ready for each other," he said simply.

The spell of the garden, the timelessness of Capri itself was close upon us. It seemed a long way at that moment from Rochdale when a small child of twelve named Grace Stansfield would go to school in the morning, work in the mills in the afternoon, and sing in club concerts most evenings, little dreaming of the ultimate fame that was to be hers, or that her final home would be an island set in the Mediterranean sea.

They had announced their engagement on Christmas Day at the party which Gracie always gives now, to her neighbours on the island. All day long they drop in upon her at the villa, bearing and receiving gifts, exclaiming at the beauty of the burgeoning Christmas tree, drinking, on this occasion, not the traditional toast of ABSENT FRIENDS, but of the bride and bridegroom, soon to plight their troth. For although their hostess was not able to give them a definite wedding date, she was absolutely certain about something else. This time she would be married in a church. It was a choice springing from a conviction deep within her.

As a small girl in the back streets of Rochdale, Grace Stansfield was taught by her mother to believe in a benevolent Deity. She has never faltered in that belief ever since. Every night she kneels down to pray before turning out the light. Of course, she did not tell me that herself: instead her husband spoke with the kind of sincerity which makes such a confession, not a matter for embarrassment, but a sudden challenge. Gracie is good, he said, and the statement had a meaning far beyond that moment of conversation.

And Gracie is grateful, too, he might easily have added. So very grateful for all that life has given her.

I remember most vividly the afternoon when I sat with her soon after the death of her second husband, Monty Banks. She had been compelled to come to London to fulfil a broadcasting contract and she wore a very old black skirt and jumper, because in Capri, she never wore black, she explained, while, since her return to England she had almost lived in the recording studios.

After her work for the day was over, we had tea together alone in a quiet flat far removed from the noise of the traffic and the world outside. Nevertheless, my companion had been unable to relax but kept on fidgeting as she listened instinctively for the telephone to ring.

Only a few weeks before Monty Banks would have been at the other end of the wire, and his warm, exuberant, southern voice would have been right inside the room, asking how the recording had gone, or, if she had been singing in a concert, how the audience had been, and what dress she had worn and all the other things that a woman wants a man to ask her about herself.

"Supposing he was in California, and I was singing in a Miami night club. The moment I got back from the show, the bell would ring just the same, and they'd say 'You're wanted on long distance.' You see, Mario did all my business for me, I liked it that way. To be managed."

And then the woman who has always been prepared to look life full in the face added something that has stayed in my memory ever since, She said: "Now when I look back over the twelve years that we were married, I think of all the women who through no fault of their own have so little share in any man."

She had no inkling then of what lay ahead. Numbed still by the shock of his sudden death upon the platform of a wayside Italian station, how could she possibly imagine that, after all, and so soon, she was to be given yet a third chance to attain happiness.

Of course there are many definitions of that word and Gracie Fields would be the first to admit that in the case of the man whom she often called by his native name of Mario, there had been passionate quarrels and equally passionate reconciliations.

"Sometimes we'd be arguing in the wings, with the band striking up my opening music, arguing our heads off as to what songs I was to sing. I like being managed, lad, but not that much!"

There can be no fear of that happening this time. Boris will be master in her house, but that will be all. Theirs will not be a theatrical partnership, lived largely in public, but instead a marriage, based on mutual respect and a desire for that kind of tender companionship which means so much to any man or woman, when the miracle happens and love is reborn in the September of one's life.

And that was why, in her gratitude, Gracie wanted passionately that the moment of dedication, when they exchanged gold rings, should be blessed by a priest.

In contrast, the first time that she had been married as a girl, with her hair done in a fringe over her forehead, to Archie Pitt, the owner of the show, 'Mr. Tower of London', that was to make her a name and him a fortune, it had been a very hurried, unromantic ceremony in a registry office. There had been no time for her and her manager to have a honeymoon. The show must go on, and she played two performances that evening in a suburban music hall. That was in 1923.

The second time she was married she was no longer a provincial *soubrette* with a voice whose full potentialities she had hardly yet realized but a star, a great star on both sides of the Atlantic. The second time she was married was in a room in a Hollywood house, and afterwards there was a party, with plenty of drinks for the guests. That was in 1940.

This time it would be in a church. She made up her mind from the start. And it was in a church, with Boris's patron, the white-bearded Edwin Cerio as best man, and a last-minute audience of Capri friends, who had not been told the day or time in advance, because the newly engaged couple were so worried about the behaviour of the gaping sightseers. In consequence, everything had to be kept secret till the last second and Gracie wore the bright violet cloth coat that she wore all that winter, because in a typical fit of generosity she had given away all her fur coats, one after the other. So, although she had meant to be married in something new, in the end she simply tied a scarf round her head in the same way as she used to go to work as a very young girl, in the mills.

Still, the ceremony was this time in a church, in the seventeenth-century cathedral with its striking baroque dome that fills one side of Capri's Piazza, as picturesquely as something painted on a backcloth. But such a very different backcloth from the one against which Grace Stansfield spent her youth.

I do not know if Boris has been to Rochdale yet, but in some ways his visit would be a surprise. Not surprise at the warmth of the welcome Gracie always receives there, but surprise at the glimpses of beauty he will find. Rochdale is often described as a 'mucky' town. In actual fact, it has a fine park, and many clean, well-laid-out streets.

As for its people, I am sorry that Boris has come too late upon the scene to meet old Bob Brierly, who made all Gracie's clogs ever since she first came to his workshop, as a kiddie, singing for her supper, singing for her workmates, singing for anyone who would listen as she clattered down Molesworth Street.

I paid a pilgrimage to Molesworth Street, and to meet Bob Brierly myself, the same year as Gracie was married for the second time. And to talk to the cobbler as he bent over his bench was a very moving experience. For here was none of the glitter, the concealing tinsel of the footlights. Here was simply an old man talking of a woman whose fame meant less to him than her character and her heart.

"She moves in grand places these days, our Gracie," he said. "But she has never forgotten Rochdale and her old friends. Every time she is in a new show in London, she always writes to invite me to the first performance. I went once and her dressing-room was full of smart folk, but it was me she spotted straight away."

You cannot deceive folk like Bob Brierly, the clog-maker of Rochdale, now gone to his rest. And as I talked with him, I remembered how the first time Gracie had visited London, and went up in the lift at Selfridge's, she asked the attendant at the top, what was the fare, like the Tower at Blackpool. And how when she attended her first cocktail party at the Savoy, she asked for a port and lemon. "I thought it was the posh thing to do." But most of all I remembered something that she had told me at our own first meeting.

"You know I believe I was given this talent by God to do my best with it, and I have honestly tried, though at heart, I am really lazy. There has always been someone to prod me along. When I first started in show business, I was quite content to be one of a troupe of kids. And later I was quite content with my imitations as a budding *soubrette*, till another youngster in the show challenged me. 'You couldn't sing a song straight,' she said, 'You haven't enough personality. You *have* to imitate someone else.' And by gum, I was so mad at that, I went out to show 'em."

So she has been showing them ever since, though it would be false to suppose that her career took an upward sweep from the start. On one occasion, in a show called 'It's a Bargain' the audience at Aberystwith was so meagre that the whole takings for a three hour performance was eleven shillings. Of that Gracie's share was exactly fourpence. A bargain, indeed.

Gracie of course was still in her teens then. By the time she was twenty-six, she was leading lady at the Alhambra, earning a hundred pounds a week. But during the long years of her apprenticeship in between she toured up and down the country in 'Mr. Tower of London', playing small dates and hopeless dates, playing any dates, but always sustained by the belief of the man who was her professional boss.

Archie Pitt kept the flame alive and for that she will always be eternally grateful. As for Monty Banks, he was later to play a Svengali without sinister intent to her Trilby. For he groomed her from a leading lady of the theatre who, away from the footlights was inclined to be careless about her clothes and her appearance, and sometimes content to imitate the hoyden that convulsed every audience, into a confident and elegant woman of the world. Yet though her first husband gave her ambition and her name in lights, her second husband poise and maturity, she has always felt alone in her career.

"Other stage folk like the Oliviers and Beatrice Lillie," she confessed to me, "have their own little group of friends inside the theatre. But somehow I've stayed outside it all. I seem to have spent my life walking on to a stage, or into a recording studio, alone."

I had been watching her at one of those broadcasting sessions when her schedule would entail putting half a dozen programmes 'into the can' in a couple of days.

"How do you manage about your voice?" I asked.

"Oh, I take care of that. I have all the numbers put down half a tone these days. That's better than straining after notes I can't be sure of reaching any more."

That sentence contains your whole philosophy of living, I thought. It makes for inner peace, and now there will be someone to offer you another kind of peace, who has also known what it is to be alone, who has no predilection for the world of the theatre: someone who will urge you with all his might, to stop living in a suitcase, to stay secure upon the terrace of the *Canzone del Mare*, in the Capri sunshine.

The producer was calling, obediently she went back to the microphone like a young trouper. The red light flickered, and she began to sing, with the look one sometimes surprises in a church.

> "And the days grow short when you reach September,
> And the autumn weather turns the leaves to flame,
> And I haven't time for the waiting game. . . ."[1]

[1]September Song: Kurt Weill and Maxwell Anderson. Chappell & Co., Ltd.

FOURTEEN

THE SPRING BRIDE

It was a Saturday morning. I could afford to lie, luxuriating, a little later in bed: there was time to read the correspondence columns of the newspapers. A letter printed in *The Daily Mirror* read: "Malaya, Korea, Indo-China, A and H Bombs, and now the football season is at an end. The news is very depressing, but I suppose it will all come right one day." I found myself laughing out aloud, a rare occurrence for me in the early morning, and I felt the mood of the day had been set.

Nevertheless, the impulse that had lead to the putting of pen to paper, in this instance, was a very sound one, I had to agree. For had there not always been pestilences and wars and floods and still the human race survived, still fell in love, still plighted its troth, one to another, in marriage. Unmindful of experience, of what had happened to other generations, in the long line. We know better: we won't make the same mess of things as our parents have: we have the armour of our youth: and above all, we believe in the eternal bounty of life.

Wasn't that the constant cry which echoed down the corridors of Time? Instinctively I found my eyes turning away from the newspapers towards the group of photograph frames beside my bed. Propped up against them was an oval miniature of my mother on her wedding day, with lilies of the valley against her white dress. Very small and easy to pack away, the picture had for many years travelled everywhere with me, as a kind of surety of faith in living: it had even journeyed backwards and forwards to Russia in the war, through the bleak, hostile wastes of the Barents Sea.

How far away all that seemed now: my Geordie mate, whose dialect was Greek to me, tipping me out of my hammock, because I would be drowning in sleep, and never heard the bugles summoning me to keep the middle watch, my midnight tryst in the eyrie of the port director, out through the tarpaulin flaps on to the ice-covered decks, and then up, up in the devil's own darkness, with the wind and the bitter spray beating me awake: how far away all that seemed now, beside the contrast of dressing with care and formality in one's wedding garments. A sudden debilitating thought struck me. I wonder if I can still get into the No. 1s that I had designed for me with such optimism and such a streamlined finish to the tunic, at Barnard's in Chatham High Street. I had them stowed away somewhere as a souvenir of my bell-bottom days. It was best to wonder and not put the challenge to the test. Memory softened everything. I shall hear myself boasting one day that I really enjoyed the Russian run, like school, I decided, while I manœuvred a new grey tie brought to me as a present from Italy, where our late enemies are busily capturing the silk markets of the world.

Of course, I was not the bridegroom. As usual, my rôle was that of the spectator, but today a very ungrudging one, except that my mother would not be able to come with me to see Amanda wed in the village church of Lurgashall. For I knew that she had been looking forward to this first Saturday in May, ever since, the August before, I had driven her one afternoon to visit Amanda's mother in their country home, on the edge of the Downs, nestling under Blackdown Hill, and with an unparalleled view from their garden terrace of the whole of Sussex spread out in the misty blue of a MacWhirter watercolour.

I think we were both remembering that view and that afternoon, when, before I left London, I stopped to see her in the hospital where she had already been lying for many weeks. From her anonymous bed in the private room, so unlike the four-poster she had slept in all her married life, she looked up at me with her still unclouded, very blue eyes, but her face on the pillow, so unfamiliar compared with the eternally young image I had always carried, not only in her miniature, but in my mind: and I, in my wedding garments, so unfamiliar a figure to her. "Give my love to the bride and to Mary," she said brightly, making a great effort not to cough. "I am so glad they have a fine day. That always makes such a difference, somehow, though it is silly to judge it, as an omen. I am sure Amanda will look lovely. I do hope they have kept her wedding-dress very simple. She is so young and fresh. . . ."

And then I was certain that we were both reliving the same moment of that August afternoon, when we were sitting, after tea, in the new garden room, at Blackdown Cottage. Amanda's mother, Mary, and her maternal grandmother, who had just published an enchanting collection of her Letters,[1] written when she had been Amanda's age, and another Queen had sat upon the throne of England, my mother whose wedding day, when she married my father, had been in the first year of the century, and myself, the perennial bachelor. There we were, talking not about the hazards of the married state, but about books, in a mood of tranquillity and contemplation when suddenly from out of doors came Amanda, in a cotton dress, bareheaded, barelegged, with such radiance in her eyes that it was like a bright light, almost blinding. Whereupon, she stood in front of us, and without embarrassment or coyness, told of the wonderful thing that had transformed the world for her: how she had met a neighbour's son, home on leave from the Far East, and like Romeo and Juliet, on a still, summer's night, they had fallen in love at first sight: and how she must somehow contain her longings until the spring when he would return to claim his bride. Then take her back with him to a new destiny, far across the sea.

"How long will you stay in Java?" I asked.

"Only a few months, alas. I hear it's a heavenly spot. Then we shall be moved. John is not sure where to. Perhaps Malaya, perhaps Pakistan, perhaps Kashmir." Her tone made it abundantly clear that she was completely indifferent as to the locale—what civilization, what climate, what kind of colony she would find herself dumped down in, on an alien shore—henceforth she would have eyes only for John, who had brought this flower of happiness and placed it in her hand.

"Please come to my wedding, with Godfrey. It's going to be in our village church and we are going to have a marquee on the lawn afterwards." Now she was speaking directly to my mother, who she was meeting for the first time, and I had the odd fancy that she was trying to pour some of her youth and ardour into the other woman's veins. I watched and felt her warmth reach out and bring colour to my mother's cheeks. "A village wedding, and a marquee on the lawn. That *does* sound nice," she exclaimed.

Then we drove home. The lanes were dusty and the foliage of the hedgerows had a curiously heavy, blind look. There was a thundery sky and my mother seemed suddenly weary. "Another summer is almost over," she said sadly. Perhaps the seeds of her illness were already stirring in her body. . . .

[1] *A Blessed Girl*, by Lady Emily Lutyens.

I tried not to think about that when I drove now the other way, down past Guildford, where, when I climb the hill with the shell of the new cathedral on the left, I never fail to ponder on the same mental sum of arithmetic. If all the money which had been collected for that grandiose landmark, had been divided and redivided among the numerous parish priests of the diocese: to exchange the Victorian mausoleums, in which they are mostly imprisoned, for compact, labour-saving dwellings: to give them and their exhausted wives and children the annual holidays that all workers have today a right to expect: above all, to increase their miserably inadequate stipends until they possess at least some relation to the present cost of living scale and thus free the ministers of Christ from their everlasting struggles to keep up appearances, struggles which indeed were a blot upon the conscience of the community at large. Would not that abound infinitely more to the glory of God?

However, it was not a day for passionate outbursts against the monstrous injustices, the stupid follies of mankind. It was a day of peace and communion. The nagging east wind that had shrivelled the promise of April had miraculously died with the birth of a new month and this May day was wreathed in blossom everywhere. A few miles later I turned off to take the road to Petworth, and it was to find Chiddingfold living up to its claim to be the prettiest village in Surrey, while nearby a young avenue of double cherry trees seemed to be blooming specially for Amanda, to be at their very best, at this hour when she would be seated at her dressing-table, calm and serene, as she always was, no matter how much her nuptial attendants might fuss about her. Secure in a world of her own imagination, like the day that we had all set out for a walk in a group after Sunday lunch, but she had soon lagged behind, indifferent to the grown-ups' chatter, eager to be left alone with her cherished, loving thoughts: eager, too, to examine the fauna of the countryside, in minute detail, step by step. "You all walk too fast," she had complained, as though that was the real reason for her solitariness.

Now in a few moments, the wedding march from Lohengrin would be pealing out once more and she would be walking on her father's arm as slowly as she could manage with her dancing heart, and her veil shrouding her child-like innocence from the pews of family friends and relations who had invaded this tiny village church, from all corners of the county. Only the bride when she came at last, with a huge white bow tied at the back of her *broderie anglaise* dress, made it seem like the first wedding I had ever attended, almost as though there had never been another wedding since the world began. The intensity of her happiness reached us all, and I could understand now why Mary had shown no anxiety, no maternal qualms that her only child should become engaged when she was seventeen. All the same I felt a stab of pity myself, remembering that when another spring would burgeon, Amanda would be far away from all the blossom which decked the pulpit, far away, too, from the green lanes and the Downs where she had so rejoiced to ride her pony, her first love. Instead the oriental sun would blaze down, arid, implacable: would she wilt, her spirit quenched? Or would it still seem, for ever after, a wonderful adventure?

I turned my eyes from the pair of young lovers kneeling at the altar to where in the choir stalls a distinguished selection of Amanda's relations were grouped, including the matriarch, whose own father had once upon a time taken his place in the honourable succession of Viceroys. And now his great-grand-daughter might find herself, in the near future, in such a different India, and if that came to pass, I had no doubts that in her own way she would do her best to uphold the legendary prestige of the Raj. Tiffin time: as many English recipes as possible, served on the Spode china that I knew to be among her wedding presents: making a garden, however inhospitable the soil for European flowers: determined, no matter what failures, to grow roses like the beds of *Peace* and *Étoile de Holland* and *Madam Butterfly*, on the terrace beside the marquee. A scented memory of her childhood.

I prayed as they exchanged their vows at the altar. I prayed for the guest who had been prevented from coming by circumstances outside her control and who long ago had made such a lovely bride herself. Then as I watched John turn, with quiet deliberateness towards Amanda, while he made his holy promise to love and to hold her from this day forward, for better or for worse, in sickness or in health till death should them part, I prayed again that disillusionment might never touch and sear them, as it had so many of those gathered together in the church: even Amanda's own parents until like my mother, they had both found a new lease of happiness, in a second marriage, a second chance to love and cherish all over again.

The cynics might sneer and pointing to the ever-increasing divorce figures suggest that all church weddings were a mockery and a waste of time. But I do not believe that anyone who watched Amanda and John offer their mutual love so humbly and trustingly, to be one more hostage to mortal frailty, would at that moment have given any support to such a thesis. All of us were washed clean: all of us, to lesser or greater extent, had our faith in the solemn beauty of the marriage service renewed and rededicated, even as the bride and bridegroom moved down the chancel steps towards the signing of the register, and the choir, like a chorus of angels, took up their cue triumphantly to sing:

"Praise, my soul, the King of Heaven
To His Feet thy tribute bring
Ransomed, healed, restored, forgiven,
Evermore His praises sing:
Alleluia! Alleluia!
Praise the Everlasting King!"

The wedding procession was reforming. The tiny attendants, in their delicious Kate Greenaway costumes, the little girls wearing gloves as green as the spring outside, and carrying shallow wicker baskets filled with white stephanotis flowers, who had been as quiet as mice throughout the service, perched upon their stools, inside the chancellery, were being shepherded by the two grown-up bridesmaids, themselves as pink and white as the church decorations. Be good, just a few moments more, their eyes pleaded, and then the other March, the Mendelssohn, equally hackneyed, equally, triumphantly right, struck up, and Amanda and John, moving as one person, went forth down the nave, to greet their new destiny, with the aura of their spiritual surrender still upon them.

Quietly we all followed and something of the perfume and the grace still lingered when we found that, while we had been inside the church, white figures had come and taken possession of the village green and now were performing other sacred rites, the first cricket match of the season.

How meet and proper that it should be so, I thought, with a vision of all the other village greens so employed this shining afternoon, and all the other village weddings being solemnized up and down the country. It had all been so perfect, I was afraid of shattering the spell. My instinct was to slip away with the music and the impact of Amanda's radiance still fresh in my mind. All the same, I am glad now that I didn't.

For though the marquee, huge as it was, became very hot and very overcrowded, and though two complete strangers, as I imagined, came up to me in swift succession to inform me that though we had not met for over twenty years they had—wasn't it amazing?—recognized me—but you've put on weight, one said, and you've lost some hair, said the other—yet the overall effect was hugely enjoyable.

It has often seemed to me that the worst thing to happen to our country since the war has been the fostering of class hatred and class consciousness. Within the marquee that doctrine, too, would have received short shrift. Amanda's nursery maid, her grandmother's housekeeper, resplendent in furs, her monthly nurse of long ago, the gardener, the village choir, a good time was had by all. Tongues were loosened: cheeks became flushed: everyone was at their ease.

And then there was the cutting of the cake: such a cake, tier upon tier, stretching, like a conjuring trick towards the green and white striped canvas roof. I always imagined it was made of cardboard, someone exclaimed behind me. But this one wasn't. And here the Master of Ceremonies, very grand in his tail coat, took charge. I watched him grow in stature before my eyes. After all, this was his great moment. Members of the Cabinet might argue with each other, behind closed doors, husbands and wives might argue with each other, only too often in public, but no bride or bridegroom would dare to argue with this demi-god as he called for silence, commanded the presence of the best man, and placed the knife in the hands of his newest acolytes. From years of practice—I'm booked fully up through the summer, he told me—he knew the exact spot where the cardboard ended and the real cake began. Cut *here*, he commanded, in ringing tones. Meekly Amanda and John, their hands entwined, obeyed.

Again, it was as though I had never seen the mystical rite performed before. Or the barbaric custom of throwing confetti and rice upon the departing pair, when an hour later they ran the gauntlet from the steps of the house to the waiting car. Amanda in a going-away coat that was the colour of the great rhododendron tree that, towering outside the drawing-room windows seemed in its scarlet magnificence to be blooming, too, specially for the bride upon this happy day. Amanda, her hair free to the sun and the sky: John, looking almost as young as she, in his shy, grey suit. A salute of waving hands, a mingled chorus of 'Good Lucks' and broadening laughter, as the car turned down the drive and everyone perceived that on the back someone had not forgotten to pin the traditional notice which read: 'NEWLY MARRIED'.

I turned to find Mary at my side. Even in her fabulous mink jacket, her wedding finery, she was still the same very dear friend. For a second the gusts of laughter enveloped us, making a tent. How is your mother? Coming back to life, but slowly, slowly. How is your daughter? Driving away down the hill, out of sight, into a new life. Instinctively we clung together, the warmth of our friendship very strong at that moment. Then her other guests came crowding in on her, queueing to say goodbye.

I kissed her quickly. "Thank you for asking me," though there was no need for conventional phrases between us, ever. "I shall always remember the spring bride," I said.

And I always shall. The blossom, the singing and the gold. . . .

FIFTEEN

THE ADDICT AND THE NOVICE

IT was a road such as you find duplicated over and over again in any suburb outside a large town in our country. This happened to be London, but the backcloth could just as easily have represented Leeds or Birmingham, Manchester or Glasgow. A long row of semi-detached houses, facing each other, with small neat gardens, and here and there a touch of spring bursting out on a newly painted front door or fence. To match the crocuses round the porch of the home that I was visiting where the front door-step itself had been freshly scrubbed.

I could not help noticing that particularly and thinking to myself how so far it was all completely normal and true to type, even to the comfortable appearance of the middle-aged woman, in a knitted cardigan, who answered my ring. "You've come to see my daughter, haven't you?" she said. "Well, she's in the back room. It's been one of her bad days." And suddenly her voice that had been bright and guarded trailed off into hopelessness, as she led the way through the hall and opened a door.

Here again my first impression was how very normally furnished, like a scheme in the showroom of a suburban store, the sitting-room seemed with its grand piano, and velvet curtains, soon to be drawn against the dusk, and the latest model in electric fires burning in the hearth. Any family would be very cosy here, I thought, but that was before I became fully conscious of the figure, bending over the grate, whimpering to herself. On her hands and knees, she was trying desperately to scrape some liquid powder off the tiles. "It's no use, Lorna. I've told you it's gone. You must try not to be so careless next time."

The mother spoke not angrily but patiently and slowly as you would speak to a child of six who had broken a toy. But this was not a toy. This was a shot of pethidine, a synthetic form of morphia, which this poor drugged creature had spilled as she was transferring it to her hypodermic syringe. More precious to her than gold, it represented the only kind of life she would ever know now.

"But the doctor won't believe I spilled it," she moaned. "I'll be a dose short tomorrow." And I saw again the queue inside the all-night chemist's shop that might well be described as the unhappiest queue in the world. For it is formed by the hopeless, incurable drug addicts who steal in round about midnight to replenish their supply—for the next twenty-four hours.

The Head of the Drugs Section at Scotland Yard explained to me that the victims could only be trusted with a prescription that gives them one or two days' supply at a time. However, they receive their heroin and their morphia, their pethidine or their cocaine, under the National Health Act, just as anyone else might ask for a bottle of aspirin.

Indeed, if its implications were not so tragic, that ironic comparison would make one smile. But I was not smiling as the girl, with the great gashes under her eyes, and the hands like claws, whom I had watched the night before coming swaying towards the counter of that West End chemist, now rose uncertainly to her feet, clinging to the overmantel of the fireplace.

All along its painted surface were black marks made by her cigarette ends. Like scars, I decided. But that was before the daughter insisted on showing me, almost as though there was some pride attached to the demonstration, the real scars; her black-pitted veins from her wrists right up her arms and her desperately thin legs where above the knees, in the wider expanse of her thighs, there were great lumps of hardness, the colour of bruises. Here day after day her hypodermic syringe had penetrated the flesh.

"Hit me there, if you like," she muttered, her voice slurring. "I shan't feel it." I realized, of course, that she wasn't boasting: she wasn't really challenging me: it was simply a statement of fact.

"Lorna," her mother cried in protest, but she was gazing past her daughter's figure, with its skirt grotesquely raised above her knees, at the other black scars, the cigarette burns along the mantelpiece. "It was spotless this morning, I did it myself," she added unhappily, "and now look . . . ."

"It's just the same in her bedroom," she continued, as though her daughter's presence was no more than an insubstantial ghost.

"I patch and patch but all her blankets have holes in them from her cigarettes. She goes to sleep and lets them fall. Sometimes I'm afraid she'll set the house on fire at night. It's like one long nightmare. . . .'

P

The mother meant the ten long years since Lorna, a young steno-grapher of nineteen with a secret taste for excitement not to be assuaged in her quiet, respectable suburban home, started staying 'Up West' in the evenings, searching out the dance halls where the saxophones wailed and the drums became the tom-toms of some primeval forest. While the best partners, since they made Lorna feel that she herself was such a wonderful dancer, were the coloured boys who seemed always to move to the sound of music, full of passionate, intoxicating rhythms, even when the band itself was silent.

Soon the disintegration, so imperceptible at first, so headlong later, had set in, and she had migrated from the comparative security of the larger dance halls to the sweaty, sexy intimacy of the little clubs that lurk, usually in basements, off the streets that surround Piccadilly Circus and Tottenham Court Road.

I had been taken to such a 'dive' only a few nights before by someone who had made a life-study of the drug traffic in Europe. Because my companion had a familiar face, the doorman let us pass and we made our way down the stairs to the cellar where the club premises were shut away behind a grille. I could hear the muffled beat of the orchestra wailing, and taste the first stench of the atmosphere within, an atmosphere where daylight never penetrated.

The next moment the door had opened and since my guide was an old club member we were greeted with friendly grins by the proprietor, ever on the watch out for the police. I tried to look as nonchalant and off-guard as possible, even when my eyes registered on the wall a notice with these words:

ALL GUESTS MUST BE PREPARED TO BE SEARCHED AT ANY TIME FOR DOPE OR CIGARETTES.

Unusual, to say the least of it, though no one, who had succeeded in reaching that inner sanctum, seemed to glance at it twice except myself. Searched for cigarettes? That could mean only one thing. Marijuana, and in my mind I heard again what my expert guide had said earlier that evening as we drove towards this meeting place for addicts and novices, pimps and pedlars, those who came to dance and those who came for other reasons.

"If you were a girl, specially if you were young and fresh, you might get your chance of a smoke quickly—too quickly.

"They go in couples to these clubs, because they are mad about the music. I suppose it *is* rather different from pounding a type-writer all day. They wait for someone to ask them to dance, then to have a cigarette. The first few cigarettes are all right, even perhaps the first few visits . . . and then the bait is offered."

The cigarette, filled with hashish, that has been smuggled ashore by Indian seamen in some dark corner of the docks, is later offered to a white girl for two reasons. First, to make the novice emotionally dependent upon the giver: secondly to make her 'high'—which in this underworld so full of shadows is their euphemous word for the effect of the drug—'high', meaning in this case a different kind of intoxication from ordinary drunkenness, though at the same time similar in its reactions to the intake of several double whiskies.

All inhibitions, it was explained to me, are broken down, and the smoker feels that she is walking on air, dancing in the clouds. A delicious sensation while it lasts, so delicious, that despite the hang-over, the depression afterwards, the novice always comes back for more. And more. And more. . . .

Soon she will be helpless. Not because marijuana is in itself a habit-forming drug but because gradually, as its effect wears thin, its sexual potency dims, the craving sets in for stronger drugs, like a 'pop' of heroin. Now the new victim is in the toils. Now she has to give in return for the cigarette, the tablets and the injections, everything that she possesses. Her wages are mortgaged, her trinkets are sold, and finally herself.

The long journey into despair, the hopeless flight from reality has commenced.

That evening in the club which for so many has served as the starting point, I could glimpse through a mist of tobacco smoke, a bar with many figures leaning against it. Some, to my surprise, were in uniform—the uniform of the United States Army and Air Force, though the majority of the other male guests were coloured.

However, it would be very wrong to suggest that the present craze for smoking marijuana cigarettes can be blamed entirely upon the coloured population of London, or of any of our seaports. That would be demonstrably unfair since an official report in the United States, where the scourge has reached still greater proportions, has proved by statistics that there are as many addicts today in the north of America as in the south.

Rather, let us keep our disapproval—and our pity—for the

white girls, who have been brought up in good, middle-class homes, but are drawn in increasing numbers to this extremely dangerous type of night club. Like the two seated against the wall at midnight, with a look of rapture on their faces, as the beat of the orchestra grew louder and still more tempestuous. "I've got rhythm, you've got rhythm," the drummer sang, and I watched the novices in their bright green reefer coats, that were as fresh and clean as their hair and skins, clap their hands while they followed with eager eyes the gyrations of the couples already on the floor, jerking and jigging like marionettes in their orgiastic rites.

How many of them were already 'high', I remember wondering? How soon would it be before those two, who looked like junior typists, would have lost their bloom, their youth, their power to define right from wrong? How soon before they ceased to care that the English translation of the Eastern word 'hashish' is 'assassin'?

I was to hear the answers to those questions, only a few days later from the lips of Lorna's mother. "At first we had no idea why she was starting to stay out so many nights a week. We thought it was just that she liked dancing. She seemed so happy and in such gay spirits at that time, we hoped it was that she had met a nice young man who she would soon be bringing home to meet her father and me. We never guessed, of course, that she had already started to smoke those horrible cigarettes. Have you ever seen one? They look so harmless. . . ."

Indeed, they look like any other cigarette that has been rolled. They showed me an exhibit at Scotland Yard, half-smoked already, and we lit it again, and I took a few uneasy puffs at it, noticing that it had a slightly acrid taste and smell, rather like one of the remedies that asthmatic patients use, inhaling with a cloth thrown over their heads.

It had no effect on me, one way or the other, and I imagine it was the same with Lorna at first. That is why the bait is such a fiendish one. The victims, unconscious that they are hooked, come back eagerly for more, until their whole being is impregnated, and then it is too late to turn back. In Lorna's case, it took two years before she started to move on down the road, becoming first a heroin addict, and then craving finally the oblivion of morphia.

When her parents found out at last what was the real cause for her intermittent bouts of depression, followed by moods of wild gaiety, above all, why she was losing weight at such an alarming rate, they did everything in their power to save her. They sent her to specialists, but the greatest expert on narcotics in Britain who has achieved wonderful results at his private nursing home in curing alcoholics, made this confession to me himself about his drug patients.

"Quite truthfully I am never anxious to take one under this roof. Not because I do not want to help, but because so often I feel defeated before I start. It is as though their minds were possessed by a devil and there is not a medicine in existence to cast out that devil.

"Now my alcoholic patients," he went on, "are easy to make friends with. You can trust them. They will tell you the truth. They know that you are trying to help them and they want to be helped. Even at their worst they remain likable human beings. You never hear of anyone speaking of an alcoholic *fiend*.

"But the drug addicts *are* fiends. They never cease to regard one with cold and hostile eyes. You never win them over. You have to watch them every second. They will lie, steal, almost murder to get what they crave. And they are far worse than any alcoholics in their desperate craving. Why, I have seen them give themselves an injection through their trouser leg. They couldn't even wait to sterilize the syringe. . . ."

"Still, at least, there are not so many of them," I had suggested, and it was then that the specialist made a considered statement which astonished me and which needs to be recorded. He said:

"No, there are not so many of them. I suppose you could say that there are five hundred thousand men and women who drink to dangerous excess in this country while there are by comparison only twenty thousand taking drugs."

"Twenty thousand?" I echoed. "But the official figures are. . . ." Whereupon he interrupted me. "I am perfectly aware what the official figures are but they take into account only the registered cases that are known either to the police or the Home Office. There are all the others who manage to hide their tragic secret because their symptoms are not yet easily discernible, like the marijuana smokers. I call them the self-assassins. They think they are being so smart. If they only knew what was to come. . . ."

That afternoon, in the comfortable suburban sitting-room, with its grand piano and velvet curtains, I recalled again how the specialist had thrown up his hands in a weary gesture, and looked away across his consulting room, towards the wall where there was a plaque, the cool, serene head of the Madonna, gazing down in mercy.

"And how do you try to cure them by the time they reach you?" I asked.

"Oh the *physical* side of the cure is not so difficult. Especially since the introduction of the drug methadone which we can substitute for whatever narcotic was being used, in the proportion of one mg. of methadone to four of morphine. We call this the Transference Period. Gradually the patient becomes solely dependent upon the methadone and this drug can then be discontinued after another ten days. . . .

"Then many doctors, too, use the insulin cure, injecting insulin to take the place of the drug to which the patient was addicted, thus encouraging a normal appetite. But it is the first few days that are such an ordeal. This is the Purgatory from which there is no escape. . . ."

"You mean what they call in America the Cold Turkey Cure?"

"I mean, the withdrawal symptoms. The sweating, the nausea, the shivering fits, the pains, like unbearable cramp, in all the extremities. I would not like to have to ask you to sit at their bedside then," he added simply.

And over and over again, in their tortured minds, I told myself, the eternal question mark. Why did I start? Why . . . did . . . I . . . start?

There were three main reasons, it was explained to me. Sometimes they became addicted through having been given a pain-easing drug after an operation and the longing for the blanket of peace possessed them. (These are the most easily cured cases.) And sometimes they started through fear—not fear of pain but fear of life, of growing old or unattractive, of poverty or war, of losing their energy and their job. Then through a sense of insecurity, they fell back on drugs and at once became doubly as insecure.

"And many," he added, "start just for the kick of it, because they see themselves as being daring or different from the humdrum life around them. They believe themselves to be the master and able to stop when they want to and then suddenly it is too late. . . ."

Too late. As it was in Lorna's case. First her parents had sent her to hospital, later they had allowed her to be forcibly detained, in prison, hoping and praying that the complete isolation from all her old haunts and companions, while at the same time she was receiving medical care and attention, would build up her body and the power of resistance in her mind. But it was no use. Only a month after she was released, she had started again down the road because the all-consuming desire was in her blood stream now and nothing but death could eradicate it.

The merciful oblivion of death. And it was at the moment, during the afternoon of my visit to her at home, when I finally became conscious of such a prayer in my own mind that Lorna's mother came back into the room, carrying three cups of tea. Whereupon the overwhelming ordinariness of that symbol seemed to make the surrounding nightmare, in which we were all of us now enveloped, even more hopelessly and horribly real.

Desperately I tried to make conversation. I admired the piano, imagining that to be a safe enough subject, but the only answer I received was that they had bought it for Lorna. "She was so fond of the piano when she was a child. Of course she never plays it now." Not bearing to look at either of them, I glanced down at the pile of music on the stool. On the top was Dvořák's familiar 'Songs my Mother taught me'.

Then I knew there was nothing more for me to say. However as I started to leave, Lorna seemed to rouse herself from her stupor in front of the fire. "If you are going Up West perhaps you would give me a lift." *Up West.* Her slurred voice clung lovingly to the phrase, as though it still possessed a kind of magic for her.

While Lorna dragged herself upstairs to fetch her coat, the mother took me into the front room to show me some pictures of the family. She opened a drawer in the mahogany sideboard, and there wrapped up in brown paper was the photograph of a handsome young man in khaki. "Your son?" I asked.

"We haven't a son. That was my husband in the First World War."

"And that?" I queried. "Is that a younger daughter?"

"That *was* our only daughter," she said.

I looked at the picture of the girl, so radiantly young, so untouched. She had the beauty of innocence and there was a jaunty feather in her hat such as Dick Whittington might have worn. Some sitters gaze shyly into the camera lens; this one seemed to be overflowing with confidence for the future.

Lorna's mother took the picture away and wrapped it again carefully in the tissue paper. For a moment, unconsciously, she held the package against her breast. "Oh why don't they put them all together on an island," she whispered, almost to herself. And then as if to justify that tortured protest which really needed no justification, she added: "Last Christmas Dad said would she like to ask two of her friends to dinner to try and cheer her up. So she did. But do you know how they spent the whole afternoon? Why giving each other 'plops' as they call it, in the bathroom upstairs. Of course, they get it through their doctors . . . but Christmas Day."

The overwhelming sadness in her voice followed me down the neat front path with the crocuses on either side, followed me for days, until it became merged in another confession brought forth this time by the despairing anger of a father.

Again the background could have been any conventional suburban home though in actual fact our meeting took place in the waiting-room of a colourless public building. A few hard chairs and a plain table across which two strangers, who were also two human beings, faced each other.

The father preferred it that way. It was easier for him to lose his identity, to conquer his shyness and pour forth the pattern of words that he had locked away, in the family safe, for so long. He kept on repeating over and over again. "Put it all down on paper, publish it in a book later, let's hope it may save some other family from the same fate. . . ."

This was his story.

At seventeen, Doris, a bright and intelligent girl with a flair for languages was sent by her father, a City clerk, to France for the summer holidays, so that she might seek to improve her French with the prospect of getting a better post, on her return.

Theirs was an arrangement that is often made. After some correspondence, Doris was placed *au pair* with a French family in Boulogne, and for the last week of her stay, the two girls were allowed to visit Paris on their own.

What happened there the father does not know except that on her return Doris was restless and unsettled and started going out on her own in the evenings. The only clue that she gave was when she exclaimed enthusiastically how she wished she could find in London the equivalent of the café life she had enjoyed so much in Paris.

"First it was only one or two nights a week," the father told me. "Then it was three or four: finally she took to staying out all night.

And when her mother remonstrated with her she always replied that she had spent the night at the home of a girl friend from the office, who lived in the centre of London, and there was nothing to worry about. But, of course, we did worry. So much so that I took her latch-key away from her."

"Did that make any difference?" I asked. "Did that make her come home?"

Sadly the man opposite me shook his head. In his dark blue suit and mackintosh with his umbrella and bowler beside him, he looked like any other business man facing one in the Tube on his way home from the City in the rush hour. No one would have guessed his secret. Or that beneath his stoical expression, used to the examination of ledgers all day long, an intolerable burden pressed down upon him, like a sick and melancholy stomach ache.

There was a pause while he stared down at his clenched fists upon the table. Then he made himself continue with the next chapter of the story which he had finally decided must be told. And to the world, at large, who knew nothing of such things.

"For months now," he went on, in a quiet, steady voice, that was deliberately drained of all emotion, "we haven't been sure what will happen any evening. Her mother always lays a place for Doris at supper but we don't wait any longer. And we go to bed at the usual time, but, of course, I can't get off to sleep.

"I wait for one o'clock to strike, because then I know that in a few minutes she will either be coming home on the last train, or not at all. I listen for her feet outside in the roadway, her tap on the front door. I don't mind getting up, it's the silence I mind and have begun to dread."

He passed one of his clenched hands across his eyes which were red-rimmed like the eyes of a man who cannot sleep because of what he remembers when he lies awake.

"Then just before Christmas she stayed away for four days and four nights. Her mother was desperate and so was I. We searched her room, and we found a diary and in it a certain name kept on cropping up. She had written it over and over again, and fortunately, in one place added the address. And I recognized the address as being in the City, not far from where we have our own offices. So when Christmas morning came and still there was no sign, no word, in desperation, I took my brother-in-law and went to the address in the book. We knocked and rang the bell, but no one came. . . ."

Then they were lucky. Or at least, in one way, they were lucky. Just as they were on the point of turning away, another lodger from the same house came towards them down the street. When he reached the door and took out his own latch-key, they explained that they wanted to call on Mr. So and So, and wish him a Happy Christmas. Genially the other tenant ushered them in and they followed him up the stairs till he pointed to an attic flat, at the top. Here they rang another bell and this time the man, whose name was in the daughter's diary, came and half-opened the door.

" 'Is my daughter here?' I asked. He was as cool as you please, and he started to deny ever having heard of Doris, but between us we managed to open the door and get past him into a room where, lying on a bed in one corner, was a girl. She had the features of our daughter, but at first truthfully I did no recognize her. Not because the curtains were partly drawn, not because she was wearing a pair of man's pyjamas, but because of her hair.

"You see, four days before at home she had been a brunette like her mother, now she was a blatant peroxide blonde. Somehow that made the whole thing seem . . . impossible."

He closed his eyes for a moment, as though seeking to erase an image that was implacably engraved upon the screen of his brain. At last he added, wearily. "I said, 'It's Christmas Day and you are coming home to your mother'."

"And she came home?" I echoed, my own mind filled at that moment with echoes of that other home, that other Christmas Day, that other daughter.

The father nodded. "Yes, she came home." But there was only defeat not elation for that victory in his voice.

"Wasn't she terribly ashamed?" I persisted. "I mean . . . at your finding her like that."

"Not a bit of it. She talked and laughed through Christmas dinner as though I had dreamt it all, and she was still the girl we used to know and love. But she wasn't. She isn't. Something has happened to her. To her mind. She no longer cares about anything or anyone. Except this man and what he gives her. . . .

"Why, even on Christmas Day she couldn't spend the evening quietly at home. She was off again at five o'clock. She just went up to her room and changed her clothes. She didn't even lie down and have some rest. She didn't need any sleep because she was still under the influence of the pernicious stuff. All keyed up, talking twenty to the dozen, high, as they call it."

"And you say she's only nineteen now?" I repeated.

"She is only just nineteen. And we can do nothing. We have even been to the police. If she wants to go with this man, who is as black as soot, we cannot stop her. And if she wants to become a hopeless drug addict, we can't stop that, either. Because she has lost all sense of shame. All sense of what is right and what is beyond the pale. She has sold herself to the devil, and she was our only daughter."

Then there was silence, a final and terrible silence in that bare room, and I remember thinking: This place is like a Confessional, but I am not a priest. I have no right to judge anyone; only to record truthfully what I have seen and what I have heard, and alter nothing, except, in this case, the Christian names of the two victims: the addict and the novice.

SIXTEEN

THE BEAUTIES OF BELFAST

I LOVE flying. I am very content to have been born into an age when I can enjoy the pleasures of being able to breakfast in Paris, lunch in my London home, and have tea, if I wish, in Belfast.

I did so wish, not long ago. All the same, I must issue a warning to other travellers. Flying to Northern Ireland on the B.E.A. route is extremely comfortable and pleasant—I have never encountered a more attractive selection of air hostesses—nevertheless, arriving that way gives one a very disappointing first glimpse of Ulster. For it is a long dull drive into the terminus and one seems to look down on to nothing but factory buildings and one cannot help recalling at that moment that Belfast is credited with having the largest gasometer in Great Britain.

How infinitely better an impression one gains when one lands at Londonderry, as I did on many occasions in the war, and drives towards the capital along the Antrim coast. For what a magnificent road it is, vying with the Moyen Corniche in splendour, especially from the Giant's Causeway onwards. The hills on one side of you, the sea on the other, when on a clear day the Paps of Jura, the colour of unripe grapes, will seem so close that you feel that you can stretch out your hand and touch them.

I have passed that way, too, upon a brilliant day in peace time, having stood the previous evening beside the Walls of Derry, and listened to the gulls crying over the water and remembered with a stab of gratitude how green the banks of Lough Foyle used to seem, during the blacked-out years, to those returning to their base from an Atlantic patrol. But now revisiting that countryside, nearly a decade later, I would like to give thanks, on behalf of all of us who were temporary sailors, for the hospitality we received from the local population. They fed us, they bathed us, they presented us with the freedom of their homes.

Of course, the southern Irish have a great reputation—and a great gift—for hospitality, and, in consequence, I have heard it

228

suggested that once you cross the border and enter one of the six counties of the north the atmosphere appreciably changes and a cold wind blows. Certainly the atmosphere does change, but not, I repeat with some emphasis, where a welcome to strangers is concerned. On the other hand, I would suggest that the main characteristic of the Ulsterman—and the Ulsterwoman—is that they are 'doers', rather than 'dreamers'. "We are the music makers, we are the dreamers of dreams," could never have been written by a Belfast poet.

Perhaps that is the reason why I could happily spend a month in Dublin, but never have any desire to linger on in Belfast, the moment that my business is completed. It may be unnecessarily cruel to compare the architecture of Ulster's capital with the eighteenth-century delights of Dublin, nevertheless, I cannot help asking, not for the first time, whether there is any sufficient excuse for Belfast being quite so noisy and quite so dusty.

However, on my last visit, I was to have the good fortune of discovering another kind of beauty, when I was invited to see over the Brookfield Weaving Factory, which is part of the largest concern of its kind, in the world. For do you know what our output of cloth is in a week? I was asked the question I was not expected to answer the moment I stepped over the threshold by Major Reade, who after very considerable war service in Burma, came home to take over the reins as the youngest managing director in the linen trade.

"Our output of cloth here is approximately one hundred miles weekly, that is to say, sufficient to cover the total distance from Belfast to Dublin."

I was suitably impressed but even more so by the impact that the six hundred women employees made upon me, in the course of my tour. It is true that they had extremely up-to-date working conditions and everything was refreshingly clean. So that it could be argued that it was not nearly so difficult for them to present such a fresh and pleasant impression as it would be for their co-workers, in an old-fashioned, mucky, Lancashire cotton mill. However, let me give credit where credit is certainly due. The lack of beauty in the pavements of Belfast is certainly more than atoned for by the high standard of looks and especially the turn out, among the older women, many of whom have spent all their working lives under the same banner of the York Street Flax Spinning Company.

Indeed, some of the faces that I saw at Brookfield I shall remember long after this book is finished. I am thinking particularly at this moment of two women, one a grandmother, and the oldest worker in the mills, and the other, a woman, neither young, nor old, whose boy of fifteen, she told me, has the unusual name of Dunnelly, and whose sixteen-year-old daughter, Dolores, has already begun to be a wage earner herself.

There is for me eternally the same problem: so many strange faces, and at which bench shall one stop? But it was the unusually attractive green dress that Mrs. Malcomson was wearing that day which catching the corner of my eye, drew me to a standstill at her side. "Don't you sometimes feel like chucking your hand in now and just staying at home as a housewife?" I asked.

"I couldn't do that till the children have properly got their start in life," she replied and with that answer she had confessed everything about herself.

On the other hand, Mrs. Cree, who is now sixty-five, and has been working in a linen factory since she was eleven, has strong views about the young of today. Despite the fact that one of her daughters and two of her grand-daughters, Grace and Ellen Moore, are also successfully employed at Brookfield, she assured me that the majority of youngsters on both sides of the Irish Sea are pleasure-mad. Incidentally, she herself never goes to a theatre or cinema, has never smoked or had a drink of anything stronger than tea in her life, and is utterly positive that she hasn't missed anything.

Certainly Mrs. Cree seemed to be still in the full tide of her life and I thought that I glimpsed a twinkle behind her glasses as she held forth so vehemently. In any case, I could not help admiring her downright manner, her sense of pride in her own long years of conscientious service, above all, her infinite knowledge of everything to do with her loom, that she was now passing on to the youngest apprentice in the factory, 'wee Maudie'.

Maud Boyles was still only fourteen, on the day of my visit, they had started her off on twenty-five shillings a week, but her flaming mop of Titian hair was in itself worth more than that, I decided. Moreover every shop that I visited and everywhere I gazed there seemed to be another scarlet head directly in my line of vision.

"It's because we have so much rain in Belfast, and so few girls wear hats these days, so their heads go rusty," Mr. Jack Cinnamond, the factory's manager suggested with a completely straight face.

For my own part I found it easier to reply to that line of conversation than when it was being explained to me how at this weaving factory, the yarn is wound from hanks on to spools: then warped from spools in a bank on to dressers' beams, is dressed or slashed, drawn in, and finally put into the loom and woven.

I am afraid that up till that moment I had always taken the aesthetic pleasure of lying between linen sheets as much for granted as the equally agreeable sight of an elegant woman in a cool linen dress on a very hot day. Nor was I aware, for instance, that the finest examples of linen cambric have been discovered in the tombs of the Pharaohs: or that the manufacture of linen was unquestionably in practice in Ireland before the advent of Christianity. Foolishly, I had always connected its inception in my mind with the flight of the Huguenots from France in the seventeenth century.

One of these, Louis Crommelin, in 1699 was appointed 'Overseer of the Royal Linen Manufacture of Ireland'. And a descendant of his family bearing the same name, two hundred years later, became the managing partner of the York Street Flax Spinning Company, which has just erected upon the ruins of the blitz, the most impressive new premises, a monument of faith to the future of Ulster's chief export.

What would these two members of the Crommelin family have thought of the glittering headquarters, where I was received by the present chairman of the company, Sir Harry Mulholland? The last time I had stood there had been among the rubble, the broken glass, the shattered hopes, after Belfast's worst raid in the war. The old buildings had meant nothing to me; I was simply a war reporter, soberly assessing facts, but now I felt a personal sense of burgeoning hope as I heard about the importation of the latest machinery from Switzerland.

Yet not only the machines, surely the human instruments would have delighted the Crommelin family, too. It is a long way from the ancient hand-spinning flax wheel that you can still find in some of the cottages outside the city, to the modern drawing-in shed at Brookfield where I found two sisters, working side by side, Louie and Madge Norrell. Madge, aged sixteen, was another striking red-head, but her elder sister possessed the blue-black hair and the very white magnolia skin that is so traditionally Irish, and when they told me, in chorus, that they were two of a family of ten, where there were six sisters and four brothers, I found myself once again more interested in that personal equation than in the undoubtedly intriguing fact that the yarn is melded with sago-skin to increase its weavability.

In the same way, the high-light of the day was for me, not the lunch that the directors gave in my honour, but the afternoon break in the factory when I was joined in the little house, set apart for the nurse and her consulting room, by the young lady who had been chosen out of all the workers to have tea with me. Her name was Elizabeth—Elizabeth Kirk—she was tall and held herself with the grace of a fashion model, and they had dressed her in a green linen frock, home-produced. But I should have enjoyed her company just as much had she remained in her working clothes.

Her youth was like a banner: she was completely at ease: her attitude to life was typical of hundreds of other girls of eighteen, scattered through these islands. One night a week she set apart for washing her hair and doing her mending, one she went to the movies, one to the local dance hall with her 'Oppo', her great friend, Audrey Wright, and every night, before she went out, she took it in turns with her sister to do the washing-up, for her mother. "You see, Mum always gets our breakfast for us," she explained simply.

Elizabeth had one great ambition, before she finally settled down. She would like to travel—"really travel, I mean"—and she was making a start that summer. "I'm flying for the first time in my life, when I go on holiday," she said. "Flying?" I echoed, and I thought of the plane that would be taking me to the south of France, and the sweep at the Bay at Nice, with the sea like blue shot-silk as you come in to land beside the sand-dunes. "Yes, we've booked our passage. We're going to Douglas." "Douglas?" I echoed again. "Yes, in the Isle of Man. They say, it's a lovely bay."

Then Mr. Joe Lyttle, her foreman, appeared, announcing it was time for Elizabeth to go back and earn her weekly wage packet once more. And when we had said goodbye, like planes that pass each other in mid-air, I asked him for the definition of a good weaver. Mr. Lyttle thought for a moment and then he said. "She must be a tidy girl. She must have patience and concentration and an even temperament."

And as he spoke, slowly putting his thoughts into words, it came to me that that had been my own overriding impression, the tidiness of everything and everyone. There is a special kind of beauty

Mrs. R. A. Butler, in the drawing-room of her London home

Evening News

"Two sisters working side by side." Louie and Madge Norrell

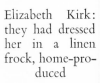

Elizabeth Kirk: they had dressed her in a linen frock, home-pro-duced

Major Reave
with Mrs. Mal-
colmson

Grannie Cree
with 'Wee Mau-
die'

TINCH

in that. However, the final memory of my visit was still to come.
On the way out, we stopped at the table of a man in a white coat,
wearing horn-rimmed glasses, who explained to me that his official
title was 'Cloth Passer'. That is to say, he examined all the finished
products to check that they were completely up to standard, and
in his hand at that moment was a tea-towel.

"Take a look at this, Mr. Winn," he said. "It is called 'Happy Days',
and we do a big turnover with it, especially in exports to America."

So I did take a look, and much to my amusement, I discovered
that the design depicted an Irish kitchen scene in which 'the head of
the house' is doing the washing-up, under duress, while his better
half, or perhaps one should say, his stronger half, is standing over him
with a rolling-pin.

"Well, well,' I temporized, "fancy that!" Expectantly I looked
towards my companion for his reaction. It was immediate and came
in one swift burst. "I don't know about the States, and what the husbands do there, but I do know about here. In Ulster, you'll never
see any self-respecting husband out pushing the pram."

Or washing-up, either, indoors . . . Mr. Bob Graham's determined,
ringing tones seemed to imply, but before I could start to argue the
toss, for I am a great believer in the sons of the house being brought
up to do their share of the domestic chores, my guides, Major Reade
and Mr. Cinnamond had moved on out into the yard, and someone
was tactfully whistling 'The Mountains of Mourne'. Like the interval
music, between the second and third acts of a play, I thought.

The Mountains of Mourne that sweep down to the sea. . . .

The last act took place the next day, and I was fortunate. For I
discovered it was one of those summer mornings which set a kind of
magic dew upon everything when a charming Ulsterwoman called
for me in her car, to rescue me from my Belfast hotel, and drive me
out to her family's summer-house at Glasdrumman, right in the heart
of the Kingdom of Mourne.

"We call it, The Hut," she explained, "and it is only a long
bungalow, but the boys love it in their holidays. They catch mackerel
in the sea for their supper and splash about all day in the stream beside
the house, and we go for picnics in The Silent Valley, where we shall
take you this afternoon, which is right in the cup of the mountains. . . ."

"Which is full of fairy folk?" I suggested.

Q

My companion gave me the sudden, sharp look of recognition one exchanges with a compatriot in a foreign land, and proceeded to tell me a story. How, years ago now, just before her first boy was born, she and her husband asked their handyman to lop off some branches from a thorn tree in front of their bungalow. Whereupon he proceeded to carry out their orders, but most reluctantly, and that same evening he came to them at supper and asked if they had moved the jacket which he had lain upon the wall while he worked. They had seen it there themselves, but now it was gone. They searched and continued the search next day, but it never came to light.

"A tramp must have slipped up the hill and taken it?" I suggested.

"We never lock our doors and windows. We have never had anything else taken," my hostess replied, adding after a pause. "Of course, our man swore it was the fairies. You see, there is a superstition never to touch a thorn tree. Or else. . . ."

"And you believe that, too?" I asked.

"Well, I don't disbelieve it," she answered with a simplicity that I greatly admired, and which was so much part of the day's timeless enchantment.

First we had a picnic beside the stream, while the mountains with their eleven peaks waited for us, like a backcloth, beckoning, and there was a small naked baby gurgling in the sunshine who looked so healthy and happy one wondered whether the fairy folk did not covet it, too.

The boy, Mark, belonged to cousins of my hostess, who were occupying The Hut at that moment, and they assured me that the secret of the baby's glowing skin was nothing to do with old wives' tales, but sprang from a diet of porridge and bread, made from stone-ground whole meal. "I used to feed the same meal to my horses in Colorado," Mr. Archer rather surprisingly volunteered.

Colorado . . . the Mountains of Mourne . . . with a spell of war-time service with the R.A.F. in Burma, thrown in . . . Stanley Archer, a strikingly fit man in his fifties, confessed that after having been a rolling stone all his life he was now more than content to settle down with his young English wife in the country of his birth. The Kingdom of Mourne once more held him in thrall.

Moreover, I understood why, that afternoon, when he became our guide. Leaving the main road, we turned up a track, where the whin, sometimes called gorse, was in full flame, a shower of blazing gold

against the white-stone cottages. These, in turn, we left behind as we reached Peddler's Brae and paused to gaze across the valley to where, eighty miles away, on a clear day you can see the faint outline of Dublin.

The Mountains of Mourne are very different from the soft blue hills of Donegal. On the side where we stood, they are stark and grey. But I had no sensation of fear that afternoon, only delight in the stillness, the atmosphere of peace as we entered The Silent Valley and beheld stretching in front of us the great waters of the reservoir. Indeed, very privileged we were to be there for the gates are closed now against chance visitors and a special permit had been obtained on our behalf.

Now as I look back to that afternoon, snatched from Time, I can see us getting out of the car, to stand upon the plateau of The Deer's Meadow, with Slieve Donard towering above us. I admit I did not make the ascent, but then we had the most excellent excuse that we must return in time to bath the baby. This was the final happiness of my day. To be allowed to lift young Mark into his tin tub, and as he lay there splashing, his eyes glowing, his small fat arms outstretched to life, I found myself exclaiming aloud:

"No, you were wrong, Mr. Graham! If this belonged to me, and I were an Ulsterman, I should be proud to push him in his pram through the streets of Belfast."

And it is true. I would.

SEVENTEEN

THE BETTER HALF OF THE BUDGET

THE hour of tea is a very pleasant time for turning back the clock. It is also a very English custom, too, and the woman whose portrait I am trying to paint in this chapter could not have been born or brought up in any other country except Britain. Our northern climate, and reticent, cautious way of life is stamped upon her brow, her high cheek bones, the strong line of her jaw.

As for her voice, that, too—like her figure and her clothes—deliberately, from long training, avoids any kind of exaggeration. It is, in fact, the kind of voice which foreigners always conjure up when they think of Englishwomen. Where is the heart, they cry.

One could answer that by suggesting that a certain degree of reserve is not a negative attribute. Indeed, it can be a very good one, for too much surface enthusiasm is as cloying as too much sugar in an *omelette surprise*. Besides, in the case of the wife of the Chancellor of the Exchequer, it is an innate, inbred shyness, not a lack of heart that can make her seem to an acquaintance at a chance meeting, aloof and austere, and most damning impression of all, patronizing.

Fortunately, we ourselves have been on Christian-name terms since the days when I was a small boy and Sydney Courtauld, as she then was, the daughter of a great industrialist, would come and stay with a school friend from Roedean, in our Worcestershire village of Barnt Green, that lies at the foot of the Lickey Hills. Today, with an ever-expanding population, it has grown into a suburb of Birmingham, but in the days when I remember it, the bluebells stretched in an untouched carpet, through the woods at the back of our garden, Cherry Hill outside our front gate was a paradise for tobogganers in the winter, and there used to be old-fashioned children's parties, unbogged down by television, in the Beazley's rambling house.

I wonder who lives in The Pump House now? The Beazleys were a large family, while Sydney, I know now, was an only child. So that looking back, I realize how much our holiday games of hide and seek, our communal pleasures must have meant to her. The chance to lose herself in an anonymous crowd of happy extroverts, to pretend for a moment, that she was the tomboy that her parents had so passionately wanted. For I know that, too, now.

Both Helen Beazley and Sydney Courtauld were several years older than I was, but I have no recollection of any feeling of being treated as someone too physically small or too mentally insignificant to be noticed. On the contrary. Moreover, one of the first people to get in touch with me when a raw youth of seventeen I took the plunge and came to London on my own, living in a students' club at Marble Arch, while I planned my assault on the West End Theatre, was the Beazley's holiday guest, now earning a considerable reputation as a blue stocking, at Cambridge.

In the vacations, she did not live at home, but in a small flat she had taken for herself in the Notting Hill Gate district. I have a feeling, though it is typical of her character that she should never speak of it, that she found her parents' home in Portman Square something of a prison, though it seemed like a palace to me, when Sydney took me there to lunch.

It was my first glimpse inside a very grand London house. Up till that time I had only read about such backgrounds in the novels of Stephen McKenna—*Sonia*, *Lady Lillith* and the others—who was the most successful society novelist of the day. Confronted by all that I had secretly dreamed of far away in Worcestershire, I was at first, for all my adolescent precociousness, overcome with shyness. Nor was my mood lessened by my sponsor's own silence in the presence of her mother.

Later, I was to come to know Lil Courtauld very well. We found that we had a mutual passion for playing tennis, and she would take me often as her guest to Queen's Club. A pretty, fair woman, who, as though she had some early premonition that her days were numbered, delighted in living every day to the full, she was utterly and irretrievably the exact opposite of her only child. In looks, in attitude to the guests who came and went, in ease of manner. There was nothing that she enjoyed more than asking twenty artists to supper, after the theatre, painters and actors and writers, and we would sit talking till long after midnight, in the vast dining-room, with its fantastic collection of masterpieces on the walls.

There was one particular Gauguin that I can never pass by, each time I visit the Tate Gallery, where it forms part of the Courtauld

Collection, which was bequeathed to the nation by Sydney's father, without remembering those early days of my own youth, and being made conscious once again of how frustrated can be the lives of the overpoweringly rich.

For both Sam Courtauld and his wife longed for a son and heir: and when instead their union was blessed only by a daughter, they equally desired that she should grow up into a conventionally pretty, fashionable young lady with fair, waved hair like her mother, who would be perfectly content with the usual round of a *débutante's* existence. And she was none of these things, and wanted none of those things. In a way, she was a misfit in her mother's world, because she wasn't interested in clothes or parties, or the small talk of the Mayfair world. While the bohemians, that her mother also, in her generosity, invited to the house, made her feel doubly tongue-tied. How they talked and talked and talked about themselves. And how exaggerated were their gestures and their posturings. It made her feel completely unreal. For she possessed herself the intelligence and the mind of a male student of world affairs, though when she walked with the angular awkwardness of a youth along the heavily carpeted corridors of the Portman Square mansion, her mother viewed her approach with secret dismay, and had no understanding or appreciation that the girl instead of a boy to whom she had given birth had within her the burgeoning seeds of great promise: so that, in the future, the daughter was to fulfil herself in a manner and to a degree that her own mother, despite all the glittering activity with which she surrounded herself, was never able to achieve.

"Well, *you* haven't changed much," my hostess exclaimed with that note of relief in her voice that is instinctive on encountering a childhood friend, after a lapse of time, when one does not wish to be reminded just how much older one is oneself. However, I could return the compliment, in a different way. My tea-time companion had changed, a great deal, but for the better. She was, I decided, both far more handsome and far more complete a personality than in the days when she had first met her future husband, up at Cambridge.

As a young woman, she already had an air of seniority, a look of strong purpose that was inclined to make her seem out of place among her cygnet contemporaries, even in a university setting. Now, a quarter of a century later, her maturity, in full bloom, gives her an air of distinction that is extremely becoming. I thought for a moment to tell her so and then I realized that she would still be embarrassed by anything that seemed not so much a compliment, as an attempt at intimacy: an invasion of privacy.

"I am afraid the room may seem rather cold," my hostess was saying crisply, "but we are waiting like so many others, for the bomb gaps to be filled in next door."

I hadn't noticed the actual, physical temperature, because I had been warming myself at the glorious Seurat on the wall behind her, passionately jealous of the superb collection of Impressionists that she inherited from her father, some of which adorn now the walls of the Adam-green drawing-room of the corner house in Smith Square where the Butlers live from Monday to Friday of every week, when the House is sitting.

"It *is* lovely, isn't it?" she agreed. "When Rab comes back from the House, having had the kind of maddening day everyone has sometimes, he always looks at the pictures in here, and then everything seems to get into perspective, click into place."

I could understand that so well. There were many times when wearily I climbed the stairs of my own London house, where once I possessed a single room, and now, as landlord on a long lease, had been able to transform a whole floor into a suitable setting for my own pictures. But that knowledge did not aid me to mount the stairs more swiftly, at the end of a long day in the Street where I earn my living. Others might think with longing of the moment when they could pour themselves out a stiff whisky and soda: for me, restoration and the renewal of my life force came at the click of a light switch. There on the walls of the new dining-room I had recently created glowed the Mathew Smiths and the Graham Sutherlands, that seemed to come to life and give one a fresh welcome each time that one saved them from the darkness of the night. If I could find the time somehow just to sit for five minutes, quietly and alone with them, I could face with equanimity whatever duties the evening had in store.

"After dinner, Rab settles down to work, surrounded by a sea of papers, and I read a book, knowing that every few minutes I shall be interrupted by his throwing a paper across to me, for a second opinion. Not *now*, of course," she added hastily, "this is the close season."

By the 'close season' she meant that it was the time of preparing for the Budget when every paper, emerging from every dispatch box, came under the same classification of 'Top Secret', of which no inkling must be vouchsafed even to one's better half, however absolute her reputation for discretion.

"Does he become very irritable and exhausted about now?" I asked hopefully.

My hostess smiled and, when she smiles, her face loses its formidable look completely. "No he is no different at all. You wouldn't guess that it was pre-Budget time. He still loves seeing people for meals. He still finds time to play with Sarah—that's our ten-year-old daughter, I'll show you her later. The truth is, Rab is one of those people who are only happy when they are working at full pressure. And, of course, he's much luckier than many politicians. He has been given the post in the Government that fits him completely."

I admired her candour: her honest appraisal of someone so close to herself. She made me feel that I could ask any question and receive an absolutely truthful answer.

"Did you always believe right from the beginning that one day you would be the wife of the Chancellor?" I asked.

Sydney shook her head decisively. No, as a young married woman, when her husband had first entered Parliament, her secret day-dreams had not taken on the substance of the Cabinet Room at No. 10 Downing Street at all. It had never occurred to her that one day she would be known as the better half of the Budget. Instead, because of the distinguished career of Rab's father—Sir Montagu Butler— she had the vaguest of hopes that the son might later be offered the Governorship of some distant Province. Even, by a miracle, that he would become Viceroy. But never, Chancellor of the Exchequer.

It was fortunate that Sydney Courtauld was attracted from the start to the mystique of politics. Other professions—architects, lawyers, doctors, insurance brokers—are only too thankful to be allowed not to talk 'shop' in their leisure hours, whereas, in contrast, the whole race of politicians are utterly and implacably adamant: with them, it is politics for breakfast, politics for dinner, politics in their bath, politics in their bed. From the moment that they enter the House for the first time till the moment that they are finally rejected by their constituents they live in a blissful state of belief that every-one with whom they come in contact, and especially their own families, are fascinated by their intolerable monologues about what Who said and When, and that so far from boring their listeners into a stupor, the silence with which their harangues are received denotes enthralled interest. If only the bubble of their obsession could be pricked just once and for all time, how many grateful 'Westminster widows' there would be, who are, at present, expected to wait up dutifully for their spouse's return, at midnight, full of wind and figures signifying absolutely nothing.

When the first marriage of Anthony Eden was in the process of breaking up, and his wife had retired to Arizona, to be as far away as possible from the English political scene which had turned her marriage into a *maison à trois*, a mutual friend contrasted the landscape with her Sussex home, a long low Charles II house, nestling in a fold of the Downs. "Don't you long, Beatrice, for the green of England, now that it is almost spring again?"

Her answer was a considerable surprise. "If going back home, means all the manœuvring and the gossip of the political circus, and Anthony talking, talking politics, night and day, I never want to see England again. You will never know how bored I was!"

In the political world intrigues are notorious; it is a far more dirty game than anything indulged in by Chicago gangsters, and if one needs final proof of that, one only has to read the passage in Duff Cooper's autobiography that describes the backstairs betrayal of his Foreign Secretary by Neville Chamberlain. The tragic irony was that the betrayer soon afterwards was to die from a particularly painful form of cancer, while the man whose head he had offered on a charger to Mussolini has, after three major operations on his liver and gall-bladder, been returned to his post, fighting fit once more. The whirligig of time takes many strange revenges and today Eden is once more in direct line of succession for the Premiership, with the Chancellor as his only close rival.

But the Chancellor's wife, even within her own intimate circle, gives no sign that she is conscious of the struggle that is going on behind the scenes, a struggle in which her husband is behaving with exemplary good manners. Someone very close to the tug-of-war, said to me the other day: "In the House, they think Rab is a cold fish of a fellow. He never stays long in the Smoking Room. It is notorious that Winston admires his brain on ice, but has no warmth of affection for him as a man, as he has for Anthony, and yet I have never heard Rab fight back except with praise of Anthony that sounds absolutely sincere. Even when Anthony was so ill, and it looked as though his political career might be over, at one moment, one felt that his greatest rival was genuine in his grief for the possible great loss to the Party."

Hearing that tribute, I found myself wondering how much of this omniscient attitude on the Chancellor's part sprang from the stem of his wife's own philosophy, the extraordinarily objective attitude to life that she first adopted as an armour of protection in the days when she was made to feel so aware of her own inadequacy at home.

The nearest that she will come to discussing the very delicate balance of power relationships inside the Cabinet is when she tells the story of a time recently when her husband was staying with his leader, in a villa in the South of France, and he had the temerity to set up his own painting easel a few feet away from that of Winston Churchill.

"I need hardly add that the results, though the view and their angle of vision were exactly the same, were utterly, unrecognizably different," his wife told me, with once again, that sudden smile which completely changes her personality and made me feel, for the moment, that we were both children again, ourselves playing with paints.

Her own favourite relaxation, apart from a great joy in classical music, is an unexpected one. A day out, hunting with the Essex farmers, near her other, country home at Halstead. "There is no waiting on ceremony there," she explained. "I am just one of the crowd."

She likes enormously that feeling of anonymity, though, in a different way, she equally enjoys committee work, especially her voluntary enrolment on the executive of the Marriage Guidance Council, whose practical influence for good she believes in with all her heart and all her intellect.

"I wish you would write about *their* work, instead of about me," my hostess suggested, as she poured me out another cup of tea. And I knew that she meant it. Because though she has grown used to publicity she has never sought it, like some politicians' wives.

There was something else she wished I would write about, too. The burning need for more women M.P.s. "And we shall only get them, if the constituents, especially in seats outside the London area, encourage their standing and support them when they do. Too many women," she added with vehemence, "are disloyal by nature to their own sex. They regard every other woman as a rival of some sort or other. And yet, unless women do back each other up, how can we ever expect our husbands and our families to take us seriously, in or out of politics?"

Lady Maxwell Fyfe, who besides being the Home Secretary's wife, is also Vice-Chairman of the Conservative Party Organization, feels equally strongly on the subject. In this year of the Silver Jubilee of the Flapper Vote, there are only a score of women M.P.s in the House, and she insists that such a small number is tragically disproportionate, not only to women as a sex, but equally to the general quality of women politicians.

She believes, too, that many women candidates, both Conservative and Socialist, are only offered constituencies where the hope for their particular Party is an absolutely forlorn one. However, for this most unfair state of affairs, it is not the men on the adoption committees who are so much to blame as the women. It is they who show the least inclination to work in support of a woman candidate. No wonder that many women assert that the emancipation of the sexes is still an empty phrase, I decided, as I deposited my empty cup on the tray. "Have you ever thought, Sydney, of standing yourself, for Parliament?" I asked.

"Yes, I *have* considered it, since I have received more than one offer, but I always turn them down, because whether I was successful or not, I am sure my first job is looking after Rab and the children. Of course, Richard is married now, and farming in Norfolk, and Adam is at Cambridge, and James at Eton, so I am not so busy as I was but somehow there is always so much to do in the constituency, as the Member's wife."

"The power behind the throne. . . ." I said, teasingly. Then I leant forward and my voice changed. "Despite being so career-minded yourself as a girl, despite all you say about the urgent need for more women to take up politics seriously, do you still believe that your sex fulfil their destiny best of all by becoming wives and mothers?"

"Come and meet Sarah . . ." my hostess replied, as though that were the whole answer.

In a panelled room off the narrow hall, a child with dark hair and wide solemn brown eyes was seated at the piano, not playing, but inscribing notes on a piece of paper.

"Are you going to be a composer?" I asked.

Sarah met my question with the candour of her mother. "I can't compose much," she said, "but I can play the violin as well."

"Which do you like best?" I persisted.

"I like it best when Daddy comes to tea. He put the cake in the waste-paper basket last time, and Ma *was* angry, weren't you, Ma?"

"Mr. Winn was your age, Sarah, when he and I first met," her mother broke in hastily.

"Were you *really*?" Sarah echoed, so that I went forth into the spring dusk, feeling momentarily as old as Methuselah. However, I was greatly comforted by my reunion over tea with a woman who has made an equal success of her public and of her private life by believing that the happiest marriages are made on earth, not in Heaven: and that if you wish to end up with something on the credit side of any budget, you must be prepared to put more into the melting-pot than you can ever hope to win back, across the years.

EIGHTEEN

'TINCH'

THE snow has gone at last from the hills and this morning I can see the bare line of the Downs very clearly once more in front of my writing-room window. But the time when the lower reaches will be burnt gold with gorse still seems a long way off, though Jim, working down in the field, on the other side of the road, wears no head covering and only the old postman's jacket that is a kind of winter uniform for him. Although he must be a hundred yards away from me, once when I look up from my typewriter, he seems suddenly quite close, as though my eyes have assumed the magical power of a pair of binoculars. His dark hair, blown now this way, now that, gives him a wild and primitive air, belied by his gentle manner when he speaks. Now he has straightened his back, and is raising his right hand, in salutation. Instinctively, I do the same, for this has become a custom with us, a friendly morning greeting between neighbours, to give us both reassurance at our respective tasks. Sometimes it happens when Jim is passing in the roadway, in his cart, but always the gesture is the same, our own version of a kind of Mussolini salute, though heaven knows there is nothing fascist about the Sussex village where Jim farms the smallholding round The Mill House.

As I break off, very conscious of the thick glass window between us, I find myself wondering what Jim thinks of my way of earning a living compared with his. Out there in the keen east wind that has been left behind by the snow, the line of his jaw aching from the cold as he cuts down the tall cabbage plants for cattle forage, my life in contrast, leaning at this moment against the back of an arm-chair, in a warm parlour, must seem an 'easy number' as we used to call it in the Navy. In those days, in the mess, there were constant, raucous arguments over the arduousness of all manual labour compared with any sort of pen-pushing. Certainly when I was on watch at midnight in the port-director, and the atmosphere of those Arctic wastes was so many degrees below freezing point that I had long since lost all contact with the extremities of my limbs, I used to find my own convictions wavering. Could anything be worse than this, I used to tell myself, or, again, working on a farm, in all weathers?

Now that I am back again in Civvy Street, chained to my desk by invisible handcuffs, I am not so sure. I waver once more towards the pen-pushers, though I am also remembering Tinch, at this moment. But then Tinch is a girl, like Jim's bonny fair wife, whom I miss very much in the fields, in her breeches and leggings and bright shirt, the epitome of all land girls. Alas, she is no longer there, stooping at her husband's side, working the same hours, always at the beck and call of the Seasons. Instead, she is indoors, most of the day, minding the baby. So when occasionally she passes on her way to Mr. Clark's shop pushing the perambulator, for its afternoon's airing, and looking like any young matron in Lewes High Street, I have to suppress a desire to dash out and interview her on the doorstep as to her own inmost feelings. Which truly was the more arduous job, the more concentrated hard labour? Did she sometimes feel a prisoner now and long secretly to be back picking cabbages, and driving the cows to pasturage and milking them very early in the mornings? Or despite the excess of attention that her baby demands as its right, does she no longer envy Tinch her freedom, and, in her turn, her excess of fresh air?

Of course, Jim and Ada have never met Tinch, and would give me a very puzzled glance if I mentioned her name. Indeed, I only met her by chance myself when I went to spend a weekend last summer on a friend's farm, in the Kentish hop country. It was one of the few really golden patches of good weather, and as on the Sunday morning, my host and I sat in deck-chairs on the lawn, I am sure that the occupants of the buses, streaming past between Maidstone and Staplehurst, all came to the same conclusion: how very easy and pleasant life on a farm must be, and, my dear, just think of having really fresh eggs for breakfast. . . .

I discussed this with my host who is himself a pen-pusher, and has an extremely able ex-serviceman as manager for the farm. "Sometimes when I come home from the City, in the evening, completely whacked, I am longing for sympathy, and then I see Johnny's face, or Tinch comes into the kitchen, looking like a blackamoor, and I have the sense to keep my trap shut. The trouble about a farm is that it is so damnably greedy. . . ."

"You mean in running costs and machinery?"

"Well, I was thinking of man and woman-hours, but now that you mention it," Chris continued, "you'd better stay over Monday and see our new toy at work. It will give me an excellent excuse to take a day off myself. The City pavements are not very alluring in August."

Or at any other time, I thought, but was wise enough to keep my mouth shut, too. For are we not all the slaves of our own particular search for security?

The new toy turned out to be the very latest thing in combined harvesters, a colossal machine which seemed almost human, as I watched its ponderous, implacable progress across a fifteen acre field, first mowing down the heavy crop and then within its belly sorting the grain from the chaff, before sifting it into bags. Manufactured in Germany, resembling in some ways a giant tank, it gave one a strange sense of incongruity, a stabbing sensation almost of fear, awaiting its advance towards one across the stubble.

However, it was too burnished a day for such morbid comparisons. I tried to banish them by concentrating my thoughts, not on this ironic reminder of war within peace, but rather on the machine's driver, who greatly to my relief turned out to be no figure clad in battle-dress, no solid farm labourer, either, with muscles of whipcord; instead, a very striking looking girl with delicate features and the figure of an athlete. Tinch.

Everyone at The Cross and Hand Farm called her that, though her real name, I discovered with some difficulty, was Yvonne Hales-Finch. Now in a novel if your heroine was a genuine land girl, not just an undergraduate or a shop-girl having a summer holiday on a farm, you would never christen her that, would you, the author in me, still half-asleep, had mused that morning, at seven, when he made himself keep a tryst in the cow-shed. Here I found Tinch already at work. Dressed in a very business-like white coat, and most impersonally professional, she went from stall to stall, moving the milking machines, for a splendid herd of pedigree Guernseys. My companion had brought a portable radio into one corner of the shed. "Do they give more milk to music?" I asked. "Well, it seems to keep them quiet and happy," she replied with one of the rare smiles that lit up her rather solemn expression.

Indeed, I was not surprised to hear that this girl, in her early twenties, originally had been a probationer at East Grinstead Hospital.

For she had already reminded me unconsciously of a young nurse, going round the ward very early in the morning, taking the patients' temperatures, friendly but exceedingly firm. "Now, Mrs. Harrison, you really must wake up." Instead of giving someone's shoulder a shake, warning her that another day had dawned and had to be faced, she slapped, here and there, the buttocks of one of the herd that was inclined to be recalcitrant. I noticed, however, that once the milking taps were fixed on to their udders and the process had begun once again, they seemed, with placid resignation, to accept their destiny. Far more so than human beings. And how human were their names on the special charts. Diana, Duskie, Melody, Sandra, Gay Lass . . . and Flower, who lay isolated in a stall full of soft hay, not because she was ill, but because she was waiting for her first calf to be born. Was it my imagination or had she a rather superior expression on her face?

In the end, I decided that the really superior head belonged to Spencer the bull, a truly magnificent creature, peering over the door, across the yard, passionately intent on all the comings and goings, longing to be let out as much as Yasmie, Tinch's honey-coloured bull mastiff that inhabited another stall, next door to a young heifer. I visited them all in turn, but the only animals on a farm for whom I have never been able to conjure up any affection are the pigs: in their grunting eagerness to bolt their breakfast, they trampled in their troughs, a queasy sight.

Visiting another farm last summer, this time in Northumberland, and commenting on my allergy for the pigs, I found my host disagreeing with me violently. "Nonsense," he said. "Pigs are like human beings. Do you remember all the talk there used to be about every house having a bathroom? Sheer waste, the old, die-hard reactionaries used to say, holding up their hands in horror: you'll see, they'll all keep the coal in the bath. And did 'they'? And do 'they'? Of course not. I've heard you yourself holding forth many a time about how when you lived on the mess-decks in the war, you found the average matelot to be the cleanest animal in the world. That's because he'd been given a proper chance to be clean. The Navy sees to that, it is part of their tradition. Well, I give my pigs a proper chance, too, by turning them out to graze, like the rest of my cattle. And look at the difference. They've got proper breathing space. Why, you could bring one of my baby porkers into the drawing-room."

Though I felt that was something of an exaggeration, there was no doubt about the basis of truth in his main thesis. And now every time I have bacon for breakfast I remember his passionate diatribe and feel slightly guilty. For my allergy to the living creature remains.

After breakfast that morning at the Staplehurst farm—and how different food always tastes on a farm, something to do, I suppose, with the cutting out of the middleman—I went to watch the German tractor at work, the new toy of Johnnie, who used to handle British aircraft in the war, and now manages everyone and everything at The Cross and Hand, with a permanently friendly grin, and the kind of flaming enthusiasm that submits to no trade union laws. For him overtime is simply a question of finishing a job that must be 'in the bag' before he himself can think of having his supper and going to bed.

In a moment of schoolboy metamorphosis, I pleaded with Tinch to be allowed to drive her infernal machine, but I was soon regretting my brashness, for what with the din, the vibration and the extremely complicated manœuvring at the corners I began to perceive that the trained skill of a tractor driver had a super-human strain in its make-up. Nevertheless, hours later, Tinch herself was still in the driver's seat, without even a proper midday break, nobly supported by her 'mate', an attractive blonde in blue jeans, named Ann Johnston, who a month before had been serving in a grocer's shop, but had taken to the open air life, as to the manner born.

As long as there was any light left in the field, they went on together, stubbornly, remembering what the harvest would mean in feeding stuff for the animals in the coming winter. Then satisfied, at last, looking as Chris had said, a little like a blackamoor, Tinch returned to the main building to do the evening milking. Like her boss, Johnnie, she refused to sit down to her supper until that was done and the sheds cleaned out and washed down.

"Aren't you dead beat at the end of the day?" I asked wonderingly.

"Yes, I am," she admitted ,"but I feel fine again once I've had a wash, and it's lovely having my own cottage across the road. I wouldn't swap my life, anyway," she added with a sudden rush of warmth in her voice.

I looked at her curly dark hair now full of shafts of grain and filthy with dust. "What about your hair?" I persisted. "When does that get done?"

R

"Oh, if it rains . . . then sometimes I take an afternoon off, and pop into Maidstone . . . but I must get back for milking time."

Such a very simple sentence, so quietly spoken and yet it has stayed in my memory with far more significance than many of the grandiloquent phrases poured out to me at different times by self-important politicians and the presidents of industrial corporations. *I must get back for milking time.*

The snow has gone at last from the hills and this morning when I came into my writing-room it was to find a wider landscape, a greater brilliance of light shining upon my desk in the window that made me believe for a moment that the winter was over. But it was not so. It was simply that the great elm had vanished overnight from the border of the field opposite where every spring it has been a resting place for the starlings, every summer its shade has cast a shadow across the lawn in front of the house, and in an agreeable manner interfered with my view of the Downs. All the same, although I am conscious that old elms can prove to be dangerous enemies, I cannot help feeling a pang to see so gallant a tree lying low, its roots naked to the pale sky, its conquerors swarming over it with axes and saws.

No wonder there was a great soughing and sighing, as I lay in my bath this morning, postponing as long as I dared the hour of composition again. It came to me like a primeval cry for help, a sound unheard on land or sea, and I cowered down in the water, taking refuge behind the clouds of steam. Yet it was only the death-pains of one more tree falling to the ground. Something as ordinary, as much part of the countryside routine as that. How fearful the mind can become, when the spring of action is out of sight, I tell myself, watching the woodcutters go about their business, as slow and methodical in their movements, as professional grave-diggers.

First they lop off the light-weight twigs, of little use for burning: then they tackle the bigger branches, sawing and shaping them into lengths suitable for carting away and selling at a good price. Finally there is only the paternal trunk left, and this they use as their sitting-space, when quietly out of their pockets they bring their 'elevenses'; certainly they have well-earned their respite, since zero hour for the operation must have been soon after dawn. I notice that there are no young men among them. They all look old enough to be Jim's father:

perhaps older than that, several of them. Yet these veterans have already accomplished almost a full day's work. Is the art of woodcutting and tree-slaying a dying art like so many other country accomplishments? Do the sons, like the majority of the miners' children, emigrate to the cities, preferring any kind of job there? And what about the girls? Both those who performed such valiant service in the official Land Army in the war years, and those who, like Tinch, have chosen farming as their vocation today. (In the same way as other girls train to be models, or take courses in commercial French, or some other kind of diploma of value in the Labour Exchange, like the one that my niece obtained for herself recently, as a dietician.) Now that we are at peace again, how do the older farmers react to the idea of employing feminine cow-hands? I would like to be able to believe that they are all as happily placed as Tinch.

Of course, I have no idea how many girls are earning their living on British farms today—and I doubt if there are any official figures— but I have a sincere admiration both for those who performed such unglamorous tasks—and wore such an unglamorous walking-out uniform—during the State of Emergency, and for those who have volunteered since, having decided that with all its drawbacks, a life in the open is preferable to the slavish routine of working behind a counter in a shop, and strap-hanging to and fro from work. I think these young women have both courage and imagination. On the other hand, what I deplore is the stupid snobbishness of those parents who would rather that their daughter was exposed all day to the querulous and selfish nagging of the customers in some small business where there is little hope of advancement for her rather than that she should take a job in a modern factory, or as help to the over-worked wife in a higher wage-bracket family. Such social caste distinctions seem utterly unreal today. Yet strangely enough it is among the various strata of the middle classes that they persist and have their most stultifying effect. So that I felt very pleased and proud when I heard that my niece was enjoying hugely the practical cooking part of her course in an Oxford hospital. So much so that even after her diploma was achieved, she did not want to leave.

In the middle of it all, Jane came of age, and my elder brother and my sister-in-law gave a party in her honour. Whereupon Jane dashed up from her Oxford kitchens and appeared in a very lush white dress as though she had done nothing else in her life since leaving Cheltenham College, except perform the conventional *débutante* round. Yet how much happier she is because she had such a very different kind of existence, I decided, when the moment came for her to cut the cake and blow out her twenty-one candles. The keys of the door. It made me feel a bit of an old fogy to watch her, receiving the congratulations of all her contemporaries (some of whom looked exceedingly grown-up), still I enjoyed myself hugely.

There is supposed to be a great deterioration in manners today among the post-war youth: but personally I do not find it so. After all, some of us could not have seemed very exciting that evening to the school friends who were crowding round Jane: but they made us all feel, the uncles and aunts and elderly cousins, as though we had just been receiving the keys, too.

A few days after her party I took Jane out for a private celebration of our own. We went to the theatre and then we had supper together, and again I felt extremely proud of my niece because she made such a very pleasant companion for the evening. She talked well, without being self-conscious or trying to show off: equally important she listened well, without fidgeting or taking out her compactum every five minutes: best of all, she seemed genuinely interested in everything and everyone. And after I had deposited her at midnight again on the parental doorstep, I had to admit to myself that the generation of young women who have grown to maturity since the war are a splendid vintage.

Of course, there are thousands of others like Jane—and Tinch—who were only small children when the bombs fell on London and Coventry and Plymouth: yet somehow, whether they were evacuated to the farming countryside or not, came through unscathed and are now as alert and independent as their brothers, insisting on taking up a career when they leave school and keeping themselves on the proceeds: even if it means, as it often does, living in digs or a hostel, far from home.

Are they, on the whole, happier than their grandmothers were, who if they were not married at twenty-one, automatically stayed at home and helped with the domestic chores? Or is life more difficult for them, not so much where money as where standards of behaviour are concerned? All the complications of having to compete on equal terms with young men at work, and then in their off-duty hours, transform themselves into gentle and feminine creatures once again.

I know that the young women of today have the reputation of being very sophisticated and streamlined in their reactions, and utterly unshockable, into the bargain, but my own impression the evening I took my niece out—and I would suggest that she is absolutely average—was that underneath her façade she was just as ingenuous and uncertain of herself as her own mother had been at her age.

The truth is, the fundamental problems in the relationship between the sexes do not change across the years. There is still one law for men and another law for women. Emotional experience for a young man of twenty-one more often than not simply increases his adult stature and enhances his sex appeal; whereas for a girl it always and inevitably removes something of the bloom from her youth. That precious bloom, that dew on the grass which stays there such a brief, brief time.

I wanted to speak of these things to my niece the other night, but at the last moment I was too inhibited. Perhaps she will read this, perhaps she has already come to the realization of this truth but if she has, then she is one of the luckier members of her generation. For most girls of today seem under the impression that because they pass their 'Matric' or obtain a college degree and afterwards a well-paid job in the open market that they can compete with men on equal terms in private life, too, and not get their wings badly singed.

They can't: and that is why, if I had a daughter of the same age as Jane or Tinch I should try to be honest with her and say: "If you are searching for happiness, my dear . . . and we all are . . . do realize that though men may pretend to welcome you, as a co-partner at work, secretly our sex resent your emancipation and your success, in your career, most bitterly. We are so vain, as a sex, that we hate to admit that we are no longer your intellectual superiors, and out of working hours we are determined to prove to ourselves that we still have the whip hand."

It so happens that I myself am an ardent feminist. I have always enjoyed working side by side with women. I find my countrywomen on the whole far more conscientious than my own sex, and just as intelligent. I should like to see very many more women in key positions in industry. But I am very much aware that I am in a minority, and that it will take another hundred years, perhaps another thousand, before there is any real change of heart where the majority of my sex are concerned. At any rate, in this country.

Let me be completely honest. Englishmen are terrified of women with brains. A young man of twenty-one likes a girl who is what is called a bright talker, that is to say, someone who just babbles on about this and that, but he hates to be cornered by a woman in a cold-blooded, intellectual argument and will turn from her in disgust towards someone who gazes at him with blank, adoring eyes. Moreover, no matter how much a young woman may boast about her desire for independence the fact—another fact—remains that being married is still in this country considered the highest form of success for any girl, whatever her background, or her circumstances.

Again, I feel like making a personal protest, for many of the most memorable and fulfilled women that I have ever met have chosen to remain spinsters all their lives: nevertheless, there still remains a faint sneer inherent in that title, and so long as it is so, it is imperative that anyone's daughter, at the moment of having her keys placed in her hand, should make up her mind realistically, about certain things.

For instance she must realize, I would suggest, that when the male of the species is seeking a life-partner he admires a young woman who is strong and healthy far more than one who is merely beautiful. The impact of the advertisements on every page of every newspaper has warned him far too many times that the beauty may be only skin deep and diminish disastrously with closer contact. While it is as true today, as it was in our grandparents' time, that most Englishmen marry, first and foremost, for a home of their own, the passing-on of their heritage by the act of having children, plus the perpetuation of their mother's cooking.

Equally, it must be realized that the pursuing male puts the same price on his prospective mate as she puts on herself, and respects her accordingly: and that all through history, the women who have made the most successful alliances have been those who have been able to flatter their consort into believing himself to be twice the man he really is.

In short, no man can be flattered enough. Lay it on with a trowel. Let him wallow in it. Clever men and stupid men, young men and not so young, all alike are knock-overs for flattery of any kind. That may sound embarrassingly crude, obvious, even, but if that is so, why are there not more successful marriages? It is because few brides have troubled to learn this elementary lesson in masculine psychology.

Had I a daughter of twenty-one, there are other things, inconsequential though some of them may seem, that I would want to tell her, at this moment when she stands upon the threshold, and is assumed, officially, to be grown-up. But not so grown up that she does not still need a lot of sleep. Two nights a week in bed at ten-thirty. That would be my prescription. So many of the youngsters I know who are the daughters of my friends, look, most of the time, as though their eyes are propped open with matches. Indeed, I am convinced that half the nerviness of this age—and who will deny how nervy we all are these days—comes from a shortage of sleep. Though old enough to be Jane's father, I practise my own recipe, and also make a habit of spending, at least, one evening a week, in my own company.

There is an idea that if a female of marriageable age isn't 'dated', as it is called in America, every evening of the week, she is a social failure. That is nonsense, and barbarous nonsense, at that. We all need time, reassuring portions of solitude, to refill the reservoir: time to stand and stare, as the poet W. H. Davies has described it for all generations: time to get our bearings once again, and to think.

Of course, it is only too easy not to like what one does see when one stops quite still at last and becomes aware of all that is going on around one in the world today. It is easy, too, especially for the members of a new generation, to grow cynical and adopt a 'couldn't-care-less' attitude, though that gets one nowhere in the end, nowhere at all. Surely what is important is not what is wrong with the world, but what each one of us can do to try and put it right. And if I had the power to speak to all of Jane's school contemporaries, I would suggest that they made a start by giving up one evening a week to some kind of social work—the exact opposite of a social date—something constructive and positive, for a worth-while cause, such as helping to run a youth club, in the poorest part of their neighbourhood. Something unselfish, something unpaid, even if it is no more than acting as a baby-sitter so that the young married couple next door can go to the movies.

When I was Jane's age, the title we all aspired to earn was that of 'a good sport'. Today it surely matters more to be regarded as a 'good neighbour' and to have honourably earned that regard. For, after all, one can divide the world into two classes. Not rich or poor, not those who work with their hands and those who work with their pens, not those who talk with one accent, and those who talk with another. But the givers—and the grabbers.

In the final analysis it is as simple as that, and I have a feeling that Jane, like Tinch, is a giver. I am very glad. For that is the key which opens most doors to contentment in the long run.

When I reached the end of the chapter, and looked up at the backcloth of the world outside which I had forgotten existed, it was to find that the long field was empty of figures and that the last load of wood had gone rumbling down the lane. I had been too intent all afternoon to notice their progress and their departure or to salute them, as I salute Jim. I shall miss the faces of the woodmen tomorrow, carved and coloured from their own bark. But Jim will be back in his domain and soon, surely now, the evenings will lengthen out over the hills, my book will be finished, and I shall be able to come up for breath.

It is strange that I should feel as weary as if I have been on a route march, I record, as Carrie comes softly into the room to close the shutters and to make me comfortable for the evening's session. She fusses at the hearth and throws a couple of logs on to the fire. "A pity they had to cart all that wood away, instead of letting us have our pick first," she clucks, with the unanswerable logic of the countrywoman.

Now she is standing at the window in front of my desk, silhouetted against the dusk, a small, indomitable figure, with her dark eyes full of affection for the uncorrupted landscape. "I wonder what the starlings will do." She speaks as though we are discussing a neighbour's lease that has unexpectedly fallen in, yet there is something in her tone that reminds me that she has known that tree herself for close on forty years, and already she had the keys when she came in service to The Mill House. Has the cutting down, the day's sacrificial rites had too great a personal significance for her? I seek to comfort but once again, it is the other way round.

"I am giving you a cheese soufflé for supper, and the water is quite hot if you want a bath," she says. I lean back, luxuriating, at the prospect. It is a very pleasant moment, snatched from an inexorable time-table. Has Tinch turned on the radio for the milking yet, I think.

NINETEEN

THE HOUSEWIVES OF THE NEW ESTATE

THERE is always a moment when I know that I am home. Home from the City. It happens, strangely enough, just after I have passed the new factories, all glass and delicate steel, still lit and glittering in the darkness like some later film conception of Metropolis. That is as you come up the hill from Patcham to the cross-roads, leading one way to Brighton, the other to Ditchling Beacon, the third down the hill again, with the noble beeches of Falmer Park to the left, and to the right, a carpet of stars, the modest, welcoming lights of the new Coldean Estate.

As we turn over the crest of the hill, and slow our speed down the narrower lane, that is the moment when Bardwell and I are both very conscious that we are home. My driver, who has at last got a newly built bungalow of his own nearby for his wife and little girl, always makes the same comment. "The lights look pretty at night, don't they?" And I always make the same reply. "Yes, they do." No more than that, and yet so much more I have always felt, right from the day when we first came to have a stake in the Sussex village where I have found, so happily, a working retreat.

For in the beginning, our beginning, nearly four years ago now, there was nothing else. That is to say, nothing past the Public House at the corner of Coldean Lane, and the first line of houses on the roadway itself, already established as old residents. Beyond those outposts, where the hill began to climb sharply, there were simply the relics of an old farm, round which a team of bull-dozers were beginning to create a pattern of furious upheaval, interspersed with quiet groups of men in city clothes, pacing now this way, now that, rulers and tape measures, their insignia.

So I have been able to watch the blue-print come to life before my eyes: the walls and roofs, the roads, with their agreeably conventional names like Beatty Avenue, the carefully spaced out grass plateaux of this garden suburb have grown week by week, while we ourselves have reluctantly passed over the hill on our way to join the London Road, returning always corroded, spent, and sometimes defeated at the end of the week. For me, therefore, it has been a strong source of reassurance to think of all the families, nearly a thousand of them all told, moving not so much, month by month, as road, by road into this latest conception in housing estates, planned by a most enlightened Council that has set a post-war example to the whole country in the speed, goodwill and vision it has shown in tackling its own problems in the Brighton area. Nor has it been difficult for me to visualize each time I reach the last lap of my own homeward journey just what this transformation of the landscape must mean to all the young married couples who have never had a home of their own before but have had to exist in intolerably crowded close quarters, often in slum-condemned property, with other people's chattels, and other people's codes of living. "It is true that we had three rooms for myself, my husband and the two children," one young housewife was to tell me later, "but our landlord forbade us, with the threat of eviction, to pull the lavatory plug we shared with him after ten-thirty at night. He said it disturbed his rest."

I had been disturbed myself, in rather a different way. My imagination had been captured by what architecturally was the crowning glory of the estate, though it lay low down in the converging centre point of all the ancillary roads, its vast expanse of window space catching every drop of the sun's rays. A sanatorium? A community hall? A very modern church? How easy it would be to guess were it not that once upon a time council schools too often looked like prisons so that it was not surprising if their scholars crawled towards them as sluggishly and as unwillingly as snails. However, this was no prison. With its encouragingly modern silhouette, and its passionate absorption of light from every angle, it made me secretly long to have the right to enter there myself and, either as pupil or teacher, to play some part in such an imaginative evocation of all the progress that has been made, despite another crippling interlude of war, in the last decade.

Was I over-dramatizing the outward splendour of that streamlined façade? Would I be cruelly disappointed if I ever ventured within? That doubt, I admit, sometimes pressed in on me, even as every time we drove by I found something new, externally, to admire.

The clever manner in which each fresh road of houses was constructed on a different level, carved from the hill-side, so that there was no echo, no faint shadow of the over-familiar mass uniformity. Again, I was much struck by the different colour washes used for the front doors. A real challenge to convention. But behind those gay entrances what would I find? The same ingrained prejudices, the same pockets of isolation that have in the past driven many young housewives almost to suicide? The Suburban Blues. It isn't really the title for a dance tune but instead a very real malaise of the spirit, symptomatic of our Age.

And then, one morning, among my post, I received a letter written on a school exercise book, and headed: 'Coldean Young Wives' Group'. Would I come and address them any Wednesday night, on any subject I liked to choose? The meetings took place in the Assembly Hall of the Primary School. I am afraid it was that which decided me: the promise of being inside that tantalizing building at last, and it proved a most rewarding experience. I only hope my audience enjoyed the evening as much as I did.

In a way it was the strangest setting where I have ever found myself addressing any audience. There was such a contrast between the external and the internal mood. Inside that huge room, in a semicircle on the pale blue chairs that matched the pastel shade of one long wall, they sat politely awaiting my arrival, knitting. As long as I kept my eyes fixed upon their berets, it was like addressing a Women's Institute meeting: the moment my gaze travelled beyond their heads, either to the far wall that could magically disappear to disclose a wide stage, or to the huge expanse of glass that took up the whole of the left side, it was as though I had taken off, in a dream, and landed upon Mars. But not afterwards: not when the padre's wife took me from group to group, introducing me. Then I was right back on earth again.

Here was a wife who told me she was up at five-thirty every morning to get her husband off in time for his shift. "But I go back to bed afterwards." Here was a buxom young woman who confided she was only able to be there that evening because her husband, being a telephone engineer, had been able to fix up an ingenious arrangement of wires that would project her baby's crying—if it happened—right into her next door neighbour's house and they would rush in to the rescue. Yet a third complained that though the hot water system in her new home worked off the back of the sitting-room fire she was spending ten shillings a week on Coalite, which on top of the rent of twenty-eight shillings a week and her husband's bus fares to work and hers into Brighton every time she went to shop made her budgeting such an eternal, nerve-wracking struggle that all her original pleasure in having a brand new home of her own had long since been swallowed up in the problem of ways and means. "And to think that we were so anxious to get in, that we moved our furniture before the builders had moved out," she exclaimed.

Nevertheless her point of view was a minority one that night. Almost everyone to whom I spoke after my talk expressed most touching and overwhelming delight in their new circumstances, and had nothing but enthusiasm for the blossoming life of the community. This was a beginning. They were a happy band of pioneers. One day they would have a church of their own. A proper playing field for the older children. Meanwhile, this room made a focusing point. One night the youth club met, another night they had a cinema show, for the price of eightpence a head, on Sunday mornings Father Bess held a service with his portable altar laid out on a trestle table.

"And do many come?" I asked.

"About the same as for your talk. It varies, of course, from Sunday to Sunday. Sometimes there is only a handful." We were both silent for a moment, both perhaps sharing the same thought, how Christ had never worried how few were in His audience. "But most of my work is done during the week," he added, after a pause. His voice had a cheerful not an apologetic tone.

"Canvassing from house to house?"

"Yes, I suppose you could call it that. In a new community like this we are all equally strangers at first to one another. It is not like taking over from another vicar. We've had to start from scratch, and I am finding one gets reactions in surprising quarters."

"And surprising reactions, too," I suggested. At least, surprising to me. For Mrs. Bess, who did not look in the least like the traditional conception of 'the parson's wife' but had presided over my meeting in a smart grey costume and with great charm of manner, had told me that sometimes they were met with waves of active hostility. Not directed at themselves, but at what they represented. "It isn't simply that some of the new residents are merely indifferent. Their agnosticism is mixed up with a suspicion, a very deep suspicion that we are trying to poke our noses into their private lives, like official

was chosen, in the Festival of Britain, as being a most
strialized village. For it has succeeded in preserving
despite the encroachment of so-called progress. Walking
rectory to the meeting, we passed the church which dates
twelfth century, and possesses that type of square, Nor-
tower that always gives one a sense of security and of
uity of the pattern. "The pyramid over there is the Stanton
rks," my host explained. I looked from one to the other
vo dark silhouettes and I remembered that another shadow,
ow of the H-bomb was slowly obliterating the peace of
f the whole world. Where were we heading? What would
say if He came back to the world today and beheld the sorry use
e had made of the free will that was supposed to lift us above
asts in the fields?

did not ask those questions aloud that night. But afterwards
pectedly I received an answer. We had returned to the rectory,
children were safely asleep and we gathered, the rector and his
e and their guest for the night, in front of the fire, having a night-
p of coffee and cheese straws. It was a very peaceful, relaxed hour. Now
y hostess had not been off her feet since the early morning. Now
e sat on the floor, with her back against a chair, warming her
ands at the last precious piece of coal. I thought how striking was
er profile in the firelight. And again, not in the least like old *Punch*
cartoons of the parson's wife. From the moment of our first introduction to each other, I had been struck by her vivid colouring and that
particular variety of strong, black hair that at an early age is becomingly
flecked with grey.

The Jones seemed like any other young married couple bearing
their name, at the end of a long day, and I was curious suddenly to
know how they had met and how he had persuaded her to accept a
future so lacking in any prospects of financial ease. "I first saw Betty,"
my host confessed, "when I was a theological student at a college outside Cardiff. One day in my lunch hour she drove past me at the wheel
of an old car. She was so pretty, I found myself smiling at her, instinctively. I wasn't sure whether she noticed me or not. Then a
few days later, the same thing happened, and I saw the car slow down
round the next corner. I followed, and she had gone into a café for
lunch. I decided it was worth the last shilling in my pocket, so I

The padre's wife
with Elizabeth
and Christopher

The School

The two small
blonde daughters
of Mrs. Kirby

Mrs. Crawford's house was twice the size of the others

Mrs. Standing: "I don't know what we'd have done without the neighbours"

snoopers coming round an
A legacy of the war years,
because he hopes in time they
Used to his athletic figure
When he joined us on the Wea
biscuits interval, I was much st
and his very firm handshake. He
rugger forward, in full training: a
and just the right type, one felt instinc
roots were not yet deeply dug and
ahead. My heart had warmed to him an
younger than her thirty-two years, and w
Dartford to set up their standard in a se
bottom of Coldean Lane, a few yards away
board in the front garden headed CHURC
times of Sunday services in the school. It had
sundial.

Now it was Saturday morning, and he and
in the Assembly Hall, looking out through the gr
two possible sites for the church that was still bu
My companion pointed away to a little hill on the
been offered that site," he said, "or there is the old bar
Coldean Lane. It might be possible to convert that as a
tackled it, I am afraid the roof, picturesque though it is
to come off."

"You know what would be a wonderful idea," I heard my
"If all the householders on the estate who happen to be pl
electricians, engineers or carpenters by trade or just labourer
of their hire would give up their weekends, and the long
evenings, to build you a church. It would be really and trul
church then. It might make a hell of a difference even to the
pockets of don't care, non-believers in anything except the re
of their weekly wage packets."

He smiled broadly. I don't know whether it was at my languag
or at the apparent impracticability of my suggestion. Yet in actua
fact I had heard tidings of just such an experiment when, a fortnight
before, I had been the guest of a country rector in Nottinghamshire,
invited by him to speak in a Lenten series organized in his village hall.

*   *   *   *

Trowell
typical, ind
its rural air
from the R
back to th
manesque
the perpe
Iron Wo
of the t
the shad
mind o
Christ
that w
the b
I
unex
the
wif
ca
M
sl
l

The padre's wife
with Elizabeth
and Christopher

The School

The two small
blonde daughters
of Mrs. Kirby

Mrs. Crawford's house was twice the size of the others

Mrs. Standing: "I don't know what we'd have done without the neighbours"

snoopers coming round and asking questions from door to door. A legacy of the war years, I suppose. But my husband perseveres because he hopes in time they will get used to him."

Used to his athletic figure always dressed in a black cassock. When he joined us on the Wednesday evening, during the tea and biscuits interval, I was much struck by his strong masculine air, and his very firm handshake. He had the outward appearance of a rugger forward, in full training: a muscular and militant Christian and just the right type, one felt instinctively, for a community whose roots were not yet deeply dug and whose social history still lay ahead. My heart had warmed to him and his wife, who looked much younger than her thirty-two years, and who had come with him from Dartford to set up their standard in a semi-detached house at the bottom of Coldean Lane, a few yards away from the pub, with a small board in the front garden headed CHURCH HOUSE, giving the times of Sunday services in the school. It had taken the place of the sundial.

Now it was Saturday morning, and he and I were standing alone in the Assembly Hall, looking out through the great windows, at the two possible sites for the church that was still but a hopeful dream. My companion pointed away to a little hill on the right. "We have been offered that site," he said, "or there is the old barn down there by Coldean Lane. It might be possible to convert that as a start, but if we tackled it, I am afraid the roof, picturesque though it is, would have to come off."

"You know what would be a wonderful idea," I heard myself saying, "If all the householders on the estate who happen to be plumbers or electricians, engineers or carpenters by trade or just labourers worthy of their hire would give up their weekends, and the long summer evenings, to build you a church. It would be really and truly *their* church then. It might make a hell of a difference even to the little pockets of don't care, non-believers in anything except the reality of their weekly wage packets."

He smiled broadly. I don't know whether it was at my language or at the apparent impracticability of my suggestion. Yet in actual fact I had heard tidings of just such an experiment when, a fortnight before, I had been the guest of a country rector in Nottinghamshire, invited by him to speak in a Lenten series organized in his village hall.

*　　　*　　　*　　　*　　　*

Trowell was chosen, in the Festival of Britain, as being a most typical, industrialized village. For it has succeeded in preserving its rural air despite the encroachment of so-called progress. Walking from the Rectory to the meeting, we passed the church which dates back to the twelfth century, and possesses that type of square, Normanesque tower that always gives one a sense of security and of the perpetuity of the pattern. "The pyramid over there is the Stanton Iron Works," my host explained. I looked from one to the other of the two dark silhouettes and I remembered that another shadow, the shadow of the H-bomb was slowly obliterating the peace of mind of the whole world. Where were we heading? What would Christ say if He came back to the world today and beheld the sorry use that we had made of the free will that was supposed to lift us above the beasts in the fields?

I did not ask those questions aloud that night. But afterwards unexpectedly I received an answer. We had returned to the rectory, the children were safely asleep and we gathered, the rector and his wife and their guest for the night, in front of the fire, having a nightcap of coffee and cheese straws. It was a very peaceful, relaxed hour. My hostess had not been off her feet since the early morning. Now she sat on the floor, with her back against a chair, warming her hands at the last precious piece of coal. I thought how striking was her profile in the firelight. And again, not in the least like old *Punch* cartoons of the parson's wife. From the moment of our first introduction to each other, I had been struck by her vivid colouring and that particular variety of strong, black hair that at an early age is becomingly flecked with grey.

The Jones seemed like any other young married couple bearing their name, at the end of a long day, and I was curious suddenly to know how they had met and how he had persuaded her to accept a future so lacking in any prospects of financial ease. "I first saw Betty," my host confessed, "when I was a theological student at a college outside Cardiff. One day in my lunch hour she drove past me at the wheel of an old car. She was so pretty, I found myself smiling at her, instinctively. I wasn't sure whether she noticed me or not. Then a few days later, the same thing happened, and I saw the car slow down round the next corner. I followed, and she had gone into a café for lunch. I decided it was worth the last shilling in my pocket, so I

I had a sudden memory of the chilblains which made it scarcely possible for me to hold a pen when I was first sent away at Christopher's age to boarding school, on the Norfolk coast, so bleak in winter: and later, at Hereford Cathedral School, the sick feeling of horror and dread each time I had to brace myself to cross the quadrangle towards the set of privies in a row, all without a door. You learnt to take your own piece of yesterday's newspaper with you, and you prayed silently that you would find the one in the far corner vacant. No ordeal I have ever had to endure in later life was as bad as that, I thought. And yet none of the parents complained at such barbarousness. In those days, the system was accepted as being quite ordinary.

"From the moment that the children come to school, after breakfast, till they leave again at three-thirty," Mr. Brown was saying, "there is no need for them, if it is a wet day, to go out of doors. Everything is here for them, including their dinner, under one roof."

To my astonishment I discovered that not only did each classroom possess its own set of wash-basins, with pegs for the children's towels, which they took away at the end of each week to be laundered at home, but also their own little group of lavatories, painted in shiny pink or blue, to separate the boys and girls.

"They couldn't have better conditions if they had a suite at the Savoy," I suggested. "Do the kids appreciate it?"

"Some of them do, some of them have to be taught. Some of them, again, make you wonder what happens at home. But I keep a very strict watch. It comes in waves. Not so long ago, I suddenly found myself in the middle of an epidemic of messes, and I was determined to find out who was the culprit. Then one day I caught him. The headmaster sent for his mother and when she came it was explained that Tommy—that wasn't his name, by the way—didn't seem to have been house-trained. Do you know what she said? 'I was wondering how Tommy would manage in the toilets. You see, he always has a pot at home.' And mind you, the lad was turned six!"

We had reached the form room of the youngest children who first take the plunge when they are five and stay in the primary school, side by side with their sisters, till they are eleven. It didn't seem like a classroom, as I remembered it, at all. There were miniature chairs and furniture like something out of a Walt Disney film. And on a table, in a prize position, a tank filled with glittering, iridescent

went in and ordered the cheapest thing on the menu. Yes, I sat down at her table, and that was how it began."

She gazed into the dying embers, and her eyes reflected their brightness. "We were married when I was nineteen. That's thirteen years ago, and for seven of those years, my husband was an Army padre, and I followed him around living in a suitcase . . . that is, when he wasn't taking part in the landings at Sicily or Salerno, or on manoeuvres in the desert."

"Or conducting a service for the native population in Delhi." He took up the story again. "In a way that was my most exciting memory of the war. The church was packed, and someone translated my sermon sentence by sentence. Afterwards I was allowed to shake hands with every member of the congregation. I really felt I did some good that day."

"And you don't regret it, either of you?" I asked. "If you both had to go back, would you choose the same road, all over again?"

They looked at each other with a deep tenderness, and I knew that my challenge had been utterly superfluous. A moment later I was receiving my answer to the other question that had troubled me earlier in the evening. A very different sort of question. A kind of *montage* in my mind with the figure of Christ nailed to the Cross, and a cloud behind His head, a great deal larger than a man's hand. The symbol of the H-bomb.

Did we deserve that the whole universe should go up in smoke because of our indifference and our apathy? I had spoken that evening in the village hall, of tolerance, because it seemed to me that that was a theme suitable for a layman, living in an age when man's inhumanity to man had never been more bitterly pronounced, and now, in that sudden mood of intimacy which is sometimes engendered between fellow pilgrims, I confessed to my new friends how earlier in the day I had been to see my mother lying ill in hospital, and how she had suddenly managed to raise her voice above a whisper to exclaim: "If you are going to talk about tolerance tonight, remember to tell your audience that tolerance isn't indifference but understanding and *active* crusading."

It was then that the Rector of Trowell mentioned the Hall of another housing estate that was being built this time at Clifton, outside Nottingham. One day a meeting was held of all the householders who by chance had come to live together and at that meeting there were none of the usual complaints that are voiced when tenants assemble *en masse* to discuss what amenities are lacking. Instead, all the artisans and all the technicians volunteered to give their services freely to build one more house on the estate, not included in the original plan: a house set apart and many times larger than the rest: a house for God.

"I have found," my host that night said quietly, "that always like a sign, at a moment of doubt and anxiety about the state of the world's conscience, there comes a gesture like that, something both practical and positive to make one believe all over again in the essential goodness of human nature: that the world is still worth saving and there are more people trying to live like Christ than one would imagine from the headings in the newspapers. What a pity that the story I have told you isn't considered front page news."

His words came back to me that Saturday morning, in the school Hall at Coldean, and I found myself wishing that the two disciples of Christ, so different in physical appearance, so spiritually attuned, could meet and exchange commands for a brief while. Then Mr. Bess would have the comfort of a church in which to preach on Sundays, and Mr. Jones could tell the tenants of Coldean about the spontaneous offer that had been made upon that other housing estate outside Nottingham. Moreover, the padres' wives would find, too, I thought, how much they possessed in common, beside their heritage. Almost exactly the same age, both radiated the same quiet air of steady purpose, an aura of being at peace with themselves though there was nothing in the least smug about either of them. Indeed, if you met them shopping in your High Street, you would never imagine that they were dedicated human beings, although you might remark upon their very sweet smiles. Again, both women have three children to care for in their own homes, two boys with a girl sandwiched in between, and in each case one of the boys has been christened after the patron saint of travellers.

The Bess's Christopher came trotting into the Assembly Hall, at that moment, his face sprinkled with freckles, a sturdy small figure in his neat green blazer and school stockings with their matching green tops. From under a thatch of ginger hair he stared up at the stranger to his world with a veiled and wary but not unfriendly look. I was about to ask where he had inherited his colouring, and then I remembered that he was a foster-child whose seven years of life had

possessed no real security, no proper family background till he had come to live at the corner of Coldean Lane.

"Are you going to show us your classroom?" I suggested.

The boy was delighted and ran ahead of us from room to room. As I followed with his foster-parent he told me that although Christopher had been a difficult child to handle at first, automatically lying in the face of authority or when invited to give a direct answer to any straight question, he was devoted to the other two children in the Bess household. "He will do anything for our little girl, Elizabeth, or the baby Martin. I think they give him a sense of belonging even more than we do."

We had reached the headmaster's study, the only room I did not care for, in the whole building. Here functionalism, at its best in the layout of the larger rooms, the corridors and the washing facilities had failed badly: the atmosphere was cold and arid; a bleak little room, without any redeeming softness: no friendly bookcases: no sense of any Alma Mater: just a plain flat desk and one upright chair. Strangely, too, this sanctum seemed to lack all personality like the waiting-room for the parents next door.

"Christopher knows this room too well, don't you?" his foster-parent joked.

"He is not here so often these days, are you though, Christopher?" We had been joined by Mr. Brown the caretaker, a middle-aged man with glasses and the country of his birth stamped all over his comfortable figure. I took an instant liking to him. He was neither subservient nor officious. I felt he was even tempered, trustworthy, a gentle kind of man. He said, at once. "I understand what you feel about this room, but the answer is, I think, the headmaster is so seldom in it. He is always on the move, always about the school somewhere, usually with two or three youngsters tugging at his coat-tails. But he never seems to mind. He is wonderfully patient with them all."

"And the parents, too," I suggested.

"And the parents too," Mr. Brown agreed.

A moment later he was showing me his own pride and joy: a typical section of the 'toilets'. He was equally proud of the coil system of heating, thermostatically controlled, which kept all the classrooms and all the corridors at the same even temperature throughout and had entirely obliterated those ice-cold pockets that used to be the feature of all schools, however expensive their fees, in my youth.

went in and ordered the cheapest thing on the menu. Yes, I sat down at her table, and that was how it began."

She gazed into the dying embers, and her eyes reflected their brightness. "We were married when I was nineteen. That's thirteen years ago, and for seven of those years, my husband was an Army padre, and I followed him around living in a suitcase . . . that is, when he wasn't taking part in the landings at Sicily or Salerno, or on manoeuvres in the desert."

"Or conducting a service for the native population in Delhi." He took up the story again. "In a way that was my most exciting memory of the war. The church was packed, and someone translated my sermon sentence by sentence. Afterwards I was allowed to shake hands with every member of the congregation. I really felt I did some good that day."

"And you don't regret it, either of you?" I asked. "If you both had to go back, would you choose the same road, all over again?"

They looked at each other with a deep tenderness, and I knew that my challenge had been utterly superfluous. A moment later I was receiving my answer to the other question that had troubled me earlier in the evening. A very different sort of question. A kind of *montage* in my mind with the figure of Christ nailed to the Cross, and a cloud behind His head, a great deal larger than a man's hand. The symbol of the H-bomb.

Did we deserve that the whole universe should go up in smoke because of our indifference and our apathy? I had spoken that evening in the village hall, of tolerance, because it seemed to me that that was a theme suitable for a layman, living in an age when man's inhumanity to man had never been more bitterly pronounced, and now, in that sudden mood of intimacy which is sometimes engendered between fellow pilgrims, I confessed to my new friends how earlier in the day I had been to see my mother lying ill in hospital, and how she had suddenly managed to raise her voice above a whisper to exclaim: "If you are going to talk about tolerance tonight, remember to tell your audience that tolerance isn't indifference but understanding and *active* crusading."

It was then that the Rector of Trowell mentioned the Hall of another housing estate that was being built this time at Clifton, outside Nottingham. One day a meeting was held of all the householders who by chance had come to live together and at that meeting there were none of the usual complaints that are voiced when tenants assemble *en masse* to discuss what amenities are lacking. Instead, all the artisans and all the technicians volunteered to give their services freely to build one more house on the estate, not included in the original plan: a house set apart and many times larger than the rest: a house for God.

"I have found," my host that night said quietly, "that always like a sign, at a moment of doubt and anxiety about the state of the world's conscience, there comes a gesture like that, something both practical and positive to make one believe all over again in the essential goodness of human nature: that the world is still worth saving and there are more people trying to live like Christ than one would imagine from the headings in the newspapers. What a pity that the story I have told you isn't considered front page news."

His words came back to me that Saturday morning, in the school Hall at Coldean, and I found myself wishing that the two disciples of Christ, so different in physical appearance, so spiritually attuned, could meet and exchange commands for a brief while. Then Mr. Bess would have the comfort of a church in which to preach on Sundays, and Mr. Jones could tell the tenants of Coldean about the spontaneous offer that had been made upon that other housing estate outside Nottingham. Moreover, the padres' wives would find, too, I thought, how much they possessed in common, beside their heritage. Almost exactly the same age, both radiated the same quiet air of steady purpose, an aura of being at peace with themselves though there was nothing in the least smug about either of them. Indeed, if you met them shopping in your High Street, you would never imagine that they were dedicated human beings, although you might remark upon their very sweet smiles. Again, both women have three children to care for in their own homes, two boys with a girl sandwiched in between, and in each case one of the boys has been christened after the patron saint of travellers.

The Bess's Christopher came trotting into the Assembly Hall, at that moment, his face sprinkled with freckles, a sturdy small figure in his neat green blazer and school stockings with their matching green tops. From under a thatch of ginger hair he stared up at the stranger to his world with a veiled and wary but not unfriendly look. I was about to ask where he had inherited his colouring, and then I remembered that he was a foster-child whose seven years of life had

possessed no real security, no proper family background till he h
come to live at the corner of Coldean Lane.

"Are you going to show us your classroom?" I suggested.

The boy was delighted and ran ahead of us from room to room. As
followed with his foster-parent he told me that although Christophe
had been a difficult child to handle at first, automatically lying in
the face of authority or when invited to give a direct answer to any
straight question, he was devoted to the other two children in the
Bess household. "He will do anything for our little girl, Elizabeth,
or the baby Martin. I think they give him a sense of belonging even
more than we do."

We had reached the headmaster's study, the only room I did not
care for, in the whole building. Here functionalism, at its best in
the layout of the larger rooms, the corridors and the washing facilities
had failed badly: the atmosphere was cold and arid; a bleak little
room, without any redeeming softness: no friendly bookcases: no
sense of any Alma Mater: just a plain flat desk and one upright chair.
Strangely, too, this sanctum seemed to lack all personality like the
waiting-room for the parents next door.

"Christopher knows this room too well, don't you?" his foster-
parent joked.

"He is not here so often these days, are you though, Christopher?"
We had been joined by Mr. Brown the caretaker, a middle-aged man
with glasses and the country of his birth stamped all over his comfortable figure. I took an instant liking to him. He was neither subservient
nor officious. I felt he was even tempered, trustworthy, a gentle kind of
man. He said, at once. "I understand what you feel about this room,
but the answer is, I think, the headmaster is so seldom in it. He is
always on the move, always about the school somewhere, usually with
two or three youngsters tugging at his coat-tails. But he never seems
to mind. He is wonderfully patient with them all."

"And the parents, too," I suggested.

"And the parents too," Mr. Brown agreed.

A moment later he was showing me his own pride and joy: a
typical section of the 'toilets'. He was equally proud of the coil system
of heating, thermostatically controlled, which kept all the classrooms
and all the corridors at the same even temperature throughout and
had entirely obliterated those ice-cold pockets that used to be the
feature of all schools, however expensive their fees, in my youth.

I had a sudden memory of the chilblains which made it scarcely possible for me to hold a pen when I was first sent away at Christopher's age to boarding school, on the Norfolk coast, so bleak in winter: and later, at Hereford Cathedral School, the sick feeling of horror and dread each time I had to brace myself to cross the quadrangle towards the set of privies in a row, all without a door. You learnt to take your own piece of yesterday's newspaper with you, and you prayed silently that you would find the one in the far corner vacant. No ordeal I have ever had to endure in later life was as bad as that, I thought. And yet none of the parents complained at such barbarousness. In those days, the system was accepted as being quite ordinary.

"From the moment that the children come to school, after break-fast, till they leave again at three-thirty," Mr. Brown was saying, "there is no need for them, if it is a wet day, to go out of doors. Everything is here for them, including their dinner, under one roof."

To my astonishment I discovered that not only did each class-room possess its own set of wash-basins, with pegs for the children's towels, which they took away at the end of each week to be laundered at home, but also their own little group of lavatories, painted in shiny pink or blue, to separate the boys and girls.

"They couldn't have better conditions if they had a suite at the Savoy," I suggested. "Do the kids appreciate it?"

"Some of them do, some of them have to be taught. Some of them, again, make you wonder what happens at home. But I keep a very strict watch. It comes in waves. Not so long ago, I suddenly found myself in the middle of an epidemic of messes, and I was determined to find out who was the culprit. Then one day I caught him. The headmaster sent for his mother and when she came it was explained that Tommy—that wasn't his name, by the way—didn't seem to have been house-trained. Do you know what she said? 'I was wondering how Tommy would manage in the toilets. You see, he always has a pot at home.' And mind you, the lad was turned six!"

We had reached the form room of the youngest children who first take the plunge when they are five and stay in the primary school, side by side with their sisters, till they are eleven. It didn't seem like a classroom, as I remembered it, at all. There were miniature chairs and furniture like something out of a Walt Disney film. And on a table, in a prize position, a tank filled with glittering, iridescent fish. "That's a great feature of *our* school," Mr. Brown said. "You'll see tanks of tame fish everywhere." Each wall was a different colour: light-hearted, freshly washed. In one corner there was a Wendy hut, full of dolls, a blackamoor among them, and here, it was explained, the girls were instructed in the elements of home-making. In another corner, there was a sandpit for the boys.

As soon as summer came the windows would be opened wide, and on every possible day there would be a general exodus of classes on to the green verge outside, leaving behind the brilliant posters on the wall which informed me that 'Monday is Washing Day, Tuesday is Ironing Day, Wednesday is Baking Day, Thursday is Cleaning Day, Friday is Shopping Day.'

They should have added Sunday is Cooking Day, I decided, a morning of ceremonial dedication to the joint that will be served up in varying forms and lessening substantiality on Monday, Tuesday, and perhaps, Wednesday. But on Sunday, still in its pristine glory, it must be watched over tenderly like a new baby whose novelty value has not yet worn thin, and, in consequence, it is a considerable relief to be able to dispatch the other children to morning Sunday School. "We have a tremendous turn out in the Assembly Hall," the padre announced with rightful pride, though, at the same time, giving just and due praise to the off-stage presence of the joint, and to the on-stage presence of the Biology Mistress from Roedean, who, for a few hours, slips away from that red-brick fortress, on the front at Brighton, which is one of the last strongholds of privilege, where education is concerned. From there each Sunday morning, Miss Thompson travels the four miles—but what frontiers she crosses—to the Primary School at Coldean, where she tells the infants Bible stories far removed from the terminology of the exact science she teaches the rest of the week. Was her spirit refreshed? Was this for her the outlet that we all seek in some form or other? I thought of all the other volunteers like her, in this cause and that, who do so much positive good in the world, of their own volition, and are never known outside their own small circle, never front-page news, and thinking, I found myself eager now to know more and more about this kingdom beyond the boundaries of my own world.

"It must be a great help for the mothers also being able to park their children for lunch at school on weekdays. How much do they pay?" As I spoke I noticed that Mr. Brown and the padre exchanged a

significant glance. A moment later, I understood why. Lunches had
gone up to ninepence, and, in consequence, less than two hundred of
the five hundred and sixty-five pupils stayed behind regularly, after
morning lessons. Only on Fridays, was there much of a mustering.
"Most of the husbands get their pay packets on Thursday nights," the
padre explained, "and on Fridays the wives take a bus into Brighton to
do the weekend shopping. Wednesdays and Thursdays are very tight
days for nearly every household on the estate. I remember last summer,
when a Coronation Tea was being put up for the youngsters the
organizer had a brain wave. She went and stood beside the counter,
when all the wives on Tuesday were drawing their Family Allowances,
and asked them for their small contribution there and then. Otherwise,
she would never have got her accounts straight."

It was a simple parable of modern life. Although I had deliberately
chosen to be shown over the school, when it was empty of pupils,
so that I could concentrate on its architectural innovations, I felt at
that moment very close to the beating heart of the community.
For almost everyone, I thought, life in the end is reduced to sums of
arithmetic and you could divide the housewives of the world into
the managers and the muddlers. But how few men would ever
accomplish all that they did on their weekly budgets, I had to admit to
myself.

Certainly young Christopher was a good advertisement, both for
his school, and his foster-home. "Which do you prefer?" I asked him
now. "To lunch at school, or at home?"

He had no doubts. "At home," he answered briskly.

"Because you feel more at home there?"

He shook his head. "Because I get more," he said.

Delighted with our laughter, he ran on ahead once more to show
me the classroom which one day he hoped he would reach, leaping two
steps at a time up the only stairs in the whole building. Here in the
one two-decker section I found everything to delight the heart of a
growing boy. A cinema projection screen where once upon a time there
would have been a dusty map of the universe, and instead of a dull
array of battered desks, a sprinkling of well-equipped woodwork
benches. And once again, each wall a different pastel shade, such
as one sees in the latest design for a modern living-room in a glossy
magazine.

"Rather different from school as we remember it," the padre

remarked. "It was all green rep and monotonous brown paint, in my day."

"And mine," I echoed, stooping to look at the two framed pictures that hung, one on each side of the landing outside the senior classroom, like introductory signposts. One was a lithograph of an early painting by Utrillo, the other the reproduction of a colour-wash by Dufy.

Surprise must have shone on my face for my companion quickly explained their presence. "The Arts Council provided fifty reproductions by famous painters for the school, and the children, in each class, without any prompting were allowed to pick their own pictures for their own walls. What do you think of their natural taste?"

"I think a great deal," I said. But the words were a deliberate understatement. The whole tour had impressed me so deeply that, for a moment, I was reluctant to keep the promise that I had made to the young housewives, a few evenings before, that I would visit them in their own homes. I was nervous of the contrast between the larger and the smaller unit. Yet I should not have been afraid, I realize now, for people are eternally more important than things, however impressive. And I should have missed meeting the two small blonde daughters of Mrs. Kirby in the house at the corner of Kenwoods. Both dressed alike in striped knitted frocks with matching woollen caps, they made an enchanting picture and I almost expected to see a Bavarian forest of pine trees stretching away behind them instead of the open fields beneath the crest of the hill. Truthfully I was able to assure their mother, who had first met her husband when he was stationed after the war in the allied sector of Berlin, that they were the two prettiest little girls I had encountered that afternoon.

"And how do *you* like living here on the estate?" It was the same question that I had asked many times already but now it had suddenly assumed a deep and urgent significance. I was thankful that Julie and Hazel's mother did not falter before my frank scrutiny. "Now we have moved here, I am very happy. The neighbours are good."

I was to hear the same words, though spoken with a different accent—this time a Sussex countrywoman's accent—when the padre's wife took me to call on Mrs. Standing. It was to discover that her small daughter had just gone down with chicken-pox, so three-year-old Elizabeth Bess stayed with her mother in the fresh air, and we were alone in the parlour that also had two pictures, like signposts, on either side of the fireplace. No reproductions of examples of modern art these but instead brightly tinted photographs of a boy and a girl. One felt instinctively that the whole of Mrs. Standing's world moved round the originals of these pictures.

"What a very unusual wallpaper," I exclaimed, not just for something to say but because I really meant it. It was pink and sprinkled with dots and splodges in a Batik design. "It's only distemper," my hostess explained. "My husband did it. Do you really like it?"

The handiwork was so excellent that I had mistaken the wash for a paper. "And I like your dining-room suite, too," I added, moving through the archway that separated the sitting-room from the dining-room section of their living quarters. "I am so glad." But a shadow of anxiety crossed her face, with its healthy, outdoor colouring. "Do you notice how empty the other end of the room is?" she went on, with a rush.

"I hadn't till you mentioned it," I said.

"We've go no furniture at all upstairs. Not even a cupboard or a dressing-table or a rug of any kind. Just two beds. One for us and the other for the children. As it's so bare we all sleep together in one room. I hope they don't notice it so much that way. You see, my husband was taken very ill, over a year ago now, very soon after we moved in, and was off work for a whole year. In the end, we had to sell almost everything to keep going. But he's better at last, and started on shift again, so we are hoping soon to be able to collect a few things together again. I don't know what we'd have done without the neighbours. They were that good to us, looking after the children's clothes."

Now we were standing upstairs in the almost empty bedroom, but once again I was struck by the pattern of the distempered walls. And by something else. Overwhelmingly by something else. No other house I had entered that afternoon smelt quite so fresh and clean and good. With some emphasis I remarked upon this, and I shall always remember her reply.

"I was brought up in a very poor home but my mother always used to say. As long as you keep everything spotless, you can hold your head up anywhere. And I always have."

It was a statement of ultimate truth. Blinking a little I came out into the strong spring sunshine, feeling inadequate, but grateful, too, that I had been speaking to one of my own countrywomen. "You look as though you need a cup of tea," the padre's wife said, with her happy smile.

My instinct was to answer that I had seen and heard enough, and that I would have my tea at home. But I am glad that I did not do so for then I would have missed what proved to be the most revealing vista of all, an experiment of inestimable social importance.

The house was twice the size of all the others and stood a little apart. A handsome woman who looked to be in her early thirties opened the door. Mrs. Crawford might have been the manageress in a good class dress shop. Her coat frock was smart, but not too smart: her dark hair was freshly done. I felt at once that she would be very competent in any crisis, but I would never have guessed in any quiz competition what her profession was: an official foster-mother.

We went along the passage to her own private sitting-room. This was the domain of her husband, herself and her own small son, who came scrounging for chocolate biscuits during tea, because he knew for once he was on safe ground.

"What does he think of the seven boys and girls you have here in your charge?"

"Oh he couldn't be more pleased. You see, it was because of him that I first had the idea of putting in for the job. When I knew that I could not have another child, and Michael was always complaining that he wanted a little brother or sister to play with, at first I did not know what to do. And then I heard that in this new estate there were going to be four houses given over to foster children from local Homes. So I spoke to my husband about it."

"What does he do?" I asked.

"Well, in the war, he was in the R.A.F. First of all in England, and then instructing, in Canada. I followed him half way across the world. Later, when we came back to England at last, he was for a time the manager of one of the Mecca Dance Halls."

"Rather a different kind of life from this?" I suggested.

"Yes, all our friends made the same comment at first. But we've settled down, and we love it now. What's more, we feel we really are getting results. The children go to the school here, just like the others, and I take as much part as I can in all the community activities, so that the children get invited to our neighbours' homes, and feel that they really belong. Of course, some of them are only with us for a few months, till their parents get sufficient accommodation on their own, but they can stay till they are fifteen."

"Who are more difficult to cope with . . . the boys or the girls?"

"Oh, I wouldn't like to generalize, but I would say the girls. And some of the parents," she added frankly, remembering the times when one or two of her charges have returned on a Sunday evening in a filthy condition and a very obstreperous mood, after a few hours of over-parental indulgence.

"Unfortunately, the parents sometimes are jealous of me—I suppose it's only natural—and think I am trying to usurp their children's affection, when I am only doing my best to be fair all round. The children always call me 'Auntie', never 'Mother'. Actually, my own boy often complains that I am firmest with him. I have to be."

At the other end of the passage was the sitting-room given over to her young lodgers, and we peeped round the door, and I was immediately enveloped in the nostalgic mood of any comfortable childhood playroom. What a wonderful change, I thought, from the usual atmosphere of most Institutions for homeless children.

"Thank you very much for my nice tea," I said, but I was really thanking my countrywoman for so much else, above all, for giving me the chance to see what progress was being made, in humanity, as well as in the arrangement of bricks and mortar.

As though a final proof was needed, a pin-pointing of the day, for ever in my mind, when I drove my guide and her little daughter home, we passed young Christopher trotting down the hill, with his arm affectionately round the shoulder of one of his contemporaries, a fellow inheritor of this visionary new world.

They were too intent in their secret communion to notice our passing and I was deep in my own discoveries, so that the padre's wife mistook my silence and said apologetically that she was afraid I hadn't had a very exciting afternoon.

"Don't you believe it." I answered. "If I owned a newspaper, it would be all over the front page what I have seen today."

And I meant it, so much, indeed, that deliberately I have made this the last chapter, feeling that here was the essence, the distillation of all that I have sought to record and capture in this mirror of the contemporary scene. For now each time that my car reaches the cross-roads at the top of the hill, and we see the lights of Coldean spread below us, more than ever I shall feel that I am in sight of home.

The Mill House, Falmer.
November, 1953—May, 1954.

THE END

INDEX

L